Internet Histories

In 2017, the new journal *Internet Histories* was founded. As part of the process of defining a new field, the journal editors approached leading scholars in this dynamic, interdisciplinary area. This book is thus a collection of eighteen short thought-provoking pieces, inviting discussion about Internet histories. They raise and suggest current and future issues in the scholarship, as well as exploring the challenges, opportunities, and tensions that underpin the research terrain. The book explores cultural, political, social, economic, and industrial dynamics, all part of a distinctive historiographical and theoretical approach which underpins this emerging field.

The international specialists reflect upon the scholarly scene, laying out the field's research successes to date, as well as suggest the future possibilities that lie ahead in the field of Internet histories. While the emphasis is on researcher perspectives, interviews with leading luminaries of the Internet's development are also provided. As histories of the Internet become increasingly important, *Internet Histories* is a useful roadmap for those contemplating how we can write such works. One cannot write many histories of the 1990s or later without thinking of digital media – and we hope that *Internet Histories* will be an invaluable resource for such studies.

This book was originally published as the first issue of the journal *Internet Histories*.

Niels Brügger is Professor of Internet Studies and Digital Humanities at Aarhus University, Denmark.

Gerard Goggin is Professor of Media and Communications at the University of Sydney, Australia.

Ian Milligan is Associate Professor of History at the University of Waterloo, Canada.

Valérie Schafer is a Historian at the French National Centre for Scientific Research (CNRS), France.

Internet Histories

Edited by
**Niels Brügger, Gerard Goggin, Ian Milligan
and Valérie Schafer**

Routledge
Taylor & Francis Group

LONDON AND NEW YORK

First published 2018
by Routledge

2 Park Square, Milton Park, Abingdon, Oxfordshire OX14 4RN
52 Vanderbilt Avenue, New York, NY 10017

Routledge is an imprint of the Taylor & Francis Group, an informa business

First issued in paperback 2019

British Library Cataloguing in Publication Data
A catalogue record for this book is available from the British Library

ISBN 13: 978-1-138-57042-9 (hbk)
ISBN 13: 978-0-367-89247-0 (pbk)

Typeset in Myriad Pro
by RefineCatch Limited, Bungay, Suffolk

Publisher's Note
The publisher accepts responsibility for any inconsistencies that may have
arisen during the conversion of this book from journal articles to book chapters,
namely the possible inclusion of journal terminology.

Disclaimer
Every effort has been made to contact copyright holders for their permission to
reprint material in this book. The publishers would be grateful to hear from any
copyright holder who is not here acknowledged and will undertake to rectify
any errors or omissions in future editions of this book.

Contents

Citation Information   vii

Notes on Contributors   xi

Introduction: Internet histories   1
Niels Brügger, Gerard Goggin, Ian Milligan and Valérie Schafer

1. What and where is the Internet? (Re)defining Internet histories   8
Janet Abbate

2. Hagiography, revisionism & blasphemy in Internet histories   15
Andrew L. Russell

3. A common language   26
Marc Weber

4. Can we write a cultural history of the Internet? If so, how?   39
Fred Turner

5. Searching for missing "net histories"   47
Kevin Driscoll and Camille Paloque-Berges

6. Out from the PLATO cave: uncovering the pre-Internet history of social computing   60
Steve Jones and Guillaume Latzko-Toth

7. Internet histories: the view from the design process   70
Sandra Braman

8. The Internet as a structure of feeling: 1992–1996   79
Thomas Streeter

9. Precorporation: or what financialisation can tell us about the histories of the Internet   90
Greg Elmer

10. Internet in the Middle East: an asymmetrical model of development   97
Ilhem Allagui

11. The unexplored history of operationalising digital divides: a pilot study   106
Bianca C. Reisdorf, William H. Dutton, Whisnu Triwibowo and Michael E. Nelson

CONTENTS

12. Early challenges to multilingualism on the Internet: the case of Han
    character-based scripts   119
    Mark McLelland

13. African histories of the Internet   129
    Herman Wasserman

14. Notes from/dev/null   138
    Finn Brunton

15. Archaeology of the Amsterdam digital city; why digital data are
    dynamic and should be treated accordingly   146
    Gerard Alberts, Marc Went and Robert Jansma

16. Doing Web history with the Internet Archive: screencast documentaries   160
    Richard Rogers

17. Breaking in to the mainstream: demonstrating the value of internet
    (and web) histories   173
    Jane Winters

18. For a dynamic and post-digital history of the Internet: a research agenda 180
    Leopoldina Fortunati

19. Tell us about . . .   188
    Valérie Schafer

    Index   197

Citation Information

The chapters in this book were originally published in *Internet Histories*, volume 1, issue 1–2 (January 2017). When citing this material, please use the original page numbering for each article, as follows:

Introduction
Introduction: Internet histories
Niels Brügger, Gerard Goggin, Ian Milligan and Valérie Schafer
Internet Histories, volume 1, issue 1–2 (January 2017), pp. 1–7

Chapter 1
What and where is the Internet? (Re)defining Internet histories
Janet Abbate
Internet Histories, volume 1, issue 1–2 (January 2017), pp. 8–14

Chapter 2
Hagiography, revisionism & blasphemy in Internet histories
Andrew L. Russell
Internet Histories, volume 1, issue 1–2 (January 2017), pp. 15–25

Chapter 3
A common language
Marc Weber
Internet Histories, volume 1, issue 1–2 (January 2017), pp. 26–38

Chapter 4
Can we write a cultural history of the Internet? If so, how?
Fred Turner
Internet Histories, volume 1, issue 1–2 (January 2017), pp. 39–46

Chapter 5
Searching for missing "net histories"
Kevin Driscoll and Camille Paloque-Berges
Internet Histories, volume 1, issue 1–2 (January 2017), pp. 47–59

Chapter 6
Out from the PLATO cave: uncovering the pre-Internet history of social computing
Steve Jones and Guillaume Latzko-Toth
Internet Histories, volume 1, issue 1–2 (January 2017), pp. 60–69

Chapter 7
Internet histories: the view from the design process
Sandra Braman
Internet Histories, volume 1, issue 1–2 (January 2017), pp. 70–78

Chapter 8
The Internet as a structure of feeling: 1992–1996
Thomas Streeter
Internet Histories, volume 1, issue 1–2 (January 2017), pp. 79–89

Chapter 9
Precorporation: or what financialisation can tell us about the histories of the Internet
Greg Elmer
Internet Histories, volume 1, issue 1–2 (January 2017), pp. 90–96

Chapter 10
Internet in the Middle East: an asymmetrical model of development
Ilhem Allagui
Internet Histories, volume 1, issue 1–2 (January 2017), pp. 97–105

Chapter 11
The unexplored history of operationalising digital divides: a pilot study
Bianca C. Reisdorf, William H. Dutton, Whisnu Triwibowo and Michael E. Nelson
Internet Histories, volume 1, issue 1–2 (January 2017), pp. 106–118

Chapter 12
Early challenges to multilingualism on the Internet: the case of Han character-based scripts
Mark McLelland
Internet Histories, volume 1, issue 1–2 (January 2017), pp. 119–128

Chapter 13
African histories of the Internet
Herman Wasserman
Internet Histories, volume 1, issue 1–2 (January 2017), pp. 129–137

Chapter 14
Notes from /dev/null
Finn Brunton
Internet Histories, volume 1, issue 1–2 (January 2017), pp. 138–145

Chapter 15
Archaeology of the Amsterdam digital city; why digital data are dynamic and should be treated accordingly
Gerard Alberts, Marc Went and Robert Jansma
Internet Histories, volume 1, issue 1–2 (January 2017), pp. 146–159

Chapter 16
Doing Web history with the Internet Archive: screencast documentaries
Richard Rogers
Internet Histories, volume 1, issue 1–2 (January 2017), pp. 160–172

Chapter 17
Breaking in to the mainstream: demonstrating the value of internet (and web) histories
Jane Winters
Internet Histories, volume 1, issue 1–2 (January 2017), pp. 173–179

Chapter 18
For a dynamic and post-digital history of the Internet: a research agenda
Leopoldina Fortunati
Internet Histories, volume 1, issue 1–2 (January 2017), pp. 180–187

Chapter 19
Tell us about . . .
Valérie Schafer
Internet Histories, volume 1, issue 1–2 (January 2017), pp. 188–196

For any permission-related enquiries please visit:
http://www.tandfonline.com/page/help/permissions

Notes on Contributors

Janet Abbate is Associate Professor of Science and Technology in Society at Virginia Tech, USA. Her 1999 book, *Inventing the Internet*, was the first scholarly history of the Internet and has become a standard reference. Her current research investigates the historical emergence of computer science as an intellectual discipline, an academic institution, and a professional identity.

Gerard Alberts is Associate Professor for History of Computing and History of Mathematics at the Korteweg – de Vries Institute for Mathematics at the University of Amsterdam, The Netherlands. He is editor of the series *History of Computing* and a member of the editorial board of *IEEE Annals of the History of Computing*, and *Internet Histories*.

Ilhem Allagui is Associate Professor at Northwestern University in Qatar. Her research interests include Internet adoption and usage patterns in the MENA region as well as media and cultural industries in the Middle East. She specializes in teaching strategic communication courses.

Sandra Braman is Abbott Professor of Liberal Arts and Professor of Communication at Texas A&M University, USA. She teaches in the areas of law and policy for information, communication and culture; global media and technology; intercultural communication; organizational communication policy; global research methods; and qualitative research methods.

Niels Brügger is Professor of Internet Studies and Digital Humanities at Aarhus University, Denmark. His primary research interests are the history of the Internet as a means of communication, and Digital Humanities, including archiving the Internet as well as the use of digital research tools.

Finn Brunton is Assistant Professor in the Department of Media, Culture, and Communication at NYU's Steinhardt School, USA. His research centres on the history and theory of computing and digital media, with a focus on hacking, privacy, cryptocurrencies, and other forms of digital money.

Kevin Driscoll is Assistant Professor of Media Studies at the University of Virginia, USA. His research explores popular culture, political communication, and networked personal computing, with special attention to mythology, folklore, and infrastructure. He is a co-author of *Minitel: Welcome to the Internet, a cultural history of the French videotex system*.

William H. Dutton is the James H. Quello Professor of Media and Information Policy at Michigan State University, USA, where he is a Director of the Quello Center. His research on Internet Studies increasingly focuses on the Fifth Estate and related issues of cyber policy, regulation, and governance.

Greg Elmer is Bell Media Research Chair and Professor of Professional Communication at Ryerson University, Canada. He is also founding Director of the Infoscape Research Lab in Toronto.

Leopoldina Fortunati is Director of the Research Laboratory on New Media, NuMe at the University of Udine, Italy, where she teaches sociology of communication and culture, and laboratory of social robotics. She is an associate editor of the journal *The Information Society*, and along with Rich Ling and Gerard Goggin, is an editor of the series *Studies in Mobile Communication*.

Gerard Goggin is Professor of Media and Communications at the University of Sydney, Australia. His research focuses on social, cultural, and political aspects of digital technologies, especially the Internet and mobile phones and media.

Robert Jansma is a master student at the joint MSc Programs Computer Science of the Vrije Universiteit Amsterdam and University of Amsterdam, The Netherlands. He is also a Research Assistant at the Amsterdam Museum involved in sustainably preserving De Digitale Stad in the project "DDS herleeft".

Steve Jones is UIC Distinguished Professor of Communication at the University of Illinois at Chicago, USA. He is also Adjunct Research Professor in the Institute of Communications Research at the University of Illinois at Urbana-Champaign, USA. His research interests range from Internet to audio technologies, and from Internet to popular music studies.

Guillaume Latzko-Toth is Associate Professor in the Department of Information and Communication at the University of Laval, Canada. He is particularly interested in how individuals and groups integrate digital communication technologies into their everyday lives.

Mark McLelland is Professor in the Sociology Program at the University of Wollongong, Australia. He is co-editor (with Gerard Goggin) of the *Routledge Companion to Global Internet Histories*.

Ian Milligan is Associate Professor of History at the University of Waterloo, Canada. He's currently exploring how historians can use web archives and other large digital repositories.

Michael E. Nelson is a master's student in Media and Information Management at Michigan State University, USA. His thesis research focuses on team and organizational transactive memory on enterprise social media.

Camille Paloque-Berges is a Research Engineer at the History of Techno-Sciences lab (HT2S) at Conservatoire National des Arts et Metiers (CNAM), France. She is also an Associated Researcher at the French National Centre for Scientific Research (CNRS), France.

Bianca C. Reisdorf is Assistant Professor in the Department of Media and Information at Michigan State University, USA, and the Assistant Director of the Quello Center. Her research revolves around digital inequalities in highly connected countries and the effects of these inequalities on vulnerable groups.

Richard Rogers is Professor of New Media and Digital Culture at the University of Amsterdam, The Netherlands.

Andrew L. Russell is Professor of History and Dean of the College of Arts & Sciences at SUNY Polytechnic Institute in Utica and Albany, New York. He is the author of *Open Standards and the Digital Age: History, Ideology, and Networks* (2014) and co-editor of *Ada's Legacy: Cultures of Computing from the Victorian to the Digital Age* (2015).

Valérie Schafer is a Historian at the French National Centre for Scientific Research (CNRS), France. She is currently studying Internet and web development in France in the 1990s and issues of digital heritage.

Thomas Streeter is Professor of Sociology at the University of Vermont, USA, and the author of books and articles on the intersections of culture with media law and policy.

Whisnu Triwibowo is assisting research at the Quello Center. He is a doctoral student in the Department of Information and Media and on leave from the University of Indonesia, where he is a Lecturer.

Fred Turner is the Harry and Norman Chandler Professor in Communication at Stanford University, USA. He is the author of several books on media technology and cultural change in post-World War II America, including most recently *The Democratic Surround: Multimedia and American Liberalism from World War II to the Psychedelic Sixties*.

Herman Wasserman is Professor of Media Studies and Director of the Centre for Film and Media Studies at the University of Cape Town, South Africa. He is editor-in-chief of the journal *African Media Studies*.

Marc Weber is the Curatorial Director of the Internet History Program at the Computer History Museum, USA. He established Web history as a topic starting in 1995 with help from Sir Tim Berners-Lee and other online pioneers.

Marc Went is a master student at the joint MSc Programs Computer Science and Information Sciences of the Vrije Universiteit Amsterdam and University of Amsterdam, The Netherlands.

Jane Winters is Chair of Digital Humanities in the School of Advanced Study at the University of London, UK. She has led or co-directed a range of digital projects, including most recently Big UK Domain Data for the Arts and Humanities; Digging into Linked Parliamentary Metadata; and Traces through Time: Prosopography in Practice across Big Data.

Introduction: Internet histories

Niels Brügger, Gerard Goggin, Ian Milligan and Valérie Schafer

> Internet history has progressed from a history of the technology to a history of modern communication. It is now intimately entwined in all aspects of our lives, so "Internet history" will shortly be indistinguishable from "human history."
>
> (Crocker, 2017)

> Journalist: Can you describe for the reader the D-day, or the H-hour or the M-minute, the precise moment when you invented the World Wide Web?
>
> Tim Berners-Lee: [His expression suggests he is lost in memories]. Well, I was coming down a footpath in the Swiss Alps... [silence] ... Then the clouds started getting thicker... and darker... [silence] ... There was a flash of lightening, a peel of thunder, a storm was beginning to blow, when suddenly the clouds parted and...
>
> Journalist: *And?*
>
> Berners-Lee: And nothing! I'm making this up... Ideas never arrive like that, you're not suddenly struck by an illumination or a revelation, everything you read about Newton's apple or Archimedes shouting "Eureka!" in his bath-tub, these are fantasies!
>
> (Berners-Lee, in Calixte, 2014)

For more than four decades, the Internet has grown and spread to an extent where today it is an indispensable element in the communication and media environment of many countries, and indeed of everyday life, culture and society. These precipitous changes have called for the understanding of the innovations, actors, changes and continuities involved in these evolutions, from a technical, but also from a social, scientific, politic or economic point of view. Although the history of the Internet has not been yet very predominant within the academic literature, an increased number of books and journal articles within the last decade attest to the fact that Internet history is an emerging field of study across a number of scholarly disciplines and fields. This is most evident in Internet and new media studies, but also is clear in culture, media, communication and technology research, across the diverse settings and institutional locations where such work may be encountered. A central issue for the advancement of the field is that historical studies of the Internet have mostly been published in journals related to a variety of disciplines, and these journals only rarely publish articles with a clear historical focus. The situation has greatly improved with the various recent issues dedicated to Internet and web histories, as well as edited volumes, but these have tended to have only a limited number of contributions.

In the face of this perceived gulf, what we felt was needed is a journal where history of the Internet and digital cultures took pride of place. Accordingly, we are very pleased to present the inaugural issue of this new journal from Taylor & Francis: *Internet Histories: Digital Technology, Culture and Society*.

In opening up this publication venue, we foresee a journal where historical studies are presented, and methodological, historiographic and theoretical issues are debated, with a view to fostering the history of the Internet as a field of study in its own right.

As the journal's name signifies, we assume that the Internet is here to stay. We are also mindful that the technology and its various entailments are not a closed box, meaning that its uses, devices, technologies, protocols, not to mention the Internet's other constitutive social, economic, cultural, political, linguistic and its other coordinates, persist in a continuing process of evolution and innovation. We are convinced that it becomes still more pivotal to have solid scholarly knowledge about the development of the Internet in the past with a view to understanding the Internet of the present and the future. On the one hand, past events, structures, artefacts, assemblages and their associated concepts, meanings and feelings, constitute important preconditions for today's Internet. On the other hand, knowledge and critical understanding of the mechanisms behind the developments in the past may prove very helpful resources for understanding what is about to happen with the Internet today. With such a rapidly developing technology, knowing where we have come, what the histories of Internet and associated technologies are or might be, and how their uses and abuses unfold, helps equip us to contemplate where it might go and for what particular futures.

Interest in a growing Internet field

Internet study is a varied field of study, but in the main, it emerged out of the social sciences and the humanities in the mid-1990s. In the beginning, the focus was mainly on studying the online Internet and its genesis and specific communities such as the engineers, the scientists, the first virtual communities that developed, sometimes outside the Internet, within the Well, newsgroups and so on (especially under the banner of cyberspace and cyberstudies).

With the rise of the Web, the focus emerged on developing the adequate theories and methods to study the Internet. A key moment, for instance, was the inaugural conference of the Association of Internet Researchers, which held its inaugural conference in Kansas in 2000. In these early years, historical studies of the Internet were practically not on the agenda. This can hardly be seen as a fault – there simply was not that much history to write about on such a seemingly contemporary topic, very much still in the making! There were various early essays and important studies of the Internet's development, especially beginning as we entered the new millennia. First, because a few scholars became interested in the historical developments that formed the basis for the rapidly evolving Internet, adding to work already blossoming in computer history – piqued, among other things, by the societal visions and implications of concepts such as the information society; second, as more archives – Web archives, of course, but many other new kinds of archives also – and approaches became available which made it possible to preserve –

and study – past Internets. Within the last decade, this tendency has gathered considerable momentum, with more and more historical studies of the Internet appearing to the present day.

A few characteristics make this new wave of Internet history especially interesting. Concerning this research, consider: the considerable international breadth and depth, including, to give just one example, special issues of journals now appearing on histories of the "cyber-orient" or Internet in the Middle East; the range of aspects of Internet and associated media and technologies receiving study (for example, histories of the religious Internet, gaming, search, spam and so on); new conceptualisations of the Internet as technology, media, communication and cultural form; in general, a growing conceptual, methodological and theoretical sophistication in emergent research.

A large field open to diverse methods and approaches

As the Internet grows, the historical field dedicated to Internet history and the history of computer networks expands as well, and diachronic studies are also more and more of interest for other disciplines – an interdisciplinary field, useful in a wide range of curricula too. At present, there are emerging and already well-organised communities and several approaches (such as visual studies, web archives, infrastructure studies, digital cultures) that make claim for a field that is not restricted to the Internet defined by the emblematic and operational technical definition of TCP/IP (Transmission Control Protocol/Internet Protocol), but also for broader scholarship interested in digital cultures, applications and genesis as developments and uses.

In embarking on this journal project, we are conscious that this field of history is large as well: there is not a single way to start and write this history, one single founding momentum, event or one space, one kind of archived materials. We are keen to solicit work that explicitly engages in historical research: diachronic studies, particular histories, use of archives, new creative ways to consider, generate and critique histories. In all of this, the journal aims to be a central platform for ferment in the field, rather than favour a single method or approach.

We consider the boundaries around the field that we chose to be as expansive as the uses, contents, applications and imaginaries of the Internet are. We do not want to limit historical exploration to the Internet in a particular epoch (especially, say, from the 1980s with TCP/IP). Rather, we consider the technology as a complex system which emerged and developed in a rich and dynamic environment too, that is of course not only technical, but political, economic and social, porous to many applications, not sealed but still evolving – just as the ways we conceive, write and express its histories are still a work-in-progress. In all this, we are conscious that no single history is adequate to do justice to the Internet, so wish to foster research that conjures with different ways and approaches influenced by history of technology, innovation, digital cultures, Science and Technology Studies (STS), Internet and code studies, digital humanities and so on.

This is *Internet Histories: Digital Technology, Culture and Society*, an international, interdisciplinary peer-reviewed journal concerned with research on the cultural, social, political and technological histories of the Internet and associated digital cultures. The journal embraces empirical as well as theoretical and methodological studies within the field of the history of the Internet broadly conceived – from early computer networks, Usenet and

Bulletin Board Systems, to everyday Internet with the web through the emergence of new forms of Internet with mobile phones and tablet computers, social media and the Internet of things. The journal will also provide the premier outlet for cutting-edge research in the closely related area of histories of digital cultures.

A hallmark of the journal is its desire to publish and catalyse research and scholarly debate on the development, forms and histories of the Internet internationally, across the full global range of countries, regions, cultures and communities. Importantly, the journal draws on a wide range of disciplines within the humanities and the social sciences. *Internet Histories* will also be open to interdisciplinary studies of history of Internet and digital cultures, from computer, information, engineering and other science and technology researchers. To inform and steer the journal, the founding editors will be ably assisted by the eminent members of our international editorial board – to whom we are very grateful for their support for this venture.

The first issue: reflecting the variety of the field

To set the scene for the new venture, the first two issues of the journal, vol. 1, no. 1–2, comprise short thought-provoking pieces that invite to discussions, raise and suggest the issues, challenges, opportunities, tensions, conceptual and research terrain, cultural, political, social, economic and industrial dynamics, distinctive historiographic and theoretical underpinning that characterise the emergent field of Internet histories.

We took up the challenge of embracing a large scope of approaches, methods, sensibilities by inviting the members of the international editorial board to reflect upon the scene, terms and possibilities for doing Internet histories. We are grateful to the authors of these opening sorties, especially for the way in which their papers richly represent the journal's ethos of openness. We asked that contributions address key questions in the field, such as:

- Why Internet histories, now? What is the role and function of historical or diachronic Internet studies in terms of current issues for our societies, the historical field, university curricula and present framing of the development of the Internet?
- How would you describe the major theoretical, methodological and/or empirical gaps in existing research on Internet histories?
- What are the conceptual and methodological opportunities of doing Internet histories?
- What are the limits of Internet, versus other kinds of media, information, communication, technology forms?
- What are the challenges for doing Internet histories that are genuinely international in character, given the wide variety of languages, cultural locations, social contexts and institutional settings?
- What are the archival and material conditions of the material of Internet histories?

These resulting short articles are neither exhaustive, nor they provide a complete state of the art of the tendencies.

The opening quintet of papers raises key questions about how Internet histories are typically defined and approached, and offer potent suggestions for reframing the terms of future research. Janet Abbate's "What and Where is the Internet? (Re)defining Internet

Histories" considers the stakes in defining the Internet in terms of technology, use and local experience, rather than the reflex, implicit way of seeing the Internet in narrowly cast material terms (hardware and software) that entails a diffusion from a very specific place of origin, the United States. In "Hagiography, Revisionism, and Blasphemy in Internet Histories", Andrew L. Russell continues this thread by provocatively likening many available Internet histories to hagiographies, and by contrast, arguing for a reorientation via a broader notion of histories of networking. For his part, Marc Weber argues for a systematic broadening of online information systems, so we can inventory and better understand their concepts and precedents and study their comparative architectures across the axes that really matter for societies now, such as questions of regulation, economy and liberty. Fred Turner's, "Can We Write a Cultural History of the Internet? If So, How?" grasps the nettle of one of the most difficult challenges – the question of culture. Puzzling out how we can acknowledge and explore the different kinds of culture the Internet involves, as well as its role in the dynamics of cultural change, Turner returns to four classic studies of earlier technologies and cultures as a source of still relevant insights and guidance. Kevin Driscoll and Camille Paloque-Berges push these lines of questioning further with their "Searching for Missing 'Net Histories'" contending at the heart of Internet history lies an epistemological conundrum, that falls apart in the comparative, critical historian's hands. To find a way through the maze of mythologies and shared narratives that shape the Internet as much as the technical aspects, they plump for the cultivation of occluded histories, less obvious and neglected sources and networks.

Along similar lines, Steve Jones and Guillaume Latzko-Toth uncover the pre-Internet history of social computing by recovering the history of PLATO, a pioneering educational computer platform developed at the Computer-based Education Research Laboratory at the University of Illinois at Urbana-Champaign in the 1960s and 1970s. The next two papers take a similar tack in addressing Internet histories through epistemological reflections. Sandra Braman studies Requests for Comments (RFCs) and the way that they can be used as primary sources, entwining the technical and social. By demonstrating the value of incorporating the history of the Internet as understood by those responsible for its design, she has written a stimulating article, which can originate from data and the way we question them, or from the use of a creative conceptual framework as shown by Thomas Streeter in his analysis of the first period of the World Wide Web. Streeter demonstrates, as do the last two papers, that technologies are best understood, "not so much as agents in their own right, but as thought-objects for the collective enactment and exploration of hopes, desires, and political visions." Greg Elmer closes this section with an alternative historical perspective on one of the best-known contemporary Internet companies – the time before the 2012 public listing of social media giant Facebook. Elmer draws attention to the importance of the pre-market, financialisation period of Internet companies, as a crucial, yet overlooked period where decisive aspects of the technology are shaped.

After an exploration over time, our articles then move into exploring space. Ilhem Allagui aims at using a critical as well as a historical analysis of policies and usages to map Arab countries' Internet development. Bianca C. Reisdorf, William H. Dutton, Whisnu Triwibowo and Michel Nelson trace the (no longer, thanks to them) unexplored history of operationalising digital divides. Mark McLelland explores the early challenges to multilingualism on the Internet with the case of Han character-based scripts. Herman Wasserman offers a pioneering article on rich and largely unwritten African histories of the

Internet, contending that the "challenge for Internet historiography focusing on Africa is to attempt a holistic grasp of these multi-facetted, complex and contradictory developments while acknowledging wide divergence in local specificities." Each of these articles helps us to look beyond a sometimes US-centric history and to broaden the scope.

We then move from some unexplored or less-known spaces to forgotten or unexplored archives, materials and resources. With Finn Brunton's piece, we enter into a stimulating debate about conservation and oblivion, preservation and deletion of digital materials, a current that extends with Gerard Alberts, Marc Went and Robert Jansma's study of the amazing De Digitale Stad, launched at the beginning of 1994, which evolved from a bulletin-board-like system to a full virtual city. Finally, this section closes with Richard Rogers' study of Web archives through a particular approach called "screencast documentaries."

These three papers invite us to deeply think about methods, sources, born-digital heritage but also the choices, issues, imaginaries, deeper motivations that they disclose and reveal and their impact on our researches, objects and subjects, on the cultural heritage and on our memories, our history and the way we write it. They demonstrate the value of Internet and Web history but the complexity of archival material too, which echoes the questions aptly raised by Jane Winters: how can researchers in the humanities and social sciences more generally be persuaded to integrate Internet histories into their research? And how can this value be demonstrated to the wider general public? No doubt that, in addition to her fine analysis of the issues that the historians and institutions will have to face in the future, some answers are already present in the research agenda that Leopoldina Fortunati suggests for a dynamic and post-digital history of the Internet too.

Taken together, these papers reveal a treasure trove of issues for now and future investigation and debate, notably how to articulate a non-centric history, open to new actors, spaces, disciplines, archives. Most importantly, we hope that they can hopefully spur further discussion in the coming journal issues.

In the same way, we asked some pioneers and actors of Internet history to briefly contribute to a section seeking to given them a voice by inviting oral histories. We also made the choice for this first issue of an audacious tone, a far cry from long-form interviews. In doing so, we wished to associate the voices of actors to this history that they wrote in the past (and some of them are still part of it) with those who write it today as historians.

In launching this new journal, we are conscious of many debts of gratitude to a range of people, organisations and institutions who have offered support. We wish to thank our publisher, Taylor & Francis, for warmly welcoming this idea, and to our publisher Sophie Wade, and various members of her team, for their excellent assistance in establishing the many elements required. We thank our institutions for their support, especially Aarhus University, as the host for the managing editor and our excellent editorial assistant Asger Harlung.

We look forward to the journal taking on a life of its own, giving its readers a voice and place, as we are open to proposals and very excited to discover the ideas and submissions that come forward for articles, interviews, reviews and special issues. "The Web as I envisaged it, we have not seen it yet. The future is still so much bigger than the past," said Tim Berners-Lee (Silva, 2009). This condition invites historians to work hard, as the past is already big and becoming bigger and bigger as new approaches proliferate!

Disclosure statement

No potential conflict of interest was reported by the authors.

References

Calixte, L. (2014, June 17). Tim Berners-Lee: "Oui, le Web est né en France" [Tim Berners-Lee: "Yes, the Web was born in France"]. Challenges. Retrieved from http://www.challenges.fr/high-tech/20140617.CHA5082/tim-berners-lee-oui-le-web-est-ne-en-france.html

Crocker, S. (2017). Tell us about… Internet Histories: Digital Technology. Culture and Society, 1(1–2).

Silva, D. (2009, April 22). Internet has only just begun, say founders. Phys.org. Retrieved from https://phys.org/news/2009-04-Internet-begun-founders.html

What and where is the Internet? (Re)defining Internet histories

Janet Abbate (ID)

ABSTRACT
The ways in which historians define the Internet profoundly shape the histories we write. Many studies implicitly define the Internet in material terms, as a particular set of hardware and software, and consequently tend to frame the development of the Internet as the spread of these technologies from the United States. This essay explores implications of defining the Internet alternatively in terms of technology, use and local experience. While there is not a single "correct" definition, historians should be aware of the politics of the definitions they use.

1. Introduction

Over the past two decades, the field of Internet history has produced a sophisticated body of research with a global scope. Empirical studies in different national and regional contexts have opened up a broad understanding of what networks can be and the decisions and contingencies that have shaped them. For example, Schafer's (2015) research on French and European networks demonstrates how design choices were tailored to local and regional user communities and regulatory environments; studies by Gerovitch (2008) and Peters (2016) analyse how networks in the former Soviet Union mirrored the organisational and political dynamics of the Soviet state; and books by Gottlieb and McLelland (2003) and Franklin (2005) demonstrate how Internet technologies have been appropriated and naturalised by residents and diasporas of Japan and the Pacific Islands. Such diverse accounts challenge the US-centric narratives of heroic invention, expansion and transfer found in much popular writing and go beyond genealogies of technical innovations to trace histories of Internet use and governance.

Yet the object at the centre of this collective research effort remains strangely elusive. Haigh, Russell, and Dutton (2015) raise the question, "What is the history of the Internet the history of?" and find answers ranging from a narrow, technical definition of the Internet as a set of routers and protocols enabling network interconnection to a broader notion of the Internet that encompasses "the contents of the networks being interconnected and their users, social practices, and skills" (pp. 143–144). Can we write Internet histories if we do not know what the Internet is? I suggest that it is time to reconsider not only what defines the Internet but the politics of such definitions. The ways in which

8

historians define the Internet shape the geographic and temporal scope of our narratives, the activities we include or ignore, the dominance of certain countries and social groups and the marginality of others. This essay will consider the strengths and limitations of three broad ways of framing Internet histories.

2. The Internet as technology

In actors' accounts and popular culture, the Internet is defined in terms of hardware and software; a typical example is Wikipedia's description of the Internet as "the global system of interconnected computer networks that use the Internet protocol suite (TCP/IP)."[1] This framework, which was shared by early histories that sought to explain the origins of network hardware and software, has several advantages. A close focus on technical components allows historians to reconstruct the social shaping of design choices, while not precluding serious consideration of national politics or user agency (Abbate, 1999). Using the framework of systems theory (Hughes, 1987), historical accounts of network creation have raised important questions about the politics of standardisation, interoperability and governance mechanisms (DeNardis, 2009).

More recently, infrastructure studies have offered a rich body of theory and research for unpacking how the Internet – and the more specialised information systems layered over it – function and are defined within social relations. Star and Ruhleder's (1996) classic definition of infrastructure highlights its socio-technical characteristics: infrastructures depend on the human labour of standardisation in order to interact seamlessly with other systems; infrastructures shape user practices, and vice versa; once learned, infrastructures become transparent to their users until a failure abruptly makes them visible again. But Star and Ruhleder also point out, crucially, that these infrastructural characteristics are not inherent in the technology but only exist in *relation* to a social group that uses the infrastructure for a shared purpose and whose members have integrated the technology into their conventions of practice. This usefully raises the historical question of how – and for which people and purposes – the Internet has taken on the character of an infrastructure.

Theorising how infrastructures develop over time, Blanchette (2012, p. 33) proposes several "infrastructural dynamics," such as "persistence" and "drift," that can help historians explain aspects of the Internet's technical evolution. *Persistence* means that "computing resources are repurposed rather than merely replaced" and that change "proceeds conservatively through mutation and hybridisation, rather than outright break with the past," while the concept of *drift* acknowledges that infrastructure change is "only partially responsive to rational control" and subject to "the push and pull of competing stakeholders working to shift its evolution in the most advantageous direction" (p. 34). Such propositions about the general characteristics of infrastructure can help counter tendencies to see the Internet as unique or exceptional and invite historians to situate Internet infrastructure in a larger economic or institutional context.

The invisibility of infrastructure described by Star and Ruhleder simultaneously promotes ease of use and difficulty of social or political accountability. Recent work on the politics of algorithms reveals how the hidden calculations behind search engines, news feeds and ad placement can violate privacy and perpetuate social bias (Gillespie, 2014; Halavais, 2008). Labour is often invisible online as well, whether it is the unpaid labour of forum moderators and social media content providers or the obscured labour relations of contingent workers who contract through online labour markets (Scholz, 2012). Making infrastructure invisible is a social and historical process that involves phenomena as diverse as protocol standards, trade secrets, user interfaces and user training. Internet histories can and should unpack how such invisibility is achieved and its social and political consequences.

One limitation of defining the Internet as a large technological system or infrastructure is that this tends to frame the Internet as a channel for transmitting data, rather than as a field of social practice. A systems approach also privileges the role of system builders over users in historical accounts. Perhaps most problematically, tracing the Internet's history to a particular set of hardware and software innovations reinforces a perception of the United States as the Internet's centre. The computer communications system that first bore the label "Internet" grew out of the Advanced Research Projects Agency Network (ARPANET), which was funded by and located within the United States; but the persistence of the name "Internet" for today's global data network should not imply that the ARPANET has been the sole source of its technology, practices or meaning. An instructive example of a non-US-centric infrastructure study is Medina's *Cybernetic Revolutionaries: Technology and Politics in Allende's Chile* (2011), which follows a nationally networked computing project called Cybersyn. Challenging the notion that all innovations in computer communications originate in the global North, Media describes how Cybersyn was locally conceived in 1971, independently of the US ARPANET (which was not yet operational). The fact that Cybersyn did not survive Chile's political upheaval long enough to join today's Internet does not negate its significance for Internet history: what did persist were social visions for networking, technical capacities and individual actors who went on to other projects.

3. The Internet as content and social space

While it is clearly important to understand the history of technical infrastructures, much of what is culturally interesting about the Internet involves applications, content, services and interaction – social media, shopping and games, rather than switches, packets and protocols. Early studies of "cyberspace" and "virtual community" highlighted how social groups constructed the Internet as a virtual space for social interaction and individual expression (Rheingold, 1993; Turkle, 1995), and more recent studies of social media and gaming explore similar issues of identity and community (Corneliussen & Rettberg, 2008). Framing the Internet as content or social space usefully highlights the active role of users as content creators as well as the political role of information and its implications for democracy. It shifts the focus away from hardware innovation and thereby potentially decentres the US and highlights local or subcultural content and practices. On the other hand, since many online communities require paid memberships and leisure time, there may be a bias toward economically privileged groups, early adopters (especially young people) and recreational uses of the Internet.

Much of this online content and social activity previously existed offline, which raises questions of periodisation. Should the history begin when the activity in question was first moved online, which could imply historical discontinuity or Internet exceptionalism, or should the online version be positioned within a longer history of the activity? And should the historical trajectory centre on technology, providers or users to explain the success and form of online practices? For example, a technology-focused history might include the development shopping-cart software, delivery services and banking and credit systems with their attendant regulations. A business history of e-commerce might examine the economic rationales behind business plans and how online and offline enterprises both compete and complement each other (Aspray & Ceruzzi, 2008). A history focused on how users came to trust and value e-commerce could include mail-order catalogues as a familiarising precedent, lower prices as an incentive to buy online, the ability to locate and economically buy or sell hard-to-find goods (such as used or hand-made items) and mechanisms that lower the perceived risk to buyers (such as secure payments and return policies). Different histories offer different policy lessons.

One important framing of online social space theorises the Internet as a "public sphere," with political significance as a place in which a collective understanding of public issues can be formed and political action organised (Benkler, 2006). Attention to political activism highlights the connections between online and offline identities and behaviours. The framework of the online public sphere can be used critically to analyse ways in which the Internet fails to measure up to this political ideal, as when social media platforms create "filter bubbles" (Pariser, 2011) that prevent users' exposure to diverse views. As a historical framework, the concept of the public sphere could also reposition the Internet within the history of the press or of social spaces for information exchange, such as cafes and public squares (Darnton, 2000).

4. The Internet as locally situated experience

The Internet's infrastructure may be global, but for its users, the Internet is always local. Users experience the Internet through specific, locally situated machines, programs, service providers and cultures, and their service providers respond to local markets and regulatory regimes. Economics partially determine what forms of online experience are locally accessible: the geographical coverage of Internet service is highly uneven and reproduces existing power disparities. Castells (2004) has argued that the "network society" is based on "a binary logic: inclusion/exclusion. Within the network, distance between nodes tends to zero... Between nodes in the network and those outside the network distance is infinite" (p. 4). These disparities also exist within local contexts: where access is mediated by the market, class position shapes which of many possible Internets one experiences. As Warschauer (2003) has argued, meaningful access also requires social capital, which could include competency in English or another language not native to the user and an understanding of what types of online services are available and how they might benefit the individual.

Qiu's (2009) study of working-class network users in China illustrates how local constraints on physical interfaces can shape what the Internet means to users. While drawing on Castells's theory of the network society, Qui goes beyond Castells's binary logic of inclusion/exclusion to argue that access is a matter of degree – his subjects are "have-less" rather than "have-nots" – and that different levels of access produce different user experiences. Qiu illustrates how the machines that working-class Chinese use for access (mostly low-end phones) constrain their experience and perception of the Internet's capabilities; many have never used email or search engines and do not regard these communicative and information-seeking tools as part of their Internet. The issue of low-cost interfaces is not unique to China; mobile phones are the primary means of Internet access in much of the developing world (Katz, 2008). Focusing on local access capabilities and practices can force us to reconsider how we define the hardware and software that constitute the Internet. As Dutton (2013) points out, "Internet" is increasingly an umbrella term for "computing, telecommunication, cable and satellite, mobile, and other ICTs," which form a larger "ecology of media and ICTs within which the Internet is embedded" (p. 13).

To see the Internet as local is to see it as multiple. Defining the Internet by local user experience undermines any notion of a singular Internet by showing how users can experience radically different "Internets" based on the technologies and content that their political environment, social position and personal capacities make available. The user's physical ability (sight, hearing, ability to manipulate a keyboard) and fluency in the language(s) used for content and interface software also constrain Internet access and shape user experience. Gender can be another defining factor, since the spaces available for online access, such as Internet cafes, may be off-limits to women in some cultures. These factors mean that the "same" infrastructure can produce extremely variable experiences between users and even for the same user in different situations.

Political issues such as privacy are also defined in important ways by local social settings. A user's privacy depends in part on whether the machine is shared or individually owned and whether the local provider (such as an employer) asserts a right to inspect network traffic. Government censorship and surveillance are another local factor that shapes the type of information available to users as well as the types of interaction and personal expression they feel safe engaging in. Users in a public library, a family living room or a Chinese Internet cafe may face human as well as electronic surveillance.

Another important local variable is the real-world social environment in which the Internet is used, which could include groups of friends, family, classmates or strangers in an Internet cafe. Socially situated Internet use can provide additional capacities to users, such as informal training. Local cultures also colour the meanings users attach to their Internet use. For example, Miller and Slater's study of Internet use in Trinidad shows how national discourse about the Internet draws on local histories and politics; for example, the meaning of "freedom" online is understood in relation to both the nation's history of slavery and its current ideology of neoliberalism (2000, p. 18). While defining the Internet in terms of situated resources and practices highlights the role of social capital and culture, the limitations of this approach are that it does not address the larger, supra-local forces shaping infrastructure and content or the similarities, connections and shared experiences across the global user base.

5. The politics of history

I have argued here that the content and boundaries of "the Internet" depend on the activity, community or issues we wish to focus on in any given case. This means that the definition – and therefore the history – of the Internet depend on why we are asking the question. For example, Streeter (2010) has traced how ideas about the purpose and promise of computer networks have reflected the political and economic ideologies of different decades. He argues that dominant framings of the Internet often reflect the perspectives and interests of those in power; definitions are not innocent. Likewise, questions about the purpose and meaning of history are raised not merely by historians but also by advocates of particular policy positions who would harness history to certify that their views represent the true nature of the Internet. As Haigh et al. (2015), p. 146) warn:

> Tracing a particular practice back to its prehistory in the ARPANET or arguing that a certain philosophy was clearly formulated in the creation of the Internet and has guided it ever since is a way of giving oneself the moral high ground.

Histories that focus on the dominant players, those with the resources to create expensive new technologies, run the risk of privileging their visions in a contemporary Internet system that has, and should take into account, a much broader scope and constituency. Definitions that locate the defining features of the Internet in situated social practices can help challenge the claim of hardware- and software-builders to speak for the Internet. In the arena of public policy, histories that frame the Internet as the evolution of the public sphere can support arguments for protecting freedom of speech or subsidised public access in a way that histories framing the Internet as an entertainment service or a vehicle for private expression would not.

Given the multiple meanings attached to the Internet, it may be misleading even to speak of "the" Internet. Yet the dominance, at least in popular English-language usage, of "the Internet" indicates that there is also a cultural reality to its status as a single global system. Part of the historian's role is to explain how public and expert understandings of "the Internet" have been formed and to what extent these understandings are tied to historical periods, places and cultures. Using "Internet" as an adjective – "Internet histories" instead of "histories of the Internet" – is one way to signal a shift in historical focus from a singular technical entity to its myriad cultural manifestations.

Note

1. Wikipedia, accessed 3 June 2017.

Disclosure statement

No potential conflict of interest was reported by the author.

ORCID

Janet Abbate http://orcid.org/0000-0001-8230-6334

References

Abbate, J. (1999). *Inventing the internet*. Cambridge, MA: MIT Press.
Aspray, W., & Ceruzzi, P. (Eds.) (2008). *The Internet and American business*. Cambridge, MA: MIT Press.
Benkler, Y. (2006). *The wealth of networks how social production transforms markets and freedom*. New Haven, CT: Yale University Press.
Blanchette, J.-F. (2012). Computing as if infrastructure mattered. *Communications of the ACM, 55*(10), 32–34. doi:10.1145/2347736.2347748
Castells, M. (2004). Informationalism, networks, and the network society: A theoretical blueprint. In M. Castells (Ed.), *The network society: A cross-cultural perspective* (pp. 3–45). Cheltenham, UK: Edward Elgar.
Corneliussen, H. G., & Rettberg, J. W. (Eds.) (2008). *Digital culture, play, and identity: A world of warcraft® reader*. Cambridge, MA: MIT Press.
Darnton, R. (2000). An early information society: News and the media in eighteenth-century Paris. *The American Historical Review, 105*(1), 1–35. doi:10.1086/ahr/105.1.1
DeNardis, L. (2009). *Protocol politics: The globalization of Internet governance*. Cambridge, MA: MIT Press.
Dutton, W. H. (2013). Internet studies: The foundations of a transformative field. In W. H. Dutton (Ed.), *The Oxford handbook of internet studies* (pp. 1–23). New York, NY: Oxford University Press.
Franklin, M. (2005). *Postcolonial politics, the internet, and everyday life: Pacific traversals online*. Abingdon: Routledge:.
Gerovitch, S. (2008). InterNyet: Why the Soviet Union did not build a nationwide computer network. *History and Technology, 24*, 335–350. doi:10.1080/07341510802044736
Gillespie, T. (2014). The relevance of algorithms. In T. Gillespie, P. Boczkowski, & K. Foot (Eds.), *Media technologies* (pp. 167–194). Cambridge, MA: MIT Press.
Gottlieb, N., & McLelland, M. (Eds.) (2003). *Japanese cybercultures*. Abingdon: Routledge.
Haigh, T., Russell, A. L., & Dutton, W. H. (2015). Histories of the Internet. *Information & Culture, 50*, 143–159. doi:10.1353/lac.2015.0006
Halavais, A. (2008). *Search engine society*. Cambridge, MA: Polity Press.
Hughes, T. P. (1987). The evolution of large technological systems. In W. E. Bijker, T. P. Hughes, & T. Pinch (Eds.), *The social construction of technological systems* (pp. 51–82). Cambridge, MA: MIT Press.
Katz, J. E. (Ed.) (2008). *Handbook of mobile communication studies*. Cambridge, MA: MIT Press.
Medina, E. (2011). *Cybernetic revolutionaries: Technology and politics in Allende's Chile*. Cambridge, MA: MIT Press.
Miller, D., & Slater, D. (2000). *The internet: An ethnographic approach*. New York, NY: Bloomsbury Academic.
Pariser, E. (2011). *The filter bubble: What the Internet is hiding from you*. London: Penguin Press.
Peters, B. (2016). *How not to network a nation: The uneasy history of the Soviet Internet*. Cambridge, MA: MIT Press.
Qiu, J. L. (2009). *Working-class network society: Communication technology and the information have-less in Urban China*. Cambridge, MA: MIT Press.
Rheingold, H. (1993). *The virtual community: Homesteading on the electronic frontier*. Cambridge, MA: MIT Press.
Schafer, V. (2015). Part of a whole: RENATER, a twenty-year-old network within the internet. *Information & Culture, 50*, 217–235. doi:10.1353/lac.2015.0010
Scholz, T. (Ed.) (2012). *Digital labor: The internet as playground and factory*. New York, NY: Routledge.
Star, S. L., & Ruhleder, K. (1996). Steps toward an ecology of infrastructure: Design and access for large information spaces. *Information Systems Research, 7*, 111–134. doi:10.1287/isre.7.1.111
Streeter, T. (2010). *The net effect: Romanticism, capitalism, and the internet*. New York, NY: NYU Press.
Turkle, S. (1995). *Life on the screen: Identity in the age of the internet*. New York, NY: Simon & Schuster.

Hagiography, revisionism & blasphemy in Internet histories

Andrew L. Russell

ABSTRACT

As a whole, existing histories of the Internet's creation and development are stories of success and triumph. In this respect, they resemble hagiographies, a literary genre that consists of accounts of Christian saints and their miraculous deeds. Internet historians should break free of their familiar hagiographic mode, and treat their historical subjects more critically. The starting point for revisionist histories of networking is an acceptance that the Internet is flawed, dangerous and ephemeral.

Introduction

Evidence mounts daily that the Internet is at best an ambivalent force in the twenty-first century: its core technologies are insecure and often unreliable, and unsavoury elements in our society rely on the Internet to promote visions of abuse, discrimination and hate. However, our existing histories of the Internet's creation and development are, as a whole, stories of success and triumph. There is a significant and jarring tension here – a disconnect between lived experience and historical accounts – that is compelling terrain for historical inquiry.

The enthusiasm woven into the Internet's origin stories is not difficult to understand, given the genuinely transformative possibilities that Internet and Web technologies afford. Moreover, many founding figures of the Internet and Web are charming people, and have made themselves available for journalists and historians to interview and consult. The journalists and historians, in turn, have been all too eager to write narratives of triumph – a common phenomenon with the first generation of accounts of new technologies. As a result, these stories tend to converge on a formulaic plot, with the creators and developers of the Internet cast as heroes, and the bureaucrats in monopolies or governments cast as villains. The bureaucrats lost because they did not embrace the swaths of destruction reaped by the Internet's creation – how silly of them!

This collection of stories – existing academic and popular Internet histories – thus resemble hagiographies, the literary genre that emerged in Europe as accounts of Christian saints and their miraculous deeds. Our hagiographic histories of the Internet need revision, but a revisionist agenda faces significant challenges and resistance. Historians should confront these challenges directly so that our accounts reflect the critical and analytical distance that all professional accounts should embody. This essay proposes a way forward, first by drawing comparisons between hagiographies and Internet histories. I then consider some obstacles to a revisionist agenda for Internet history, such as the co-construction of triumphant narratives of the Internet's success alongside the archival record that documents this purported success. One way to confront this challenge is to create distance between historians and our subjects, which can be accomplished by setting the Internet's history into broader conceptual frames. I propose one such frame, *histories of networking*, before concluding with some suggestions for revision and reinterpretation that may strike some readers – especially the devoted followers of Internet evangelists – as blasphemous.

Hagiographies, past and present

Hagiography is the "name given to that branch of learning which has the saints and their worship for its object" (Delehaye, 1913). One modern authority on the subject is the Jesuit scholar Hippolyte Delehaye, author of the 1907 book *The Legends of the Saints: An Introduction to Hagiography*. Delehaye explained that the practice of hagiography began in the early Christian Church, and took on a more elaborate form throughout Medieval Europe. In the process, hagiographers generated a "considerable number of documents" that range from a list of martyrs and calendars of anniversaries to narratives such as historical memoirs, literary compositions and liturgical texts. These texts eventually grew alongside the genre of secular history, and the two practices shared similar concerns about errors in the classification and analysis of documents as authentically historical. Nevertheless, Delehaye took pains in *The Legends of the Saints* to make clear distinctions between hagiography and history:

> The work of the hagiographer may be historical, but it is not necessarily so. It may assume any literary form suitable to the glorification of the saints, from an official record adapted to the use of the faithful, to a poetical composition of the most exuberant character wholly detached from reality. (Delehaye, 1907)

In his 1913 contribution to *The Catholic Encyclopedia*, Delehaye defined a second definition of hagiography as "scientific hagiography", which is the critical study of the sources and production of hagiographic texts. Some scientific hagiographies investigate the paucity of sources (including archaeological evidence), others scrutinise the details of hagiographic texts and martyrologies, and still others seek to address the accounts that erroneously conflate the lives of saints with myths and legends. This scientific tradition within hagiography came into closer alignment with the scientific approach to history that emerged in the nineteenth-century Europe and the United States, manifest in the work and teachings of Leopold von Ranke. But the crucial difference remained with the analyst's view of the ontological status of their subjects. Critical and scientific hagiographers did not engage in heresy: they did not undermine the sanctity of the saints and martyrs that they studied. Even the most rigorous and sophisticated examination of hagiographic sources and texts accepted the fundamental theological premises of Christian doctrine. Such overt displays of faith toward their historical subjects are the defining differences between the eternal reverence of the hagiographers and the occasional irreverence of secular (what von Ranke called "scientific") historians. One canonical example of such irreverence can be found in revisionist interpretations of the American Revolution of the 1770s and 1780s. In contrast to nationalist interpretations that cast founding fathers such as Washington and Jefferson in marble, John Bach McMaster attacked these figures with his 1896 essay "The Political Depravity of the Founding Fathers" (see generally, Novick, 1988; Wood, 2006)

I invoke the contrasts between hagiography and secular histories because they shed light on professional and popular accounts of the Internet's history. Hagiographers do not call into question the fundamental status of the saints or the tenets of the Christian faith itself, such as the belief in the Holy Trinity or the inspired and infallible status of God's word as given by the prophets. Similarly, Internet histories reify the status of the TCP/IP Internet as a triumph, and construct an air of infallibility about the people and institutions that created it. These histories contain no trace of the possibility that the core technologies of the ARPANET or Internet are fundamentally flawed, or that protagonists in Internet history such as Paul Baran, Robert Kahn or Tim Berners-Lee might have been acting out of selfish ambition.

Among the historical accounts of the Internet treat their subject with deep and unquestioning reverence, some use terminology that is explicitly spiritual. For example, Jack Goldsmith and Timothy Wu's influential 2006 book *Who Controls the Internet?* features a chapter titled "The God of the Internet". The chapter profiles Jon Postel, whose long white beard and ever-present sandals made him an especially memorable character in the early Internet's technical community. Esther Dyson, chair of the controversial Internet Corporation for Advanced Names and Numbers (ICANN) from 1998 to 2000, actually has referred to Postel as a "saint". (Roush, 2012). Such religious language has deep roots in programmer communities, as Christopher Kelty has demonstrated through his discussion of affinity that "geeks" have for allegories of the Protestant Reformation, "religious wars", and "holy wars" among programmers with different points of view (Kelty, 2008). These metaphors persist in popular and corporate culture, such as in the role of corporate "technology evangelist". To give one example of deep significance, Vint Cerf, co-creator of the Internet's foundational TCP/IP standards, joined Google in 2005 and chose the title of "Chief Internet Evangelist".

Internet histories, as a whole, are rife with an implicit sense of admiration and deference (Greenstein, 2015; Hafner & Lyon, 1996; Hauben & Hauben, 1997; Rheingold, 2000; Segaller, 1998; Veà, 2013; Waldrop, 2001; Wu, 2010). In Mariana Mazzucato's *The Entrepreneurial State*, for example, DARPA's sponsorship of the ARPANET and Internet appears as a paragon for innovation – a process that, like the Internet and its development, the author assumes to be a universally good thing. It is precisely this approach, where authors can safely assume that their audiences will accept that particular subjects are beyond criticism or reproach that should give professional historians pause.

Fortunately, there are ARPANET and Internet histories that bring a more critical and sophisticated reading to their subject. These authors broke out of the hagiographic mode precisely because of their immersion in critical scholarly traditions, and their distance from having any personal stake in the outcome of the stories they told. The most authoritative history of the ARPANET and Internet, Janet Abbate's *Inventing the Internet*, deploys a social constructivist approach that refrains from any explicit moral judgments – even if the book clearly sits more comfortably into a genre of "success story" than "failure story". Paul Edwards' *The Closed World* comes from a similar constructivist tradition, but takes a stronger critical stance by situating the growth of the ARPANET within the context of American Cold War militarism and "the deepening crisis of culture in an increasingly root-less world". (Edwards, 1996). The moral ambiguity of computer networks in general and the Internet specifically are also highlighted in Neil Randall's *The Soul of the Internet: Net Gods, Netizens and the Wiring of the World*. Despite the divine allusion in his subtitle, Ran-dall was deeply anxious about the Internet's "soul", drawing repeated comparisons between the Internet and Frankenstein's monster. These three accounts should have planted seeds in the minds of attentive readers, and can support further reinterpretation of the Internet's development as something other than the work of gods, saints and evangelists.

Obstacles and archives

One obstacle to a revisionist (or blasphemous) history of the Internet is the available record of primary source materials. These materials exist as hybrids of paper and digital documents, with some paper documents now scanned and available online, and some "born digital" documents now available only in printed copy. The challenges to digital preservation are well understood, but formidable nevertheless. Likewise, the challenges to creating traditional archival collections for Internet history are well understood, and several efforts are currently underway to preserve the documentary traces that institutions and individuals created since the early days of packet switching in the 1960s.

Although the existing archival record is a perpetual work in progress, there are a few general patterns worth noting. First, there is a significant body of oral history interview transcripts available from institutions such as the Charles Babbage Institute, IEEE History Center, and Computer History Museum. While these transcripts continue to be mined by historians, as a corpus they carry an implicit bias: they consist only of people who histori-ans have deemed necessary to interview, and therefore, omit people who, for whatever reason, have not made themselves known to interviewers. Some people passed away before they sat for interviews; others moved away from the networking field and have escaped the notice of historians; and still others either do not want to speak on the record, or do not want to speak to historians at all. As a result, the record is rich with recollections from ARPA and Internet insiders such as Vint Cerf, Larry Roberts and Leonard Kleinrock – and many other insiders, such as Alex McKenzie, have donated personal copies of rare documents for archival collections. There are some encouraging signs that historians can reinterpret familiar sources, such as the ARPANET network maps, in creative and genera-tive ways (Fider & Currie, 2016). Nevertheless, there are striking gaps and silences in exist-ing oral histories and archival collections, and some important people have been rendered all but invisible. As with all archival and oral history collections, the very act of collecting constructs, new hierarchies of power and importance that did not necessarily exist in the past. At the same time, this process can marginalise individuals as well as entire sections or demographics of people who, for various reasons, do not fall into the gaze of historians (see generally, Perks & Thomson, 1998).

Because they take an active role in shaping the archival record and its interpretations, Internet insiders have been able to whisper in Clio's ear. Many Internet pioneers are alive, active and eager to shape the histories that describe their accomplishments. Some disre-gard professional norms through interpretations that flatter themselves and their friends while ignoring contrary evidence (Partridge, 2016). Museums are equally eager to publicise pioneer stories and create exhibits for public consumption. In the process, it is normal for everyone involved to leave out unsavoury or unflattering aspects of the past. Internet history is being written, tweeted, blogged and podcasted by the victors, through accounts that celebrate themselves and vilify their vanquished rivals.

My own experience with oral history interviewing provides a case in point. When I started graduate school, I was lucky to meet and learn from Internet pioneers such as Vint Cerf and David Clark. My first oral history interview was with David Mills, an early participant in the Internet Engineering Task Force who made crucial (and still underappreciated) contributions to routing and network time synchronisation. Mills described a conflict between charismatic Internet leaders – "Priests of the West" – and the "Priests of the East" who developed Open Systems Interconnection, a rival system of the Internet. Mills characterised the latter group as "European Union [...] They're faceless". I grew curious about this group of faceless Europeans, and eventually interviewed some "Priests of the East" including the French computer scientist Louis Pouzin, thinking that I would encounter the petty and clueless villains of Internet history. I was wrong, of course, and the brilliant and charismatic Pouzin explained that the real villains were the engineers working in telecom and computing monopolies. Subsequent interviews with some of those engineers – the IBM veteran Marc Levilion and Rémi Després of France Telecom – helped me understand that their technical choices were reasonable and creative responses to their institutional constraints and priorities. Indeed, by their accounts, it was the technical approach implemented in the TCP/IP Internet that was careless and naïve. My interviewees had spun me completely around; I often think about them as standing in a virtual circle, all wearing "I'm With Stupid" tee shirts, forming an infinite loop of contempt (Després, 2012; Levilion, 2012; Mills, 2004; Pouzin, 2012)

Histories of networking

Many of the omissions and blind spots in the source material for Internet histories – as well as the historiography of the Internet – could be addressed by confronting a category error in historical conceptualisation. The category error operates in the following way: curiosity about the Internet prompts questions about where the Internet came from, which, in turn, prompt investigations into the Internet's history. The story then is researched and written in a teleological fashion: what were the forces in the past that led to our present moment in its current configuration? This dynamic appears, for example, in accounts that sketch the history of "Net Neutrality": they excavate the past for an anachronistic genealogy of the present moment, cruelly stripping ideas and practices from their formative contexts (see, for example, Madrigal & LaFrance, 2014).

The very title of this journal reflects a welcome (if partial) rebuke to such category errors. The name *Internet Histories* carries the notion that there are many ways to tell the Internet's story, and that our existing histories of the Internet have only scratched the surface. I would take this rebuke one step further, and suggest that we could benefit from situating the Internet's past in an even broader conceptual frame, *histories of networking*. The histories of the ARPANET and TCP/IP Internet fit within this broader frame, but there also is space for histories of other networks and the people who built and used them. Some of these networks are computer networks that fit neatly next to the Internet and ARPANET in terms of chronology and technology, such as Usenet, Fidonet, Minitel, Cyclades and so on. Histories of networking also include developments in data networking, telecommunications, railroading and wireless transmission that do not fit neatly into the narrative of the Internet's success. In other words, this enlarged category encompasses projects that are not necessarily part of the established linear history of the Internet but are, nevertheless, relevant for historical assessments of social and technological phenomena that we associate with the Internet (Campbell-Kelly & Garcia-Swartz, 2013; Driscoll, 2016; Russell, 2012, 2013)

One advantage to the "histories of networking" concept is that it compels Internet historians to engage more directly with accounts that do not deal with computer networks. Two examples are Nicole Starosielski's *The Undersea Network* and Venus Green's *Race on the Line*. The former book investigates some historical and theoretical issues related to undersea cables, which enabled intercontinental communication far before modern computers or the Internet. Starosielski's account helps scholars focused on the Internet to understand the longer colonial and material dimensions of intercontinental communications. *Race on the Line* also brings the nineteenth century into conversation with the twentieth and twenty-first through a study of race, gender and labour in the American telephone industry from the 1870s to the 1980s. Green's account introduces historical and conceptual richness in a way that is more or less absent from existing Internet historiography. This is not to say that race and gender are absent from the actual lived *history* of internetworking – rather, scholars who are focused on writing about the history of the TCP/IP Internet have not adequately represented those themes. Indeed, *Race on the Line* can help Internet historians see that historical writing about technologies can mature and change over time: narratives of invention and discovery can, eventually, give way to richer and more complex stories that historians do not hear from pioneers who are asked to tell their heroic tales.

To be sure, the expanded category of "histories of networking" raises some tricky methodological questions. For example, the category invokes some distance from the historical specificity of digital computer networks that are at the core of the TCP/IP Internet and its histories. What would such "histories of networking" use as a starting point, since, after all, social and material networks are characteristics of all human cultures? Rather than see this epistemological uncertainty as a risk, my proposal here is that it is an opportunity for Internet historians to engage more directly with questions that they miss when they use the ARPANET as their starting point. For example, Ingrid Burrington proposed that the American transcontinental railroad is a useful starting point for histories of the Internet's infrastructure and data centres. Greg Downey has demonstrated how the work telegraph messenger boys of the nineteenth century help us think more clearly about the place of labour in so-called information revolutions. In my own work, I have documented how the Internet's standards-setting process mimics the culture and process of engineering committees that were worked out between the 1880s and 1920s (Burrington, 2015; Downey, 2001; Russell, 2014). Each of these approaches pushes historians to consider continuities between the Internet era and previous eras in human history. In doing so, they chip away at the veneer of innovation and novelty painted by accounts that present the Internet as something exceptional or unprecedented.

There is reason to be optimistic that new scholarship, guided by methods from outside the historical profession, will generate source material that will help future historians reckon with the ongoing development of the Internet. Existing histories focus primarily on the production of networking technologies; future histories will reckon more squarely with the diverse groups of users who have woven the Internet into the fabric of everyday life. One example is the University College London project "Why We Post", a remarkable collective effort by nine anthropologists who each spent fifteen months living with user communities around the world (Miller et al., 2016). The lesson here is that as time passes from the Internet's origins, the subjects of our history and scholarly modes of analysis also can become more diverse and multifaceted as well.

Blasphemies and tragedies

One benefit of moving from "Internet History" to "Histories of Networking" is an enhanced ability to create critical and scholarly distance from the TCP/IP Internet itself. When the Internet is no longer the total field of inquiry, no longer the one true faith, it becomes possible to evaluate it not as a gift from the gods, but rather as a human creation – *flawed*, *dangerous* and *ephemeral*.

One does not need a computer science degree to understand that the design of the Internet is *flawed*. Spammers and scammers easily take advantage of lax security, disrupting personal communications, commercial transactions and even national elections. And Internet connections can be unreliable, as users who are in crowds, rural areas or on the move have discovered. Internet experts have known about these problems for many years, and "clean-slate" redesigns of the Internet's architecture have been seriously and regularly proposed since the early 1990s. Yet, the QWERTY phenomenon of economic and technical lock-in to a dominant standard has prevented new designs from being implemented in any significant way (Geddes, 2015, 2017).

It did not need to be this way. Several scholars have looked closely at international discussions during the 1970s, and have drawn two conclusions that are significant for the historiography of the Internet. First, TCP/IP's design did not have the majority support of the international community. That community voted in 1975 to support an alternative protocol of internetworking; it was only when the results of that vote were publicised that DARPA scientists Robert Kahn and Vint Cerf decided to ignore the community consensus and stick with their own approach (Day, 2016; McKenzie, 2011; Russell, 2014). They then turned to an implementation phase, preferring to build out a network instead of pursuing research that could have improved some aspects of their design (such as its lack of security and flawed approach to addressing and routing). The computer scientist John Day has an apt description for this approach: "engineering without science" (Day, 2008). The second significant conclusion is that Kahn and Cerf's decision to ignore the international community was driven and facilitated by political and economic considerations, rather than a mere difference of technical opinion. Fuelled by the tax dollars of Cold War Americans, DARPA had the mandate and resources to build its own network. Its leaders saw no need to get caught up in the politics of international standards, and found it to their advantage to use an autocratic style of network governance (Russell, 2014). The result is that the ARPANET and TCP/IP standards emerged more quickly than any alternatives, and at a lower cost – and thus emerged triumphant from an era of competition in internetworking standards (Pelkey, 2007). But we should not confuse this victory for a sign of technical superiority. As Day has put it: "Of the 4 protocols we could have chosen in the late

70s, TCP was (and remains) the worst choice, but they were spending many times more money than everyone else combined" (Emerson & Day, 2015).

Moving forward in time, we can see clear evidence that the Internet can be *dangerous*. Dreams of liberation from the 1990s – most famously in John Perry Barlow's "Declaration of Independence of Cyberspace" – have given way to a more realistic understanding that the Internet is being used as a tool of control that undermines individual autonomy. Many accounts of the Internet's history and design philosophy have sought to explain the Internet's promise for a new era of decentralised, global and peer-to-peer "network society" (Benkler, 2006; Castells, 2003). However, as scholars come to understand the actual conditions of total surveillance by government organisations such as the American NSA and British GCHQ and corporate behemoths such as Google and Facebook, they might take a less optimistic view of the history of networks such as the Internet. Internet trolls are no longer minor irritants on the peripheries of acceptable behaviour; they now have central roles as power brokers in business and politics (Phillips, 2015). Some conceptual and empirical grounding for a more pessimistic view of the Internet's history may be found in Edwards's *The Closed World*, Gandall's *The Soul of the Internet* and Evgeny Morozov's *The Net Delusion*. The philosopher Ken Wilber put the point clearly in the 2001 edition of his book *A Brief History of Everything*: "The Nazis would have loved the Net. The neo-Nazis certainly do. The FBI reports that hate-group activity has dramatically skyrocketed, thanks to the Net, which allows these people to find one another" (Wilber, 2001). This view put Wilber in a tiny, cynical minority in 2001, but the resurgence of organised white supremacists in 2016 makes his remarks seem, well, prophetic.

Finally, revisionist histories of the Internet could do more to emphasise its *ephemeral* qualities. Situating the Internet within the broader and longer from of histories of networking is an effective way to emphasise this point. A cursory review of other forms of networked communication, such as telegraphy, telephony, radio, television and fax, shows that routines of use or ownership rarely last more than a few decades. As a result, historians would be wise to use more critical reflection when they see journalistic or policy-oriented accounts that use the halcyon days of the late 1990s – free music downloads in a world of entrepreneurship and innovation – as a normative baseline for network histories. Feel-good slogans like Stewart Brand's "information wants to be free" were powerful motivators for historical actors, but should not be interpreted as timeless truths. Indeed, pundits have been warning for several years that a unified, end-to-end model of the Internet already has given way to a splintered, balkanised Internet, filled with dark webs and secluded islands (Gehl, 2016; *The Economist*, 2010; Naughton, 2013).

Conclusions

To call for revisionist and blasphemous Internet histories may be interpreted by true believers as a sign of disrespect. In fact, it's the opposite – it comes from a recognition that the Internet must receive the same kind of measured analysis and debate that historians employ with other developments of profound societal significance. Revisionism would be a welcome development because it would show that Internet and network historians reject the whiggish approach that is common throughout histories of science, technology and medicine (On whiggism, see Jardine, 2003; Mayr, 1990).

In his landmark 1998 review essay in the *American Historical Review*, Roy Rosenzweig argued that the emergence of the Internet "needs to be rooted in the 1960s – in the 'closed world' of the Cold War and the open and decentralized world of the antiwar movement and the counterculture" (Rosenzweig, 1998). From the intervening 20 years, historians should have learned that it is not enough to root Internet historiography merely in this binary interpretation of the American 1960s. We will need to continue with Rosenzweig's contextualist approach, but also carry it from 1970s through the present moment, and set the Internet's development into a global context. We must resist the urge to sanctify even the kindest of individuals who feature in our histories, and we should learn to view computer networks and internetworks in a more prismatic way that can account for their moral and political ambiguities. A viable critical tradition in histories of networking would take a tragic interpretation of the Internet's history more seriously – analogous to studies of historiographical debates around American foreign policy (Williams, 1959). Data networks such as the Internet have seeped into modern life in unpredictable ways, and our historical accounts should be wary of conceptual boundaries that would pin down something so flawed, dangerous and ephemeral.

Acknowledgments

I am grateful for comments from Brad Fidler, James E. McClellan III and two anonymous reviewers. They pushed me to sharpen some points in this essay and soften others. The rough edges that persist are my sole responsibility.

Disclosure statement

No potential conflict of interest was reported by the author.

References

A virtual counter-revolution. (2010, September 2). *The Economist*. Retrieved from http://www.econo mist.com/node/16941635

Benkler, Y. (2006). *The wealth of networks: How social production transforms markets and freedom.* New Haven, CT: Yale University Press.

Burrington, I. (2015, November 24). How railroad history shaped internet history. The Atlantic. Retrieved from https://www.theatlantic.com/technology/archive/2015/11/how-railroad-history-shaped-internet-history/417414/

Campbell-Kelly, M., & Garcia-Swartz, D. D. (2013). The history of the Internet: The missing narratives. *Journal of Information Technology, 28*, 18–33.

Castells, M. (2003). *The Internet galaxy: Reflections on the internet, business, and society*. Oxford: Oxford University Press.

Day, J. (2008). *Patterns in network architecture: A return to fundamentals*. Upper Saddle River, NJ: Prentice Hall PTR. p. 223.

Day, J. (2016). The clamor outside as INWG debated: Economic war comes to networking. *IEEE Annals of the History of Computing, 37*(3), 58–77.

Delehaye, H. (1907). *The legends of the saints: An introduction to hagiography*. New York, NY: Longmans, Green, and Co. p. 2.

Delehaye, H. (1913). Hagiography. *Catholic Encyclopedia,* Retrieved from https://en.wikisource.org/wiki/Catholic_Encyclopedia_(1913)/Hagiography

Després, R. (2012, May 16). *Oral history interview by Valérie Schafer*. Paris: Charles Babbage Institute, University of Minnesota, Minneapolis.

Downey, G. J. (2001). Virtual webs, physical technologies, and hidden workers: The spaces of labor in information internetworks. *Technology & Culture, 42*(2), 209–235.

Driscoll, K. (2016). Social media's dial-up ancestor: The bulletin board system. *IEEE Spectrum, 53*, 54–60.

Edwards, P. (1996). *The closed world: Computers and the politics of discourse in cold war America*. Cambridge, MA: MIT Press. p. 365.

Emerson, L., & Day, J. (2015). What's wrong with the Internet and how to fix it: An interview with Internet pioneer John Day. *Ctrl-Z: New Media Philosophy*, 5. Retrieved from http://www.ctrl-z.net.au/journal/?slug=emerson-day-whats-wrong-with-the-internet-and-how-to-fix-it

Fider, B., & Currie, M. (2016). Infrastructure, representation, and historiography in BBN's Arpanet Maps. *IEEE Annals of the History of Computing, 38*(3), 44–57.

Geddes, M. (2015). The Internet is just a prototype. Retrieved from https://medium.com/@martingeddes/the-internet-is-just-a-prototype-9adb2633d32c

Geddes, M. (2017). Let's face facts: We need a new industrial Internet. Retrieved from https://medium.com/@martingeddes/lets-face-facts-we-need-a-new-industrial-internet-ae6b382a278.

Gehl, R. W. (2016). Power/freedom on the dark web: A digital ethnography of the Dark Web Social Network. *New Media & Society, 18*(7), 1219–1235.

Greenstein, S. (2015). *How the Internet became commercial: Innovation, privatization, and the birth of a new network*. Princeton, NJ: Princeton University Press.

Hafner, K., & Lyon, M. (1996). *Where wizards stay up late: The origins of the Internet*. New York, NY: Simon & Schuster.

Hauben, M., & Hauben, R. (1997). *Netizens: On the history and impact of Usenet and the Internet*. Los Alamitos, CA: Wiley-IEEE Computer Press.

Jardine, N. (2003). Whigs and stories: Herbert Butterfield and the historiography of science. *History of Science, 41*, 125–140.

Kelty, C. M. (2008). *Two bits: The cultural significance of free software*. Durham, NC: Duke University Press.

Levilion, M. E. (2012, April 2). *Oral history interview by Andrew L. Russell*, Paris. Minneapolis, MN: Charles Babbage Institute, University of Minnesota.

Madrigal, A. C., & LaFrance, A. (2014, April 25). Net neutrality: A guide to (and history of) a contested idea. *The Atlantic*. Retrieved from http://www.theatlantic.com/technology/archive/2014/04/the-best-writing-on-net-neutrality/361237/

Mayr, E. (1990). When is historiography whiggish? *Journal of the History of Ideas, 51*, 301–309.

McKenzie, A. (2011). INWG and the conception of the Internet: An eyewitness account. *IEEE Annals of the History of Computing, 33*, 66–71.

Mills, D. (2004, February 26). *Oral history interview by Andrew L. Russell*, Newark, DE, Minneapolis: Charles Babbage Institute, University of Minnesota.

Miller, D., Costa, E., Haynes, N., McDonald, T., Nicolescu, R., Sinanan, J., … Wang, X. (2016). *How the world changed social media*. London: UCL Press.

Naughton, J. (2013, July 27). Edward Snowden's not the story. The fate of the Internet is. *The Guardian*. Retrieved from https://www.theguardian.com/technology/2013/jul/28/edward-snowden-death-of-internet

Novick, P. (1988). *That noble dream: The 'objectivity question' and the American historical profession*. New York, NY: Cambridge University Press.

Partridge, C. (2016). The restructuring of internet standards governance: 1987–1992. *IEEE Annals of the History of Computing, 37*(3), 25–43.

Pelkey, J. (2007). *Entrepreneurial capitalism & innovation: A history of computer communications, 1968–1988*. Retrieved from http://www.historyofcomputercommunications.info/.

Perks, R., & Thomson, A. (1998). *The oral history reader*. London: Routledge.

Phillips, W. (2015). *This is why we can't have nice things: Mapping the relationship between online trolling and mainstream culture*. Cambridge, MA: MIT Press.

Pouzin, L. (2012, April 2). *Oral history interview by Andrew L. Russell*, Paris, Minneapolis: Charles Babbage Institute, University of Minnesota.

Rheingold, H. (2000 [1985]). *Tools for thought: The history and future of mind-expanding technology*. Cambridge: The MIT Press.

Rosenzweig, R. (1998). Wizards, bureaucrats, warriors & hackers: Writing the history of the internet. *American Historical Review, 103*(5), 1531.

Roush, W. (2012). ICANN's boondoggle. *MIT Technology Review*. Retrieved from https://www.technologyreview.com/s/428911/icanns-boondoggle/

Russell, A. L. (2012, October). Histories of networking vs. the history of the internet. Paper presented at the SIGCIS 2012 Workshop, Copenhagen.

Russell, A. L. (2013). The Internet that wasn't. *IEEE Spectrum, 50*, 38–43.

Russell, A. L. (2014). *Open standards and the digital age: History, ideology, and networks*. New York, NY: Cambridge University Press.

Segaller, S. (1998). *Nerds 2.0.1: A brief history of the internet*. New York, NY: TV Books.

Veà, A. (2013). *Cómo creamos Internet*. Barcelona: Península.

Waldrop, M. (2001). *The dream machine: J. C. R. Licklider and the revolution that made computing personal*. New York, NY: Viking.

Wilber, K. (2001). *A brief history of everything*. Shambhala. pp. 284.

Williams, W. A. (1959). *The tragedy of American diplomacy*. New York, NY: W. W. Norton & Co.

Wood, G. S. (2006). *Revolutionary characters: What made the founding fathers different*. New York, NY: Penguin.

Wu, T. (2010). *The master switch: The rise and fall of information empires*. New York, NY: Knopf.

A common language*

Marc Weber

ABSTRACT
Both the Internet and the Web beat out numerous rivals to become today's dominant network and online system,[1] respectively. Many of those rival systems and networks had developed alternative solutions to issues that face us today, from micropayments to copyright. But few scholars, much less thought leaders, have a meaningful overview of the origins of our online world, or of the many systems which came before. This exclusivity is a problem, since as a society we are now making some of the permanent decisions that will determine how we deal with information for decades and even centuries to come. Those decisions are about regulatory structures, economic models, civil liberties, publishing and more. This essay argues for the need to comparatively study online information systems across all these axes, and to thus develop a "common language" of known precedents and concepts as a prerequisite for making informed discussions about the future of the online world. Doing so depends on two factors: (1) preservation of enough historical materials about earlier systems to be able to meaningfully examine them; (2) interdisciplinary, international attention to "meta" stories that emerge from considering the evolution of multiple networks and online systems.

Introduction

When I told people I was researching the history of the Web in early 1995, about half of them were amused: "But it's too young to have a history!" "When was it invented, last week?" Others simply took it in stride. *Everything* was surprising about this hot new medium, and the idea of somebody researching its surely flimsy history seemed no more odd – or comprehensible – than companies which sold nothing and had names like "Yahoo!" A few people were intrigued.

For most of the time since, society moved straight from that early puzzlement to a kind of incurious acceptance. The future of the online world remains perpetually ablaze with promise, fanned by the wide-eyed predictions of tech blogs and magazines. But most people know more about the evolution of the light bulb or the personal computer than of

---

*Portions of this article may be published in a slightly different form in a forthcoming book by the author from Thomas Dunne Books/St. Martin's Press.

this great transformation of our time. The online past remains a murky patchwork – a terra incognita occasionally illuminated by the reflection of one shining myth or another.

Until recently, this public ignorance was matched by tepid interest from most researchers (for more details, see Weber, 2016). But in the last few years something reached critical mass, especially among scholars. Why it happened now, and not before or later, is a mystery to me and long-time colleagues. But there is, finally, a swell of serious interest in the origins of the online world, from the wires it runs over, to networking protocols, to the Web and other online systems that help us navigate those networks. This journal is itself an important marker of that change.

Yet it is still early days. And the biggest problem is that the new interest remains highly fragmented. The work many people are doing is excellent, and appropriate to the precepts of their own disciplines. But few have a solid sense of the evolution of the online world as a whole, or the sheer variety of systems that came before. This makes it hard to have meaningful discussions about its past, but also about its future. It's as if the first generation of anthropologists was busy trying to kick-start the field of comparative studies while remaining innocent of a continent or two.

What scholars know also matters because they play a role in predigesting a new area. Obviously, the average person is unlikely to ever want many details of how the online world evolved. But the shorthand versions that *do* become common knowledge will be partly based on what the experts say and write. If they are missing part of the story, that carries forward.

To take one small specific example, the commercial networks of the 1970s – Telenet, Tymnet, General Electric Information Services (GEIS), the corporate-facing side of CompuServe – were more significant at the time than the research-only ARPANET and the experiments that eventually led to the Internet. The commercial networks spanned the globe and served paying customers of all kinds. They also hosted a huge variety of services, including unique early e-commerce and group collaboration systems. Yet the Internet *did* eventually become very important, and this has thrown its distant past into disproportionate relief. Even minor players in the ARPANET get interviewed over and over again by successive waves of researchers, journalists and filmmakers; much popular writing makes it sound like the ARPANET and Internet were the only networking protocols around back then. Savvier scholars may know there was more to the story, but are short on details. The 1970s commercial networks are remembered mostly by their own aging creators.

Closer to our time, few people realise the Web was invented to be an interactive medium with authoring as a core feature every browser, in contrast with the more consumption-oriented platform it has become as chronicled by Gillies and Cailliau (2000) among others. Web 2.0 and early social media like GeoCities were attempts to add back some authoring to read-only browsers.

Figure 1 gives a sense of the sweep of systems and standards in the shortish history of connected computing. It's a little like early maps full of blank spaces; only the handful of entries in bold are relatively well researched and preserved. Campbell-Kelly and Garcia-Schwartz (2013) also pointed out much of the missing terrain.

The current state of affairs is not for lack of trying by a number of people, including myself, colleagues, some historians, and Web and hypertext pioneers. Over the past two decades, there have been books, exhibits, history tracks at Web conferences and more than a few articles. The Internet Archive has been preserving snapshots of the Web at regular intervals since 1996.

Online History by level

Users

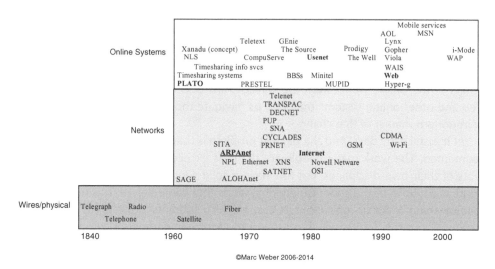

©Marc Weber 2006-2014

Figure 1. Online history by time and level. Systems shown are meant to be representative, not complete. Those in bold are known to the author to be reasonably preserved; in bold *and* underlined quite well preserved including oral histories. The ARPAnet is the only one that meets both criteria; better known systems tend to be better preserved.

But those who have a kind of "meta" knowledge of the evolution of cyberspace remain a small club. This exclusivity is not just an academic problem, since today's companies, government agencies and NGOS are now making some of the permanent decisions that will determine how society deals with information for decades and even centuries to come. Those decisions are about regulatory structures, economic models, civil liberties, publishing and more.

Our age is perhaps comparable to that of the "Victorian Internet" 150 years ago when the most basic frameworks of telegraph systems, railroads, libraries and modern journalism were hammered out. Regulatory decisions made in the reign of Queen Victoria still channel the flow of the modern world's information, not to mention quadrillions of dollars earned from its movement.

The penchant for creating monopolies back then birthed firms that now sell you bleeding-edge smartphones (AT&T, origins 1879; T-Mobile aka Deutsche Telekom, origins 1870; etc.). They are regulated by the International Telecommunications Union, founded in 1865. You read about their latest antics under a patent system shaped by the telegraphy disputes of the 1850s, in a newspaper often called some variation of the *Telegraph* – a relic of the electrically-assisted birth of modern journalism. The Western Union money transfers you see advertised in bodega windows were pioneered in 1878, when the company was 20 years old, and so on.

Back in those days of brass and steam, there were few direct precedents to study. Automated communication really was a brave new world. Today, we can look to that 170-year history, as well as the last century of what we might term "world brain" ideas[2], from H. G. Wells to Otlet to Nelson, and 60 years of actually going online with computers. That is if we bother, and if we preserve enough material. The latter is a topic I will touch on below, along with the kinds of uses we might have for what gets preserved.

Far from an immaculate conception, our familiar online world is built on shards of earlier systems. When you click on a link, you are using a concept invented as one tiny part of a grand internationalist vision of the early twentieth century for a "world brain" on microfilm and paper — a brain meant to power a new era of world peace through knowledge.[3]

The mouse whose button you click is one of the few survivors of Douglas Engelbart's poignantly ambitious 1960s effort to teach us to navigate and "play" human knowledge with the ease that a virtuoso plays music, and thus make ourselves capable of solving the world's problems.

The smartphone that brings the Web to your pocket echoes Alan Kay's 1968 vision of the personal Dynabook,[4] as well as Nikola Tesla's 1901 attempt to build a global, mobile "World System". Except that Tesla's version also involved electrifying the entire earth's atmosphere (!), as noted by his biographer Carlson (2013).

Even the Web we know is just one part of its inventors' far grander original vision (Berners-Lee & Fischetti, 2000; Gillies & Cailliau, 2000).

The fact that so many visions ran aground has left many features out there untapped, a great silent library of experiments waiting to be tried as the online world unfolds. Some have already been partly reinvented, like Wikis as a baby step towards older visions of full online collaboration by Engelbart, Nelson[5] and Berners-Lee.[6] Others, from ways of deeply structuring information to new publishing models based on micropayments, may need a future age to weigh their promise. All told, just the Web alone had well over a *dozen* direct predecessors, both visions and real-world systems.

Consider the main kinds of systems involved in the evolution of the online world, as depicted in Figure 1. The timeline is broken out by level, like a very simplified version of the networking layer model.[7] Online systems like the Web are shown on the top level. Networks are shown on the level below, and physical infrastructure on the bottom layer. Such predecessors remain some of the few detailed guides to possible futures for our own life online.

Why do such guides matter? Because online systems deal with the most basic ways we communicate and navigate raw information, and with the still mysterious processes that transform it into knowledge. This makes them far more than a set of "gee whiz" techie features. Just as a free press or its absence can shape politics, the methods we use for sharing – which also means buying, selling and controlling – information are a fulcrum that can shift history.

For instance, a world where being able to freely read and *write* on a universal medium is technically easy and legally protected (no, we're not there now) really would be different from one where a few corporations control mutually incompatible "walled gardens", like the old CompuServe and AOL or their many would-be successors. Or a world where a government monopoly runs a national "web" as in the old French Minitel system – guaranteeing goodies like security and payment while also tightly controlling software and who can run a server. Or any of a dozen other possible scenarios.

Some of the key decision points coming up are around net neutrality, governance (now moving outward from the United States), and unity – will there be one Web and Internet, or a feudal chessboard of *de facto* national ones?

Then there are the many decisions about privacy and surveillance. From a purely technical point of view, your smartphone is a perfect panopticon adapted for the pocket or purse. But who, if anyone, is on the other end watching you is the product of concrete policies.

Fake news is a perverse consequence of advertising as a revenue model – whether something is true or not is independent of its ability to draw eyeballs. How we deal with it can have consequences for some time to come.

Technology is not destiny. Many today think of the Gutenberg press as a great disruptor, by its very nature transforming traditional ways of handling knowledge at every step. This is plausible when the focus is Europe. But rarely mentioned is that the Gutenberg press – and early forms of both block and movable type printing – were absorbed by many societies all over the world with little effect on existing practices for the movement, creation or sharing of information. The essays in Suarez and Woudhuysen (2013) exhaustively detail this differential impact.

So the details of *how* we implement online systems matter. Far from being over, the InterWeb revolution is just beginning. In print terms, it's as if Gutenberg is still alive and the year is 1460. The basic shape of the book is still up for grabs, as well as who gets to read and write it, and censor it, and profit from its sale.

Or perhaps we are even further back in this analogy: in the dawn times when Sumerian bureaucrats first began to press flattened sticks into wet clay to mark cattle, wheat and ore.

Either way, there is a lot at stake.

A common language

Can we learn directly from the past? I'm not sure it matters – whether or not we draw explicit lessons, the online world's history is important as a shared frame of reference, a common language for naming and comparing the moving parts within this great revolution of our time.

When we discuss politics, or science, or literature, we use the language of the past. We talk of Newtonian physics, Euclidean geometry and Marx's vision; of an Art Nouveau sensibility, of Boyle's Law and Galileo's cosmology and Plato's republic and ideal world.

This does not mean we use them all today. But we have heard of them. They are touchstones, often proper names for current schools of thought. The scientific method itself is explicitly built around a literature of past ideas which have been proven or cast aside.

Yet when it comes to schemes for navigating all of human knowledge with machines, a process now transforming society as fundamentally as any invention you care to name (printing press? indoor plumbing? bureaucracy?), we are only starting to accumulate enough shared knowledge to even have proper arguments.

I will use myself as an example. Back in 1995, I immersed myself in the history of the *Web,* and to an extent its roots in hypertext. For a long time, my perspective on the rest of cyberspace was a bit like the famous sketch of a New Yorker's view of the world,[8] where everything beyond a richly detailed Manhattan quickly recedes into distant squiggles.

It was only a dozen years later, when I started the Internet History Program, that I tried to systematically understand the overall sweep of cyberspace as it evolved. (Figure 1 is one way of trying to visualise the results, a kind of "Whole Earth" view of cyberspace.) The

Networking, Web and Mobile galleries in the museum's permanent exhibition are attempts to turn that holistic view into a coherent narrative for a popular audience.

Part of the difficulty in seeing the evolution of cyberspace whole is that different systems were partitioned by geography, types of users (geeks, students, general public, etc.), and the hardware they ran over.

A French farmer posting questions about small engine repair from his Minitel terminal in 1989 had no reason to be aware that counterparts in Canada used something called CompuServe, or that American student geeks shared sexy images on Usenet, or that office works all over exchanged email and shared files over corporate LANs, or that mostly North American researchers and uber geeks were Telnetting into each other's computers over a growing network of networks called the Internet. And so on, and so on.

Even professionals at the time rarely had a sense of the online world as a whole; that was a bit like trying to visualise the shape of our galaxy while inside it. The historical isolation of these different "cyberspaces" is part of what makes them valuable to study, as I will discuss further on. But even today, it means that many scholars of the online world are partly bounded by their own starting points. These can be geographic, and technical, i.e. scholars coming in from a study of multimedia, or PCs, or hypertext, or UNIX. French researchers are likely to be very aware of the huge impact of Minitel, the first truly mass market "web", and of the lost possibilities of CYCLADES, an Internet that could have been. Until recently, an American researcher may have heard of neither, while being steeped in a local history of BBS's and multimedia CD-ROMs.

The patchwork knowledge I am talking about is not just around the subtleties of long-gone online systems. It reaches down to the most basic power dynamics of who controls our online life. Only 30 years after the PC revolution, few remember that it really *was* a revolution, fought against what we now fashionably call "cloud computing" – a new name for the centralised control which timesharing systems exerted from the early 1960s well into the 1980s. The last time most programmes and data lived on central servers (aka "the cloud"), users often had to pay hefty hourly fees to access them, fees to store their data, follow expensive and byzantine procedures to upload or download it, and obey strict rules about what programmes could and could not be used. As the PC dissolves in a sea of centrally controlled tablets and smartphones, will the future be so different? (Of course, the rugged isolationism of the PC also threw away a lot with the bathwater, including the best early chances for a connected world… but that's a story for another essay.)

Similarly the humble, squawking modems used on analogue phone lines[9] gave users nearly 40 years of independence from the oversight of the telecom companies who own the wires. That freedom was hard won. It took a *court order* in 1968 to force the former US telecom monopoly to permit the intrusion, and many countries never formally granted any such liberties. But once users were allowed to hook up modems to their phone lines, US telecom providers could charge only for a raw connection, and neither control nor differentially charge for what went over it. It was a technical form of net neutrality. But those days are over. Our modern connections, like ADSL and cable broadband, are provided by the telecom companies themselves. They can see – and block or charge for – every bit of data you send or receive.

Both the cloud companies and telecom companies are playing nicely for now. Connectivity providers rarely block a competing service outright, even when they legally can. Software publishers try to gently lure us from running stand-alone programmes on our machines with discounts and licensing models, rather than simply switching wholesale to the cloud. Will all that niceness persist after competing choices have faded away – when both personal computers and full control over what you connect to are remembered as relics of some quaint, frontier age?

At a less ominous level, our ignorance of the past means that programmers keep on blithely recreating past features, from Java-like applets to parts of mobile phone interfaces. Often they patent them, as I have observed as an expert consultant on half a dozen cases. For online tech, Santayana's quote should perhaps be changed to "Those who cannot remember the past are condemned to reinvent it." And sometimes, when the real past gets dredged up by the other side's patent lawyers, to fight it in court.

Fresh fields

So what are Internet histories, and what should we do with them?

I certainly hope we will take on the term "Internet" in the sloppy popular sense of the term – as a synonym for the entire online world, or what was once called cyberspace, from the wires and switches that lay its foundations to a cat video playing on a child's iPad. This is the sense we use it for the Internet History Program at the Computer History Museum.

As a base, more and more fields will doubtless look at the online world through their existing lenses. English departments are already looking at online literature, journalism and media studies departments at the rainbow of new media, i-schools at a variety of topics. Economists and business schools are analysing the development of e-commerce, sociologists the changing ways we interact online. Beyond academia, patent lawyers are combing through what records exist for possible prior art.

This is a continuation of a heartening trend. In the past five or eight years, the first wave of academics has appeared who have a serious interest in the history of networking, though less so the Web and online systems, or the infrastructure that underlies them all. Historians of technology are in the process of recognising just how little of the total history of cyberspace has been deeply researched (though not necessarily of how little has been preserved!).

The launch of this journal is, of course, a very positive sign of this growing interest in cyberspace and its origins. By bringing together people from a variety of disciplines, it may also help to avoid some of the risks that face this very young field.

One is of compartmentalisation; the current wave of interest could simply dissolve into a series of atomised narratives peculiar to each discipline, without any serious attempt to address the field as a whole.

Another is that only selected parts of the story will be remembered and emphasised. There has been a tremendous amount of myth-making around the origins of the online world. In popular culture, the ARPAnet kicked it all off in 1969 and led pretty much straight to Google and Facebook. This has channelled what little interest there has been in cyberspace history to only one or two out of dozens of key systems and standards. Figure 1 shows the few that have gotten attention against the larger backdrop.

As I have written about elsewhere (Weber, 2016), the dominant narratives have a major effect on who gets interviewed and which materials get valued and preserved, as in the example I gave earlier of the neglected commercial networks of the 1970s.

Another selection bias is around the levels of cyberspace history that get researched. As in Figure 1, we can think of that history as being split into three simplified levels, each with their own timelines. At the base are the wires or other transport media. Next up are networks, the hidden software "plumbing" that transports bits to where they need to go. At the top are online systems like the Web, CompuServe, Minitel, etc.; these are the programmes users actually see and click on. Partly because of the heavy emphasis on the ARPAnet and Internet, much of the more systematic work done on cyberspace history has been around the middle, networking level. Coverage of the Web and other online systems has been patchy, something I am currently trying to help address, and little has been done with the physical base infrastructure on which all else rests.

To study the history of networks without reference to the online systems that run on top of them is a bit like a history of television broadcasting technology without any discussion of the shows that got made, who made them, and how the medium evolved over time. You learn lots about broadcast standards and equipment, but have little sense of what it was used for, by whom, or why. Of course, to look at online systems in isolation from the networks that support them is an equal distortion. While in technical terms the Web can run over many other networks, its success was inextricably linked to that of the Internet. From the consumer version of CompuServe to Minitel, online systems have tended to rise and fall with the networks they run over.

The wires, too, can be technically interchangeable – modern networking protocols can be adapted to nearly any kind of medium from copper wires to fibre-optic cables to radio waves, even carrier pigeons in one humorous experiment.[10] Yet changes in cost and bandwidth and who controls those "wires" can occasionally shift the online world at a tectonic level; net neutrality, the breakup of telephone monopolies, the switch to 3G and the shift to home broadband are just some familiar examples.

Obviously there are many, many ways to slice the history of cyberspace. But three other important divisions are around the stories of the *makers*, i.e. the people who developed a particular system, the *users* of that system, and the *medium* that system creates – like Web content for the Web. All are indispensable when you look at the top layer of Web-like online systems.

Table 1 – Narrative layers

- Maker story
- User story
- Medium story

In addition to approaching cyberspace through the lenses of traditional fields, I believe there are a couple of areas unique to the new medium that can be fleshed out on their own, and studied in a cross-disciplinary fashion.

One we might call the comparative design of online information systems, including social, economic, literary and civil liberties implications. Worldwide, a number of institutions have been independently feeling their way towards portions of this emerging field for well over a decade, from the Web Science Research Initiative to the Oxford Internet Institute and i-schools and Internet Studies programmes of all kinds. Some have been oriented towards legal or business issues, like the Berkman Center at Harvard or the Stanford Law School's Center for E-Commerce. One emerging framework for tying many of those aspects together is concept of "social machines", or the gestalt of humans interacting with computing technology to form a dynamic system, like Wikipedia, or going further back, bureaucracies based around punched cards.

But until recently all these efforts largely ignored the past. Unsurprisingly given my background, I would argues that studying the lessons of previous systems is indispensable – both for bringing this new field to maturity, and for making intelligent decisions about current policy.

For researchers from some backgrounds, the idea of setting out to inform policy may seem alien. But that is a very traditional use of fields like sociology, and political science, and economics, not to mention harder sciences like physics and biology. It is we, as scholars, who do key initial research and in many cases frame the debates that ramify outwards to society as a whole.

It may not be a stretch to think that the policies that govern the flow of information will come to be seen as every bit as important as economic policy, with schools of thought, major prizes and so on. A free press, of course, has been seen as playing a powerful political role in democracies for several centuries. The convergence of most media onto electronic networks takes that existing power and kicks it into overdrive.

My own bias is to see the history of the online world as not just about the Web itself, or networks like the Internet, or computers, but as all of these within the long tradition of tools we have created for sharing and refining information: books and clay tablets and talking drums and more.

These tools have a very special potency since they are engines of cultural evolution, that accumulation of ideas and invention that has brought us from the flint blade to the food processor, shadow puppets to CNN. Moments of technological change in such information tools – from hand copying to printing, books to the Web, messengers to telegrams – are especially powerful. They can transform utterly the way information moves, how quickly, and who controls it.

We look at societies in terms of the movement of money, but rarely of information. Because our information now moves electronically, we can study its movement and uptake in far finer detail than ever before. In fact, if you were to design an ideal experiment for tracking the transmission of information and concepts, you might come up with something like the Web and Internet. In theory you can trace out each movement over the net, as well as whatever data ends up stored at the various end points. This could eventually make some previously abstract social, economic, political and even literary questions actually testable. The analyses of word usages in books scanned by Google are a very modest example of such an approach. If done correctly such research needs not compromise privacy, either, any more than aerial studies of traffic patterns reveal our individual journeys.

Of course, much of the way information moves – or does not – through society has to do with people. There is a pitch to be made for what we might jokingly term behavioural information theory. "Real" information theory – the math and physics kind – defines how and how much information can be transmitted over a channel, whether a radio link, wire or talking drum. But that also means it's not intended to say much about the human and institutional actors behind our own communication; why the channel is there in first place, what it's used for; who owns it. To make a very imperfect analogy, you might compare its lack of human interest to traditional economic theory before the movement to take into account human motivation and behaviour spawned so-called "behavioural" economics.

If we bother to keep records of the Web and Internet's predecessors, we can also compare how certain variables – say central control, or the mechanics of linking – play out in alternate scenarios, just as anthropologists make comparisons across cultures, or business schools assiduously study cases. A single good insight of this genre – into the often tacit ways we rate information – launched Google.

To take another example, the cost of messaging and whether anyone polices the content have enormous effects on the prevalence of spam and other sorts of unwanted communication. With decent records of historical systems, say telegraphy, CompuServe and Minitel, we could actually analyse this relationship, perhaps even begin to quantify it.

Most early online systems including Minitel were self-contained; so-called "walled gardens" where users of one system had little access to any other. While this feudalism limited their utility at the time and created the hunger for a single standard like the Web, it also made such walled gardens near-perfect as experiments – and today as case studies. Each is an alternate scenario for how to create and use "cyberspace", as it was termed then; a fresh start with new users free of preconceptions from other systems.

For instance, how does something as seemingly minor as the cost of running a server ripple outward, and shape the overall flow of information in an online system? Minitel, Gopher and Web servers are examples of three radically different price points, and outcomes – the first a system where only big players could publish sites online, the last the free-for-all we know so well, where the anarchy of open access paradoxically helps push consumers toward the familiarity of giants like Facebook and Amazon. Gopher was stopped in its tracks by a decision to start charging for the use of previously free server code.

User-generated content is another variable that differed widely. CompuServe generated most of its content from users, like blogs and social networks today. But as a corporation, it had absolute power over any content it did not approve of. It used that power to squelch porn and even limit small-scale advertising by users. Minitel relied more heavily on professionally produced content, from magazines to restaurant guides. But as a public utility, owner France Telecom had to respect freedom of speech – hence the explosion of highly profitable erotic sites, many with user-generated chat and classifieds. But as a sop to print media worried about online competition, only organisations registered as press could legally provide a Minitel service (server).

The idea that the flutter of a single butterfly's wings in Brazil can lead to a tornado in Texas has been largely discredited when it comes to weather. The flutter is as likely to get dampened as amplified. But systems for sharing information are a kind of ultimate fulcrum, where leverage over what we see, and hear, and know approaches exponential heights. Seemingly small changes in the construction or pricing of such systems really *can* ramify outwards to make – or break, or shape – an online world. And with it, the flow of knowledge for generations to come.

I hope that partly within these pages, we can together begin to identify and understand the moving parts that make up that grand arc, and to explore the many kinds of Internet histories.

But as I have already alluded to, the Achilles heel of all this is preservation. There is a very serious risk that we will collectively forge wonderful new approaches to the evolution of cyberspace just as the underlying materials we could test those approaches on melt away, like snow in a spring rain.

Unfortunately, some promising avenues for research – like, say, exploring the relationship between server costs and open access to publishing – involve having lots of detailed data. Some of that also needs to be old data. Since the triumph of the Web and Internet in the mid-1990s, cyberspace has partly become a monoculture. To examine how the same variables play out in truly different environments you need to go back to the pre-Web era, to The Source and PLATO and Usenet and CompuServe and Minitel. If agricultural researchers could not study wild and heirloom breeds of corn, they would be at a loss to understand the origins of the mono-cultured kind on your table. If evolutionary biologists did not have fossils of trilobites and other extinct lineages from the Cambrian explosion, they would know far less about how body types evolve.

But when it comes to the "Cambrian explosion" of networks and online systems in the 1960s, 1970s and 1980s, many of the supporting materials are at serious risk if not already gone. The same is true of the materials that would let us bring to the foreground the roles of under-credited groups, including women and minorities, in building our online world.

Of course, even the worst case scenario won't prevent future scholars of technology from studying the past. They will merely re-interpret the same few ARPAnet stories over and over and over again.

It is encouraging that many of the founding and other editors of this journal have a deep interest in preservation, as well as in interpretation. Perhaps this can help these pages become one of the forums for a new synthesis of the two. As I have written elsewhere (Weber, 2016), given the ephemerality of digital media we need to devise a new approach to collecting materials; more like archaeologists rushing to preserve as well as interpret what they can before a new freeway goes in than scholars taking their leisure in studying materials stably preserved in centuries-old archives.

But even if we mostly lose that race, as I think we will, the attempt to look at the sweep of cyberspace now, at the dawn, can build a conceptual framework that endures. That in turn can help us understand the many linked but still distinct cyberspaces – whether on apps, or walled garden websites like Facebook, or mobile phones, or national or ethnic communities – to come.

A truly world-wide Web

More than 50 years ago, students and researchers began chatting and sending emails over early multiuser computer systems. Today, over three billion people are connected to the Web and Internet, and the spread of cheap smartphones is about to quickly double that number to nearly everybody alive.

Who will shape this truly world-wide Web of nearly seven billion users? Will tomorrow's titans be familiar Internet companies, or more like the closed systems favoured by mobile carriers on the "poor man's Internet" of texting and flip phones that still serves *three billion* across the developing world today? Will the online world of a decade hence have been telescoped down to the needs of pocket or watch-sized screens? Or blown out into the world around us with augmented reality on walls or on head-up displays, Google Glass-style, or primitive brain-computer interfaces, – or something else entirely? Will it even stay world-wide, or fragment once again into a feudal mishmash of walled gardens?

Nobody knows, of course. But if there is any time it might be useful to study previous systems and visions, it is now.

Notes

1. "Online system" in this essay is used as a generic term for Web-like systems, i.e. systems for navigating information over networks. The origins of the term are in the 1960s oNLine System (NLS). This essay uses "online world" as a generic term for all of cyberspace.
2. H.G. Wells used the term "World Brain" as the title of his book of the same name. However Paul Olet, Ted Nelson and others had visions of a worldwide information system that I believe can be meaningfully put under a general "world brain" label.
3. Wells, Otlet and Otlet's co-founder of the Mundaneum Henri de la Fontaine and other associates were pacifists involved with the internationalist movement (see Otlet, 1934; Wright, 2014).
4. Kay has written about his Dynabook and related concepts in a number of articles (e.g. Kay, 1972).
5. Ted Nelson's Xanadu system has described both in his own writings and by many authors. For a good overview, see Barnet (2014).
6. The same sources apply as above; Gillies and Cailliau, Web was Born, Berners-Lee and Fischetti, Weaving
7. The basic idea of networking layers has been adapted to various purposes, such as Yochai Benkler's physical, code and content layers (see discussion in Murray, 2016).
8. The original 1976 illustration has been adapted as a poster and to many different purposes (Steinberg, 1976).
9. Technically, DSL modems are also used on analog phone lines. But they include high frequencies that only carry a short distance to pack in more data.
10. There may be other write-ups of this event – see BLUG (2014).

Acknowledgments

The author thanks Niels Brügger and Gerard Goggins for help and advice in the preparation of this article, and his agent Laurie Fox for helping him think through some of the material that led to its contents. He thanks Kirsten Tashev, Len Shustek, Dag Spicer, Chris Garcia, Paula Jabloner, Karen Kroslowitz, Al Kossow, and many, many others at CHM for educating him about interpretation and preservation in a museum context. He thanks Ben Segal, Jean-François Groff, Tim Berners-Lee, Stevan Keane, Jenny and Dave Raggett, and Kevin Hughes for getting him hooked on the topic in the first place.

Disclosure statement

No potential conflict of interest was reported by the authors.

References

Barnet, B. (2014). *Memory machines: The evolution of hypertext*. London: Anthem Press.
Berners-Lee, T., & Fischetti, M. (2000). *Weaving the web: The past, present and future of the world-wide web by its inventor*. London: Orion Business.

BLUG. (2014, September 7). The informal report from the RFC 1149 event. Retrieved from http://www.blug.linux.no/rfc1149/writeup/

Campbell-Kelly, M., & Garcia-Swartz, D. D., (2013). The history of the internet: The missing narratives. *Journal of Information Technology, 28*(1), 18–33.

Carlson, W. B. (2013). *Tesla: Inventor of the electrical age*. Princeton, NJ: Princeton University Press.

Gillies, J., & Cailliau, R. (2000). *How the Web was born: The story of the World Wide Web*. New York, NY: Oxford University Press.

Kay, A. (1972). *A personal computer for children of all ages*. Boston, MA: Proceedings of the ACM National Conference.

Murray, A. (2016). *The law and society*. (3rd ed.). New York, NY: Oxford University Press.

Otlet, P. (1934). *Traité de documentation: Le livre sur le livre, théorie et pratique* [Treatise on documentation, the book on the book, theory and practice]. Bruxelles: Editiones Mundaneum.

Steinberg, S. (1976). Cover. *The New Yorker*.

Suarez, M. F., & Woudhuysen, H. R. (2013). *The book: A global history*. Oxford: Oxford University Press.

Weber, M. (2016). Self-fulfilling history: How narrative shapes preservation of the online world. *Information & Culture, 51*(1), 54–80.

Wright, A. (2014). *Cataloging the world: Paul Otlet and the birth of the information age*. Oxford: Oxford University Press.

Can we write a cultural history of the Internet? If so, how?

Fred Turner

ABSTRACT

What would a cultural history of the Internet look like? The question almost makes no sense: the Internet spans the globe and traverses any number of completely distinct human groups. It simply cannot have a single culture. And yet, like the railroad, the telegraph and the highway system before it, the Internet has been an extraordinary agent for cultural change. How should we study that process? To begin to answer that question, this essay returns to four canonical studies of earlier technologies and cultures: Carolyn Marvin's *When Old Technologies Were New*; Leo Marx's *The Machine in the Garden*; Ruth Schwarz Cowan's *More Work for Mother* and Lynn Spigel's *Make Room for TV*. In each case, the essay mines the earlier works for research tactics and uses them as jumping-off points to explore the ways in which the Internet requires new and different approaches. It concludes by speculating on the ways that the American-centric nature of much earlier work will need to be replaced with a newly global focus and research tactics to match.

What would a cultural history of the Internet look like?

The question almost makes no sense. The Internet is simply too vast and too varied in the forms of life it supports to have a single culture. It hosts conversations, financial transactions, videos, industrial strength software tools, commercial development collaborations – virtually the entire range of human behaviour, or at least, those parts of it that can be turned into ones and zeros. Like the telegraph and telephone systems before it, the Internet traverses continents, stretches under oceans and extends through the stratosphere into space itself. The range of communities, nations and, for that matter, *species* whose existence it touches is almost unimaginably vast. So too is the range of human cultures with which it intersects. Hunter-gatherers, farmers, urban cosmopolitan elites – around the planet, no matter how we organise our lives, we all check our cell phones as easily as we once they looked up to the sky to check the weather.

Even so, in the late 1990s, soon after the Internet became widely available in America and Europe, scholars and pundits began proclaiming the existence of something called "Internet culture" (see, for instance, Aronowitz, 1996; Bell & Kennedy, 2000; Stone, 1991; Jones, 1997; Lovink, 2002; Moore, 1995; Porter, 1997).[1] It was a strange amalgam. It consisted partly of online interactions, partly of multimedia lectures performed at universities, and partly of the utopian pronouncements of American pundits, usually wrapped in scintillating graphics. Above all, the idea of an "Internet culture" partook of one of the Internet's founding misunderstandings: the belief that the Internet was somehow a *place*. This too was an American construction. In the pages of *Wired* magazine and the minds of those who read it, the Internet was much more than a new communication system. It was a new frontier. As such, it had to be settled, and when it was, like the fantasy of America itself, it would enjoy a culture of liberated, collaborative individualism.

Twenty years later, we may finally be ready to abandon the dream of the Internet as a great good American place. And if we are, then we might also begin to explore the ways that it has become an engine of cultural change, in the United States and around the globe. To do that, we need to agree on a few guiding principles at the outset. I propose the following: first, the Internet is not a place, nor is it merely a new platform for creative expression. Rather, it is an infrastructure: a complex assemblage of wires and switches, institutions and individuals, through which financial data and love notes travel intermingled. Second, it has no inhabitants. Instead, its streams of bits and bytes run through the lives of people who live, as they always have, in bodies, locations and societies. Third, it has no culture apart from the communities who have built, used and sought to regulate its electronic networks. In other words, there is no such thing as a single universal Internet culture.

With these precepts in mind, we are free to write the history – or really, the many histories – of the Internet's involvement in cultural changes that have taken place around the world. But how? What might the cultural history of an infrastructure look like?

To begin to answer these questions, I would like to turn back to the work of two generations of scholars that emerged during and after the 1960s in the United States and particularly, to their studies of four infrastructural systems: the railway, the electrical grid, the industrialized kitchen and the television system. Like the Internet, each of these systems reaches into almost everyone's lives, on almost every continent. And like the Net, each consists of a complex, interlinked set of technologies and social worlds, both of which interact to produce images and stories, rituals and subjectivities, which are the foundations of culture. Only one, television, is generally regarded as a communication medium, yet all act like media at times. And all have been both products and drivers of cultural change at the global level.

In the wake of World War II, scholars set these infrastructures against a changing definition of culture. As Raymond Williams explained in his 1982 volume *The Sociology of Culture*, his generation inherited an idealist, nineteenth-century view in which the culture of a people consisted of an animating "spirit" which was in turn represented symbolically in literature and the arts (Williams, 1995). The class implications of this tradition were clear: culture too easily became high culture, an aesthetic toolkit for the cultivation of elite sensibilities, and so part of the ideological weaponry with which elites defended their status. Williams and his colleagues thus took up a materialist position. They studied the social and material conditions of cultural production, the terms on which symbolic goods were made and distributed. This let them explore the ways in which culture and social order were reproduced. Williams and those who raised the banner of cultural studies regarded aesthetics as in some ways a freestanding branch of politics. Even though the arts – including the mass media arts – evolved in response to professional debates within art worlds, they explained, the arts also expressed and shaped the distribution of power within the larger social systems in which they were embedded.

I do not want to rehearse the coming of cultural studies here, or to weigh the relative merits of the idealist and materialist definitions of culture. Though they emerged sequentially in time and though materialists have offered powerful critiques of the idealist tradition, both approaches in fact offer useful ways to think about and study the role that emerging infrastructures play in cultural change. Consider one of the high water marks of American idealism, Leo Marx's 1964 study of American literature, *The Machine in the Garden*. In it, Marx tried to explain a shift in how American writers represented nature and civilisation that took place in the mid-nineteenth century. Before that time, he noted, American literature tended to treat the American landscape as a wilderness to be tamed by rugged, hard-driving adventurers. Yet, somewhere around the 1840s, a new kind of nature and a new kind of hero emerged. America became a pastoral landscape, a garden to be tended. Its inhabitants no longer needed to conquer the wilderness, but rather to balance the needs of nature against those of encroaching civilisation.

The key to this shift was the arrival of the train, Marx explained. The first train tracks in America were laid in 1829; within a year, engineers were trying to link Maryland and Ohio. By 1860, 30,000 miles of track crisscrossed the woods and fields (Marx, 2000, p. 180). "The locomotive, associated with fire, smoke, speed, iron, and noise," wrote Marx, became "the leading symbol of…industrial power" (Marx, 2000, p. 27). It represented the domination of the wilderness by man, but at the same time, it hemmed Americans in. They had won the fight with nature. Now they had to begin a new fight, to celebrate what was natural as opposed to mechanical, in this newly fenced landscape and in themselves. Walt Whitman declared that nature and man were one; so too in their ways did Emerson and Thoreau. The arrival of a new transportation infrastructure, wrote Marx, drove a generation of artists and intellectuals to rework the symbolic frameworks by which they and their readers understood where and how they lived.

Today, Marx's tight focus on literature might offend our more materialist sensibilities. Marx was writing just 15 years after the end of World War II, at a time when American intellectuals were preoccupied with tracing the emergence of what many called "the American mind". That mind was largely thought to have arrived on the continent with the writings of the Pilgrims and in the nineteenth and early twentieth centuries, to have inhabited mostly white male bodies living in and around centres of economic privilege such as Manhattan and Concord, Massachusetts. Today, it is easy to see how Marx's focusing on symbolic transformation within a literature that excluded non-elite populations in its pages – as opposed to studying the ways that symbolic systems at the time worked to exclude such populations from political power – belonged to a largely conservative intellectual enterprise.

That fact should not blind us to the tools his book offers for the study of the Internet, though. First, it reminds us that new infrastructures can and do change the symbolic frames by which societies understand themselves. As any number of anthropologists has shown, the rituals of everyday life in a given community make sense to their participants precisely because they accord with that community's guiding symbolic frameworks (for starting points, see Geertz, 1973; Gell, 1998). Second, Marx has identified at least one key group of people who transform emerging technologies into engines of cultural transformation: writers. And though he pays primary attention to canonical poets and essayists, he also reaches deep into popular literature and journalism. In other words, he looks high and low, and at each location, he shows how authors do the work of turning machines into symbols. Finally, he reminds us that infrastructures are always available as symbols: for new ways of living, new ways of organising society, new ways of being in our bodies. They need only be transformed into symbols by our storytellers.

How might Leo Marx approach the Internet? Well, he might study the ways that magazines and novels helped turn the Internet into a symbol, and how the Internet in turn may have altered widely shared symbolic frameworks (for a glimpse of what such work might look like, see Jagoda, 2016). If he spoke enough languages, he could take this approach around the globe. He could study the arrival of the Internet as a literary event and so perhaps map the emergence of a newly networked sensibility in America and abroad. Such an approach is very different from one that focuses on what happens on line. But therein lies much of its value: by stepping back from the noisy arcade of online life, Marx would have been able to trace the Internet's impact on the less visible but extremely powerful symbolic frameworks that shape our understandings of life, online and off.

Twenty years after Marx wrote *The Machine in the Garden*, America was a very different country. In the wake of the Civil Rights movement, the Vietnam War and the rise of feminism and gay rights, historians of infrastructure had lost all desire to trace the origins of a generalised American mind. They turned instead to studying the ways that technical infrastructures affected the lives of women, children, the poor and, to a lesser degree, Americans of colour. Drawing particularly on the work of Michel Foucault, they showed that emerging technical infrastructures shaped subjectivity – either through their technical operations, or as objects of debate and political struggle.

Few had more impact than Ruth Schwartz Cowan. In 1983, Cowan's *More Work for Mother: The Ironies of Household Technology from the Open Hearth to the Microwave* turned Marx's approach on its head. She too studied industrialisation, but not of the landscape. She studied the then-neglected precincts of the kitchen. Like Marx, Cowan hoped to explain a shift in American culture. In the early years of the Republic, she noted, men and women laboured together and the line between "men's work" and "women's work" was relatively blurry (Cowan, 1983, p. 18). By the twentieth century, it had hardened into the stereotyped patterns seen on Cold War TV series such as *Father Knows Best* and *Leave it to Beaver*. Having focused on labour in the marketplace and factory rather than the home, more traditional (and usually male) historians of industrialisation had no idea how this had happened. In their accounts, the story of industrialisation was largely one of steady progress: the rise of the factory system and the conglomerate organisation had made life better for all. Cowan knew better. Step by step, she demonstrated that in the nineteenth century and much of the twentieth, "industrialization served to eliminate the work that men (and children) had once been assigned to do, while at the same time leaving the work of women either untouched or augmented" (Cowan, 1983, p. 63).

More Work for Mother upended the story of American industrial progress. At the same time, it opened a series of methodological doors. First, Cowan turned her eyes away from high culture and towards the everyday world. There, like other materialists, she showed how the routines of daily life drew on, shifted and hardened cultural categories, in her case, of gender. Second, she showed how individual devices such as washing machines and electric ranges depended on networks of electricity, municipal plumbing, transportation and the like. This broke down the division between a woman's world that ostensibly lay outside the marketplace and the masculine world of heavy industry. Third, by studying how women worked with changing technologies in the kitchen, Cowan could explain both transformations in their labour and transformations in the cultural categories by which they were known as workers and people. The networked devices of the kitchen became material shapers of behaviour and so subjectivity. They also became available to advertisers, journalists and novelists as symbols of new ways of feminine being. In other words, in Cowan's account, domestic technologies became nodes on technical networks and at the same time, key elements in emerging models of culture. They exerted power both materially and ideally, much as the Internet does today.

Cowan's work has continued to shape histories of technology and culture, thanks especially to Carolyn Marvin and Lynn Spigel. When Marvin published her now canonical book *When Old Technologies Were New* in 1988, she yoked Cowan's concerns with the politics of gender to a new appreciation for the power of discourse. The result was a new way to study the integration of infrastructure and culture. Marvin set out to explore the process of electrification and to a lesser degree, the installation of new communication systems, at the end of the nineteenth century. Like washing machines and stoves, the electric system would seem to do a great deal and signify nothing in particular. It had to be made to mean. To see how, Marvin turned to the professional journals of early electricians. These men "grafted" the electrical system "onto existing rules and expectations about the structure of social relations", she wrote (Marvin, 1988, p. 233). They and others developed what Marvin called an "electrical discourse", a Foucauldian pattern of symbolic production that ranged from technical discussions of light bulbs to draping women with strings of lights on stage (Marvin, 1988). This mode of discourse travelled with electricity itself, requiring all those it touched to reinforce or perhaps rewire their own cultural assumptions.

Marvin's book offers a Baedeker of techniques we might apply to studying the cultural history of the Internet. Since the early 1990s, professional communities of Internet developers have been powerful sources of what we might call "Internet discourse". What have its engineers said the Internet should be? What sort of people have they suggested it will make us? Where have these debates taken place? And where have they been performed? What has been the Internet equivalent of the dancing lady draped in glowing bulbs? These are just some of the questions her book encourages us to ask. Like the electrical system, the Internet is an object of struggle and debate. We need to study the communities in which those struggles and debates are taking place.

In 1992, media scholar Lynn Spigel took many of the tactics deployed by Marvin and Cowan and used them to rethink the cultural impact of Cold War television in her book *Make Room for TV: Television and the Family Ideal in Postwar America*. Her work remains a model of how cultural historians of the Internet might balance the materialist and idealist approaches. In the years after World War II, television spread across the United States with the same speed that personal computers and the Internet would later move. Cultural analysts and early media historians tended to take the television itself as a simple platform and to study only what appeared on the screen. Spigel took a different approach. Much as Cowan had studied the ways dishwashers altered the daily labour of housewives, Spigel asked, "How, over the course of a single decade, did television become part of people's daily routines? How did people experience the arrival of television in their homes, and what were their expectations for the new mass medium?" (Spigel, 1992).

Such questions posed a methodological problem familiar to those who study the Internet: it is almost impossible to find records of individual viewers' internal, psychological experiences or to collate them effectively if you do. Spigel turned instead to popular magazines of the period and explored the ways they depicted television and family life. She argued that the magazines reflected widely shared views at the time. At the same time, she suggested that viewers would have made sense of television in terms shaped partly by magazine features and advertisements about it. Spigel supplemented these sources with trade journals and social scientific studies of viewers. In the process, she developed a way of understanding the intersection of a new medium with its culture that depended hardly at all on what appeared on the screen. Spigel showed that television arrived with material force. It changed the ways men and women and children moved in the household, where they ate, when and how they talked. Like Cowan's kitchen appliances, the television set both challenged and reinforced enculturated patterns of behaviour, and thereby, the symbolic organisation of American culture as a whole.

We can still see faint traces of the ways that television helped reshape gender relations in the home on TV itself. In the United States, today viewers can watch the situation comedy *Modern Family*. There they can see two gay men parenting, an inter-racial, intergenerational couple and a classic white suburban family. This range is at least in some small part a legacy of the ways that bringing televisions and dishwashers into the home simultaneously hardened existing gender categories and for some families, began to break them apart. At the same time, it is clear that a show like *Modern Family* only became possible in the wake of several generations of social movements devoted to civil rights. What did those movements have to do with television? With transportation infrastructures? With industrial kitchens and electrical systems? It is still hard to say. *Modern Family* and Spigel's work on the history of television remind us that we cannot study the cultural history of the Internet as if it moved in some separate, technological sphere, apart from everyday life on the ground. On the contrary, we need to figure out how new media infrastructures entwine with ongoing social and cultural change.

Taken together, the works of Marx, Cowan, Marvin and Spigel reveal a number of principles and tactics we might use to tell a cultural history of the Internet. They remind us that infrastructures of all kinds interact with culture materially and symbolically, at the same time. They urge us to study the communities in which technologies are turned into elements of stories, whether those are gatherings of experts, journalists, artists or performers. They point us to understudied populations, to subaltern communities as well as to powerful elites. They show us that culture is never reproduced only through symbolic work and that for that reason, we need to study the material conditions of cultural production.

At the same time, they may lead us astray in two important ways. First, each of these canonical studies focuses all but exclusively on the United States. Given the American origins of much Internet technology and the continuing influence of American engineering communities in its global deployment, it would be easy to return to the era of the early "Internet culture" debates and to tell the history of the Internet as an exclusively American story. We should not, and as recent work on communication infrastructures in Chile, the former Soviet Union, and under the seas suggests, we almost certainly will not (Gerovitch, 2002; Medina, 2011; Parks, Starosielski, & Acland, 2015; Peters, 2016; Starosielski, 2015). The Internet is a global infrastructure and its intersections with culture need to be studied globally. Even so, Marx, Cowan, Marvin and Spigel remind us that all cultures are ultimately local. Because of the Internet's global reach, it is all too tempting to imagine that a new global cosmopolis is emerging in its wires. The dream of such a technology-enabled global union is itself American. We need local studies of the Internet and cultural change, conducted in different locations around the world, with sufficient respect for and understanding of the local cultural histories that precede the Internet's arrival. Work in this area is just beginning; we need much more (Mullaney & Peters, in press)

Earlier cultural histories of infrastructure can lead us astray in another way too. Like so much writing on technology, they focus primarily on the periods in which infrastructures are new. The cultural history of infrastructure to date might even be better described as the cultural history of the *emergence* of new technologies. Yet, infrastructures have long lives. Their engagement with cultural change does not stop just because the devices themselves have assumed some seemingly stable form. Nor do the technologies stop changing. As a growing body of scholarship on processes of breakdown and repair has shown, computer networking technologies, like all infrastructures, interact with human cultures in a chronological sequence that arcs from the mining of minerals to the smashing of broken monitors and the burning of cables long after computers no longer function (Jackson, 2013; Rosner & Ames, 2014), What's more, the ways the Internet interacts with nature shapes and is shaped by its interaction with regional cultures. How should we think about server farms and their need to be cooled, for instance? How does that need shape where they are located and the lives of those already living in those places?

For all the much-needed emphasis on the material side of the Internet, we need to also remember that it remains an exceptionally powerful vehicle for the circulation of signs and symbols. As once Leo Marx traced changes in the novel and the essay, literary historians will eventually need to trace the rise of new genres of expression and new modes of literary circulation in conjunction with the Internet. Who will be the first historian of the selfie? The question sounds ridiculous until you think about the generations of art historians who have recounted the cultural history of the painted self-portrait.

Finally, we continue to face an institutional challenge that plagued earlier generations of scholars too. At the universities that are the platforms for cultural historical work, earlier centuries have bequeathed entire departments devoted to the study of media and culture (Art History, Literature, Film Studies, Communication, Music and more), whole fields devoted to the study of culture as such (Anthropology) and of history, and whole schools devoted to building new technologies (Schools of Engineering). The Internet is changing each of these fields, yet so far at least, lives at the centre of none. How can we tell a cultural history of one of the most influential infrastructures built in recent centuries, let alone decades, if those tales have no institutional home? In the years after World War II, the study of technology was largely exiled from the study of cultural history, at least in the United States. Yet as the work of Marx, Cowan, Marvin and Spigel suggests, it should not have been.

Perhaps the Internet offers us a new kind of opportunity. Maybe now we can finally put the study of infrastructural change back into the field of cultural history, where it has always belonged.

Note

1. Early alternatives to "internet culture" included "virtual culture" and the still widely used "cyberculture".

Disclosure statement

No potential conflict of interest was reported by the author.

References

Aronowitz, S. (1996). *Technoscience and cyberculture*. New York, NY: Routledge.

Bell, D., & Kennedy, B. M. (2000). *The cybercultures reader*. London: Routledge.

Cowan, R. S. (1983). *More work for mother: The ironies of household technology from the open hearth to the microwave*. New York, NY: Basic Books.

Stone, A. R. (1991). Will the real body please stand up? Boundary stories about virtual cultures." In M. Benedikt (Ed.), *Cyberspace: First steps* (pp. 81–118). Cambridge, MA: MIT Press.

Geertz, C. (1973). *The interpretation of cultures: Selected essays*. New York, NY: Basic Books.

Gell, A. (1998). *Art and agency: An anthropological theory*. Oxford and New York, NY: Clarendon Press; Oxford University Press.

Gerovitch, S. (2002). *From newspeak to cyberspeak: A history of soviet cybernetics*. Cambridge, MA: MIT Press.

Jackson, S. J. (2013). Rethinking repair. In T. Gillespie, P. J. Boczkowski, & K. A. Foot (Eds.), *Media technologies: Essays on communication, materiality, and society* (pp. 221–239). Cambridge, MA: The MIT Press.

Jagoda, P. (2016). *Network aesthetics*. Chicago; London: The University of Chicago Press.

Jones, S. (1997). *Virtual culture: Identity and communication in cybersociety*. London: Sage Publications.

Lovink, G. (2002). *Dark fiber: Tracking critical internet culture*. Cambridge, MA: MIT Press,

Marvin, C. (1988). *When old technologies were new: Thinking about electric communication in the late nineteenth century*. New York: Oxford University Press.

Marx, L. (2000). *The machine in the garden: Technology and the pastoral ideal in America*. Oxford: Oxford University Press.

Medina, E. (2011). *Cybernetic revolutionaries: Technology and politics in Allende's Chile*. Cambridge, MA: MIT Press.

Moore, D. W. (1995). *The emperor's virtual clothes: The naked truth about internet culture*. Chapel Hill, NC: Algonquin Books.

Mullaney, T., & Peters, B. (Eds.). (in press). *Shift CTRL: Global computing and new media in perspective*. Cambridge, MA: MIT Press.

Parks, L., Starosielski, N., & Acland, C. R. (Eds.). (2015). *Signal traffic: Critical studies of media infrastructures*. Urbana-Champaign: University of Illinois Press.

Peters, B. (2016). *How not to network a nation: The uneasy history of the soviet internet*. Cambridge, MA: MIT Press.

Porter, D. (1997). *Internet culture*. New York, NY: Routledge.

Rosner, D. K., & Ames, M. G. (2014). *Designing for repair? Infrastructures and materialities of breakdown*. Proceedings, Computer-Supported Cooperative Work, Baltimore, MD.

Spigel, L. (1992). *Make room for TV: Television and the family ideal in postwar America*. Chicago, IL: University of Chicago Press. p. 2.

Starosielski, N. (2015). *The undersea network*. Durham: Duke University Press.

Williams, R. (Ed.). (1995). *The sociology of culture*. Chicago, IL: University of Chicago Press. p. 10.

Searching for missing "net histories"

Kevin Driscoll and Camille Paloque-Berges

ABSTRACT

Across time, space and language, the meaning of "the Internet" is taken to be self-evident; appearing to both the scholar and the everyday user as a singular, homogeneous sociotechnical phenomenon. But the Internet, as it is generally known, is as much mythology as technology, a shared set of narratives that frame our expectations of the future. As we begin to write comparative, critical histories of the Internet, this seemingly stable object breaks apart, revealing a diversity of experiences, technologies, norms and motivations. The epistemological problem at the heart of Internet history requires us to borrow creatively from other fields and develop new historical methods. To arrive at new operational definitions of the Internet, we advocate the pursuit of hidden histories, obscure sources and less visible networks, stoking new life into vernacular terms such as "the Net."

Introduction

Finding what has not been found, patching holes in narratives and acquiring new documentation are classic problems in modern historiography. Unlike many other twentieth century technologies, the Internet arrived to most users as simultaneously brand-new and already-historical. During the late 1990s, readers in the US were likely to encounter a history of the Internet before accessing the Internet itself. Indeed, the first edition of Katie Hafner's bestselling *Where Wizards Stay Up Late* was published in 1996, the same year that the Pew Research Center estimated that 77% of US adults were not Internet users (Hafner & Lyon, 1996; Pew Research Center, 2017).

Two decades after the publication of Hafner's book, the prevailing narrative of popular Internet history is still shaped by the direct influence of those sleepless wizards. From the perspectives of these central players, "Internet history" follows a tradition of publicly funded networking research in the USA and Europe that produced ARPANET, TCP/IP and the World Wide Web. In 2015, Thomas Haigh, Andrew Russell and William Dutton raised three objections to this account. First, they argued, this history is teleological; built around an unresolvable dispute over "who invented the Internet?" further fuelling a perception that conflicting accounts of history are competing to win a zero-sum game. Second, this narrative gives privilege to the "fittest" technologies that remain in use today while leaving out the political, economic, social, cultural and geographic conditions under which technologies are adopted or abandoned. Third, the sources that give rise to the dominant narrative are primarily first-hand accounts and oral testimonies from a small coterie of networking researchers known as the "fathers of the Internet," a nickname that reflects the intimacy and fraternity of the ARPANET community, as well as the normative conception of the Internet as primarily a technological achievement.

One immediate project for critical Internet historiography is to learn how to handle the vast pre-existing knowledge that has accrued around the dominant history of the Internet. Key figures from the ARPANET milieu, authorised by institutional affiliation and audience interest, began to produce first-hand histories as early as the 1990s. We must integrate these existing narratives with the voices of other populations whose experiences and contributions add dimension and complexity to our understanding of the Internet phenomenon. As Martin Campbell-Kelly and Daniel Garcia-Swartz argue in their critique of the dominant narrative, "the evolution of the Internet is a much richer story than portrayed in the standard histories" (2013).

In addition to representing a greater range of people and places, a richer account of Internet history will also enable new analytic approaches. In the tradition of Michel Foucault (1969), the epistemological reflexivity of critical historiography may reveal unacknowledged power relationships embedded in our knowledge of the Internet's past. We should raise doubt about the prevalence and ubiquity of the Internet as a "winner" by interrogating how we understand the process of technological diffusion and its narration. In order to reframe the Internet's past, we have to move away from thinking the Internet as an "it" in favour of a plural approach.

The Internet has always been multiple. The afterlife of Amsterdam's public online service *De Digitale Stad* (DDS) exemplifies the value of thinking about the Internet in plural. Operating from 1993 to 1999, *De Digitale Stad*, or "the digital city," was a citizen-oriented network open to all Amsterdam residents through dial-in access points and public terminals. The city's vibrant squatter culture shaped the growing network by situating it within a pre-existing tradition of media appropriation, activism and organising (Nevejan & Badenoch, 2014). In recent years, researchers have revived the material history and social memory of DDS through classroom teaching, museum exhibitions, scholarly inquiry and creative re-invention. These encounters with DDS reflect a number of historiographic challenges: the reworking of internet histories through the experiences of users, the attention to digital artefacts, the concern for different temporal and spatial histories and finding ways to tackle these problems in the present.

In this essay, we reflect on the theoretical and methodological consequences of the Internet's inherent plurality. To this end, we argue that a bit of old slang, "the Net," offers some guidance for how to orient ourselves toward this emerging field of historical inquiry. While dominant histories of the Internet are organised around the interplay of technologies, standards, states and enterprises, *histories of the Net* begin with the experiences of users. This shift in perspective is not without complications, of course. For one, the definition of "user" is not self-evident. Users range from technical hobbyists, exploring the Net for novelty and pleasure, to knowledge workers, compelled to adopt this new technology as a condition of their employment. Each user renders the Net differently, a result of the circumstances within which their own encounter with this now-ubiquitous technology began.

Net histories also put researchers in contact with source materials that are difficult to interpret, rife with bias and subject to rapid decay. The search for net histories will require us to get our hands dirty, developing new methodological techniques and theoretical frames for thinking about information and communication infrastructures of the past. What is our responsibility to find and document hidden histories, obscure sources and less visible networks? Under that light, we suggest that a tighter focus on uncertain or inconsistent temporalities, archives and software will be crucial to realising a more diverse point of view in the study of historical computer networks.[1] Our aim is to encourage junior scholars not only to explore hidden net histories, but also to develop an "operational" notion of what the Internet is; a working definition in the context of an expanding and diversifying object of study.

An argument for "net histories"

The Internet is a deceptive object of historical analysis. At first, the Internet appears to be a singular, stable socio-technical phenomenon, in kind with "the television" or "the automobile." To the extent that we have been able to write histories of these other twentieth century technologies, it seems like we should know how to write a history of the Internet. Based on previous experience, a determined researcher might document experimental networks, interview the designers of protocols or trace the early interconnections that gave rise to the global information infrastructure.

But the Internet is as much mythology as technology. As a socio-technical phenomenon, the Internet is held together by a set of narratives and beliefs about how information and communication power ought to be distributed through a society (Flichy, 2007; Katz-Kimchi, 2015; Turner, 2006). As scholars have begun to write comparative, critical histories of the Internet, the Internet seems to break apart, revealing a range of experiences, technologies, norms and motivations (e.g. Brunton, 2013; Driscoll, 2014; Hargadon, 2011; Mailland, 2016; Paloque-Berges, 2011; Russell, 2014; Schafer & Thierry, 2012; Schulte, 2013). Indeed, technology is just a small part of the Internet story.

Nor is the instability of the term "internet" common to information systems as objects of historical inquiry. Systems like DDS and Geocities were discrete historical phenomena with beginnings and ends, clear boundaries from which to begin a diachronic analysis. The Internet offers no similar footholds. At its simplest, the Internet is defined as a "network of networks," a recursive puzzle that resists beginnings and endings.[2] As the Internet grows, the network of networks swallows its constituent parts, growing larger and obscuring any boundaries that might have once existed.

To address the historiographic challenges posed by the singular Internet, we suggest an alternative framing that foregrounds the plural, polysemous quality of the Internet. Consider, for a moment, *net histories*. Unlike the Internet, "the Net" is self-conscious about its ambiguity, and like "the Grid" in John Shirley's cyberpunk novels or "the Matrix" in John S. Quarterman's telecomputing atlas, "the Net" is a superset, inclusive of an ever-evolving complex of information systems and communication networks (Quarterman, 1990; Shirley, 2012). Social histories of the Internet will be composed of stories about *the Net*.

The Net is also a vernacular term of art, calling forth a memory of computer networks as sites of exploration and play. Rather than technologies or infrastructures, a historiography of the Net begins with users. Histories of the Net are concerned with the everyday experi-ence of living and working among computers and networks. From this perspective, "the Net" might refer to any number of systems: a campus network, Usenet, a local bulletin board system (BBS), a commercial online service or some combination of all of them. The Net arises out of the imaginations of its users.

Adopting a net perspective draws attention to two shortcomings in our prevailing his-tories. One is spatial, and has to do with cartography, defining borders and territories; the other one is temporal, putting things in diachronic perspective. The need for non-US net histories is clear. Emerging efforts to broaden the geographic scope of the history of digi-tal computer networks include the *Routledge Companion to Global Internet Histories*, edited by Gerard Goggin and Mark McLelland (2017), the *Asia Internet History Project*, edited by Kilnam Chon (2013–2016) and this very journal. Not all work in global internet histories takes a net historical perspective, however. For pragmatic reasons, new research often grows out of existing histories, attending to the perspectives of individuals and organisa-tions affiliated with well-known "pioneers" in Europe and the USA, such as CSNET and the Internet Engineering Task Force (IETF). We should not simply jump from region to region, re-writing the same tales of a first modem, first email, first ISP, etc. So how do we concep-tually frame net histories from different parts of the world while including the variety of user experiences?

Historical maps of the net reveal relations of authority – who or what is authorised to be connected – and hierarchy – who or what is more visible or central than others. Across the academy as well as in the popular culture, digital networks are imagined as global and transnational infrastructures, open to the world's computer owners despite their origins in the "closed worlds" of surveillance and containment (Edwards, 1997). Indeed, across many histories of the Internet, similar landmarks appear – for instance, Unix-to-Unix copy (UUCP) networks played a recurring role connecting new regions to the emerging Net (Paloque-Berges, 2017; Salus, 1994) – but these similarities are offset by richer stories of domestication and adaptation. In the pursuit of geographically diverse net histories, we must learn how global standards are negotiated locally (Negro & Bori, 2016; Russell, 2014), as well as how culture comes into play when a digital network is appropriated. In the case of Amsterdam's DDS, the "digital city" was "portal" to both a global network as well as a local virtual community, "rooted" in a specific place and marked by Dutch society, style, norms and language (Nevejan & Badenoch, 2014, p. 190). To complicate matters, not all networks follow standards or seek interconnection, and yet, their users may still think of them as "the Net." How do these isolated networks challenge the meaning of being "on the Internet"?[3]

In addition to being user-centred and geographically diverse, histories of the Net also require a spectrum of temporalities. Time is a defining quality of the Net experience, from the hard limits of a modem's transfer rate to the subjective experience of feeling like a "n00b."[4] Time zones, timelessness, microprocessor cycles and automated billing cycles are all rolled into the temporal fabric of the Net. Likewise, familiar temporal structures such as the 10-year decade do not fit easily onto the Net. We should not expect to find coherent memories of "the 1990s" across systems, spaces and socio-economic groups. Net histori-ography will therefore need to accommodate the simultaneous unfolding of multiple, incompatible temporalities as users from across the globe encounter, adopt, modify and abandon new information and communication networks.

Popular histories of the Internet tend to focus on either the 1970s or the 1990s, on experimental networks and fundamental concepts such as dynamic routing and packet switching, or the creation and implementation of now-familiar systems such as the World Wide Web. The gap in this disjoint chronology reflects the messiness of inter-networking. In Europe and North America during the 1980s, thousands of networks were built under a variety of social, technical and political-economic conditions. Store-and-forward mail systems, commercial X.25 networks, UUCP links and packet radio mailboxes each contributed to the emergence of a global infrastructure that enthusiasts began to call "the Net." In contrast to the direct hop from ARPANET to the Web, the plurality of the 1980s Net resists narratives of linear progress.

As long as we conceptualise the Internet in the singular, we will find ourselves entangled by its polymorphism. Histories of the singular Internet will always be written against the backdrop of what Thomas Streeter calls "the standard folklore" of the Internet: ARPANET, TCP/IP and Silicon Valley (2011). By adopting a *net histories* perspective, however, we de-centre the "standard folklore," making room for new origins, side quests, counterfactuals and net mythologies. So where do we look for evidence of the Net? What sources will give rise to a historiography of the Net? What new conceptual and methodological challenges do these sources present?

What do (new) sources hide?

As historical inquiry grows within Internet studies, critical methods for handling historical sources – particularly, "born-digital" materials – will become necessary skills for scholars in the field. Native to digital environments, born-digital sources do not present wholly new problems for the historian accustomed to reflecting on the epistemological centrality of archives and sources, in both intellectual and material terms. Following Lisa Gitelman, the digital is "always already new": what we consider "sources" are also structures and instruments through which history is framed "newly" with every study (2006). Furthermore, born-digital sources should not be restricted to a new generation of technologies with their unique emergent qualities, just like there is nothing natural in "web-native" culture, as Michael Stevenson recalls: they both take their meaning as positions in a field of strengths and powers (2016b). Today, born-digital sources are being acknowledged in the public sphere, and how this acknowledgment actually works reveals obvious power at stake. All eyes are on big data and email leaks; seemingly novel forms of informational power. In the context of research, however, the newness and bigness of born-digital sources are merely superficial. Instead of focusing on what is new or newly accessible, we might find that a fruitful approach is to uncover what born-digital sources hide behind the fascination to which they subject us.

First, there is digital data, which, as Geoffrey Bowker rightly reminded us, is never raw, always structured (Bowker, 2005; Gitelman, 2013). The predominant debate among researchers about big data concerns what is left out and what is not interpreted when mining very large data-sets, with a plea to consider smaller, contextualised data (Boyd & Crawford, 2012). Several other issues are not on the forefront of these debates, yet they are no less crucial when handling born-digital sources: formats, documents and archives. Because of data structuration, it is very hard to consider data outside of its digital document frame – its format. On the complex and ever-changing border between data and document, there lie many variations on the problem of what is not found: obsolete standards, constraints, re-writability and unreadability. When everyone and everything computes data, how do we read it?

Media that are hard to read or hard to reach tend to be forgotten. In one recent example, Hilde Van den Bulck and Hallvard Moe confronted historical neglect in their study of teletext (2016). In spite of being adopted by TV broadcasters throughout Europe, the teletext medium is difficult to collect and archive, and even more difficult to consult and analyse beyond an immediate live broadcast. Teletext tells the story of a failure, not the failure of the technology itself, but the failure of the conditions for explanation and value-creation in memory and history. A second example of data formatting and historical failure is the Usenet collection scattered across Google and the Internet Archive. Partly due to impractical formatting, these data are of little use to researchers and lay unexamined even as Usenet remains among the most prevalent systems in the social memory of the Net (Paloque-Berges, 2017). Attending to format thus helps us to consider not only what sources are available but also the conditions in which they are made readable and even desirable to potential researchers.

Second, there is software itself, and its family members, code, algorithms, programs and applications. What historiographic problems does software hold? First, and foremost, there is no automatic "authenticity," in the historiographical sense, when recovering, compiling and running old source code on new machines. As researchers began to re-build DDS from a preserved snapshot of source code and data, they found it almost impossible to recreate the original system, turning again and again to informed guesswork and improvisation (Bethlehem et al., 2016; De Haan, 2016). Critical code and software studies offer guidance for analysing source code and databases, revealing issues of cultural and political power in the design and operation of these technological systems (Fuller, 2008; Mackenzie, 2006; Manovich, 2001; Marino, 2006). But one peculiar question is seldom raised: what happens when the program does not work? How do we make historical sense of software failure as programs move from their "original" contexts into states of recovery, emulation and reproduction?

Beyond the materiality of software and source code, media scholars seem to agree that algorithms themselves are "ubiquitous" in society, have a "purpose" and "shape social phenomena" (to quote a recent symposium on the topic).[5] There are interesting and weird questions about agency, responsibility and anthropomorphism underlying these formulations – even if actor–network theory taught us to consider the role of non-human actors beyond a critique of anthropomorphism (Latour, 2005). But the nascent field of algorithm studies also seems to take for granted that algorithms "work," that is, algorithms are rarely thought to breakdown, crash or fail. The implementation of any algorithmic process is based on a network of conditional branches, each with a narrow range of possible outcomes, a 1 and a 0. Let us say that meeting the 1 condition subjects the user according to the primary goal of the program. Code studies tend to focus on the social, political and economic consequences of this outcome, this subjection. However, there are other dimensions to the experience of programming and/or being subjected to computer programs. When the condition for the initial purpose of the program is not met, i.e. when the program reaches 0, what happens to user experience? How do the conditions laid out by the program meet the contextual conditions of use? What other *scenarii* are forecast by the machine or invented by users? It is possible for programs to act outside of the expectations of their programmers/

designers. Efforts to re-create old net systems, such as DDS (Bethlehem et al., 2016) or the Everything Engine (Stevenson, 2016a), show that failure is fundamental when working with old software. Indeed, the limitations that come with broken, incomplete, unreliable or out-of-date software may have shaped the cultural contexts of their use (e.g. Davison, 2015). In writing net histories, we will need to characterise the autonomous and unpredictable behaviour of software agents – independent of both human programmers and users. Tales of resistance, such as users challenging or undermining the planned execution of software, should be treated with the same critical care as the dominant stories of engineering heroism, not only as celebrations of hackers' exploits.

Third, and following the previous argument about the autonomy of born-digital sources, how do computerised artefacts themselves materialise social contexts? The physics and logics of the machine, the merits of which engineers love to argue about, tend to obscure its sociality, its economics and its politics. What do people think, do and feel when there is a machine around? How do computer artefacts materialise these interactions with social structures, conventions and habits? How is the use of a machine constrained or framed by economic or political choices? Beyond the deterministic debates around technologies shaping behaviours, or techno-discourse inventing the future while predicting it, we should also not forget that networked computers encode what is already there, an imperfect reflection of existing social conditions. From a temporal perspective, this means that studying the inscriptions lingering in old machines may reveal sensitive information about the human beings who lived among them.

Net histories raise ethical questions that may be new to historians of technology. The materials that survive in the personal collections of former users were created with different expectations regarding privacy and publicity (McKee & Porter, 2009). The users of earlier networks may have assumed a greater level of privacy simply because the Net was not accessible to a vast majority of their peers; security through obscurity, as the saying goes. In the case of the experimental re-construction of DDS, researchers found a surprising amount of personal information preserved in a backup from the 1990s. Former users may have been harmed if their old data were simply put back online, suddenly linked to databases and search tools that did not exist in the past (Bethlehem et al., 2016). Of course, this risk was not unknown to early Net users, some of whom pioneered the very idea of "the right to be forgotten" as soon as the late 1990s, long before it was formalised by research or law (Paloque-Berges, 2017). But net histories require us to rethink archival studies in terms of human subjects research. A willingness to share personally identifying information in the past should not be taken as a license to identify private persons in the present.

Fourth, people also exist independently to machines. Who is talking has a tremendous importance on how we build our narratives. The "fathers of the Internet," with their prominence in popular media, leave little room for alternative accounts (Bory, Benecchi, & Balbi, 2016). But sometimes "a challenger appears," as in the case of the on-going email invention controversy. In short, an engineer named Shiva Ayyadurai registered a software system called "EMAIL" with the US Copyright Office in 1982 and is now running a professional media campaign to be recognised as the sole inventor of email. Beyond the accuracy of Ayyadurai's claims, this situation raises interesting questions as to how to include voices other than the ones producing the official narrative. Along with the compulsory biases coming with oral histories, it seems important to give attention to "wrong discourses" – that is, stories about the past that appear to be inaccurate to the pragmatic historian or researcher.[6] For instance, nostalgia is frowned upon as a form of techno-fetishism, but it may also provide an opportunity for the rediscovery of alternative histories and motivate the amateur preservation of source material (Ankerson, 2011). In memory and in the use of old artefacts, nostalgia surfaces stories of decline and endurance that challenge narratives of linear progress. Nostalgia also introduces hidden dimensions. For instance, the same modem sound that conjures a feeling of nostalgia among former users provides evidence of the social, technological and economic considerations of using dial-up Internet. Memory is not objective, memory is inconsistent and unreliable, but memory will also be an invaluable resource for net histories.

To sum up, the sources that give rise to histories of the Net require the same critical methods developed in other areas of social and cultural history. Crucially, one should never trust one source or one archive, but should confront it with other documents, keeping in mind what each source obscures, leaves out or misrepresents. With the help of auxiliary sciences, critical methodologies devote much effort to looking into the problems raised by sources, beyond what they tell at the surface. Thus, the instability of born-digital sources or the biases prevalent in nostalgic accounts of the Net are not obstacles but resources for a critical historiography of the Net.

Net.things: lost and found

The range of Net histories that will be possible to write in the future depends on the preservation work performed in the present. One reason for the predominant focus on networks sponsored by public institutions is that modern bureaucracies demand documentation. Grants must be renewed, receipts filed, initiatives proposed and proceedings published. This trail of paper provides a detailed, if skewed, account of organisational work over time. In contrast, the networks assembled and maintained by activists, artists, community groups and entrepreneurs are seldom subject to such a strict documentary regime. The material evidence of these nets suffers from a combination of neglect, decay and self-destruction. Their survival depends on the labour of amateurs and enthusiasts working outside of traditional archival institutions. If we wish to write net histories in the future, we must also be engaged with net preservation in the present.

Neglect and decay are twin threats to material history of the Net. By and large, the dominant ideology of the Internet values novelty over memory, a preference that manifests in both active and passive forms. On one hand, old versions of software are not only devalued, but seen as a liability thanks to intellectual property disputes and unpatched security flaws. On the other hand, online services often age poorly, descending slowly into a tangle of dead links, broken images and 404 errors.

The problems of neglect and decay are further exacerbated by the enclosure of large segments of the Net by private enterprise (Helmond, 2015). The corporations of the net industries have proven poor stewards of cultural heritage. In 1999, Yahoo! took ownership of tens of millions of homepages from Geocities, and in 2001, Google acquired a large archive of Usenet posts from DejaNews. Within a decade, neither Google nor Yahoo! continued to maintain the public accessibility of these archives, a failure to meet their responsibility to early net culture.

Public archival initiatives for born-digital material make long-term preservation a central concern. Faced with the frantic evolution of net technologies, these efforts struggle not only in terms of curation, but also with methods, tools and uncertain legal regimes. National libraries and other institutions tasked with a mission to maintain national web archives are caught between short-term demands and long-term priorities. One paradox is the invisibility of collected material, for legal and technical reasons – such as the fabled Twitter archive announced by the Library of Congress in 2010, yet still inaccessible today. Another paradox is the sense of emergency that motivates the collection of cultural materials.[7] They meet similar predicaments faced by pioneering amateur archivists of born-digital heritage who have developed emergency collecting strategies for moments of crisis, such as the "just-in-time grabs" of Geocities pages coordinated by Jason Scott and the Archive Team. A third paradox can be called the "time-capsule" effect: when one institution or one group decides to create a rough archive (sometimes called "dump"), leaving the future users to make sense of it. Such a solution was adopted by the city of Amsterdam to preserve the DDS project. With an operation called "the FREEZE", a snapshot of the municipal network was intentionally captured for the benefit of "archaeologists of the future" (Bethlehem et al., 2016).

Even when the material artefacts of net history are accessible to researchers and enthusiasts, there remain significant costs associated with caring for and maintaining these collections. In many cases, maintenance costs are borne by people working outside of traditional archival institutions. Vital resources for net history such as Textfiles.com, Minitel.org and the Softalk Apple Project are maintained without the benefit of formal support. To sustain the practice of net history into the future, we must find models for collaboration between researchers and enthusiasts that ensure a fair distribution of resources, labour and credit.

Beyond having to deal with urgency, accessibility, neglect and decay, some networks are ephemeral by design. In the early 1980s, BBS software for the Commodore 64 was designed to run without a mass storage system such as a hard disk drive. To make efficient use of the spare memory on a floppy disk, these systems maintained a small queue of recent messages, routinely deleting their own histories. Decentralised messaging systems such as Usenet and FidoNet presented a different sort of anti-memory design. Without a central hub to maintain an authoritative archive, the material histories of these networks survive in bits and pieces. Usenet's customs have relied for a long time on servers' administrator choices to keep or delete their newsgroup archives – which, in times of scarce server space, could be no longer than a week. Newsgroups listings and content were sometimes printed by the labs connected to the network, allowing researchers to retrace micro-histories of Usenet users even with no born-digital sources. Finally, we must consider areas of the Net designed to evade surveillance, such as the encrypted social media systems described by Robert Gehl as Dark Web Social Networks (2016). Secret, secure systems from the past leave a void in the material record in the present. Thus, researchers need to be resourceful at finding new methods, sometimes highly technical, to retrieve hidden data or supplement lost documents.

Conclusion

Internet histories represent a new field of scholarly inquiry, a transnational network of researchers attempting to understand how this network of networks diffused through so many different social, political, geographic and technological domains. One of the key challenges facing this emerging field is the elasticity of the term "Internet" itself. How can one history contain the experiences of ARPA-funded researchers at Stanford in 1976 and an elderly mobile phone user living in Beijing in 2017? In the face of the essential plurality of the Internet, we propose that researchers adopt an alternative approach to internet historiography rooted in the experience of users. Rather than pursue a strictly defined, singular Internet, we argue that the notion of "net histories" allows for a broader array of computer-mediated social worlds, unstuck from the narrow definition and US-centric history of the Internet.

To arrive at new operational definitions of the Internet, we advocate the pursuit of hidden histories, obscure sources and less visible networks, stoking new life into vernacular terms such as "the Net." Taking a net historical approach is no easier than taking a traditional route, of course. Net histories depend on a diverse array of sources, many of which challenge our conventional methodological tools and theoretical frames. In the absence of institutional collections and formal archives, we will dig through the detritus of lives lived online, engage with the complexity of social memory and learn to make peace with absences, silences and deletions. Just as the Net was imagined as an infinite expanse of gateways, login screens, file repositories and systems to explore, Net history is without clear boundaries, a tussle of meaning and mechanism.

Finally, the notion of net histories recalls a time when the cultural meaning of the Internet was still uncertain. After their first encounters with the net, many enthusiasts believed it to be a communication technology that was always-already counter-cultural, somehow readymade with an "alternativeness" to broadcast media (Tréguer, Antoniadis, & Söderberg, 2016). As naive as these early notions may seem today, amid mass surveillance by states and start-ups, net historiography will require us to find empathy with those who enlivened the early Net with dreams of freedom and openness. What was it about these modems, servers, pseudonyms and stories that so many thousands of people, across so many diverse contexts, could come to believe that a singular, unified "Internet" connected them all?

Notes

1. This essay calls for more diverse approaches to historiography without, for lack of space, detailing the critical diversity issues that will animate these histories, including differences in gender, race and ability, as well as broader environmental challenges. Among the pioneering works lighting this pathway through the history of computing, see: Abbate (2012), Ensmenger (2015) and Hicks (2017).
2. The phrase "network of networks" is one of the three definitions given by early Net chronicler Ed Krol in RFC 1462, along with "a community of people who use and develop those networks" and "a collection of resources that can be reached from those networks;" see Krol and Hoffman (1993).
3. There is actually a Request for Comments from Network Working Group member David Crocker that proposes a definition for "on the internet." Although Crocker's definition adopts the point of view of "users," it is based on the arrangement of protocols, platforms and gateways (1995).
4. An archetypal example of an Internet evolving and reflecting within and out of network time is the aptly named "nettime" mailing list, whose administrators recently started to compile a collaborative history for the 20th anniversary of the list. Ted Byfield and Felix Stalder initiated the first version on 1 November 2015 at http://nettime.org/Lists-Archives/nettime-l-1511/msg00001.html.

5. Summer School of the International Algorithm Studies Network – date: 4–8 July 2016. Stockholm, Sweden. http://algorithmnetwork.org/summerschool/
6. A search in the mailing list archives of the Special Interest Group for the History of Computer and Information systems (SIGCIS) reveals how professional and amateur historians of the field reacted, often with a strong protective stance, to the Ayyadurai's affair. http://lists.sigcis.org/pipermail/members-sigcis.org/
7. The French National Science Foundation has commissioned in 2015–2016 research projects focusing on terrorist attacks. One of them, ASAP, studies institutional web archiving in time of emergency. https://asap.hypotheses.org/

Acknowledgments

The authors wish to thank the participants in the 404 Histories Not Found workshop at the 2016 Association of Internet Researchers conference in Berlin, Germany.

Disclosure statement

No potential conflict of interest was reported by the authors.

References

Abbate, J. (2012). *Recoding gender: Women's changing participation in computing*. Cambridge, MA: MIT Press.

Ankerson, M. S. (2011). Writing web histories with an eye on the analog past. *New Media & Society, 14* (3), 384–400. doi:10.1177/1461444811414834

Bethlehem, R., Jansma, R., Koch, T., Mortier, M., Nirghin, K., Veenman, T., & Went, M. (2016, June). *DDS: De Digitale Stad Gekraakt* [DDS Plugging It Back In]. Presentation at the Amsterdam Museum, Amsterdam, Netherlands.

Bory, P., Benecchi, E., & Balbi, G. (2016). How the web was told: Continuity and change in the founding fathers' narratives on the origins of the world wide web. *New Media & Society, 18*, 1066–1087. doi:10.1177/1461444816643788

Bowker, G. C. (2005). *Memory practices in the sciences*. Cambridge, MA: MIT Press.

Boyd, D., & Crawford, K. (2012). Critical questions for big data: Provocations for a cultural, technological, and scholarly phenomenon. *Information, Communication & Society, 15*(5), 662–679. doi:10.1080/1369118X.2012.678878

Brunton, F. (2013). *Spam: A shadow history of the internet.* Cambridge, MA: MIT Press.

Campbell-Kelly, M., & Garcia-Swartz, D. D. (2013). The history of the internet: The missing narratives. *Journal of Information Technology, 28*(1), 18–33. doi:10.1057/jit.2013.4

Chon, K. (2013–2016). *Asia internet history projects.* Retrieved from https://sites.google.com/site/internethistoryasia/

Crocker, D. (1995). RFC 1775 to be "On" the internet. Retrieved from https://tools.ietf.org/html/rfc1775.

Davison, P. (2015). Because of the pixels: On the history, form and influence of MS paint. *Journal of Visual Culture, 13*(3), 275–297. doi:10.1177/1470412914544539

De Haan, Tjarda. (2016, October). *Project 'The Digital City Revives': A case study of Web Archaeology.* Paper presented at iPres 2016, the 13th International Conference on Digital Preservation, Bern, Switzerland.

Driscoll, K. (2014). *Hobbyist inter-networking and the popular internet imaginary: Forgotten histories of networked personal computing, 1978–1998* (dissertation). University of Southern California, Los Angeles, CA.

Edwards, P. N. (1997). *The closed world computers and the politics of discourse in cold war America.* Cambridge, MA: MIT Press.

Ensmenger, N. (2015). *Dirty bits: An environmental history of computing.* Retrieved from http://homes.soic.indiana.edu/nensmeng/enviro-compute/

Flichy, P. (2007). *The internet imaginaire.* Cambridge, MA: MIT Press.

Foucault, M. (1969). *The archaeology of knowledge.* (A. M. Sheridan Smith, Trans.). London: Routledge.

Fuller, M. (2008). *Software studies: A lexicon.* London: MIT Press.

Gehl, R. W. (2016). Power/freedom on the dark web: A digital ethnography of the dark web social network. *New Media & Society, 18*(7), 1219–1235. doi:10.1177/1461444814554900

Gitelman, L. (2006). *Always already new. Media, history and the data of culture.* Cambridge, MA: MIT Press.

Gitelman, L. (Ed.). (2013). *"Raw data" is an oxymoron.* Cambridge, MA: MIT Press.

Goggin, G., & McLelland, M. (2017). *Routledge companion to global internet histories.* New York, NY: Routledge.

Hafner, K., & Lyon, M. (1996). *Where wizards stay up late: The origins of the Internet.* New York, NY: Simon & Schuster.

Haigh, T., Russell, A. L., & Dutton, W. H. (2015). Histories of the internet: Introducing the special issue of information and culture. *Information and Culture, 50*(2), 143–159. doi:10.1353/lac.2015.0006

Hargadon, M. A. (2011). *Like city lights, receding: ANSi artwork and the digital underground, 1985–2000* (master's thesis). Concordia University, Montreal, Quebec.

Helmond, A. (2015). The platformization of the web: Making web data platform ready. *Social Media + Society, 1*(2), 1–11. doi:10.1177/2056305115603080

Hicks, M. (2017). *Programmed inequality: How Britain discarded women technologists and lost its edge in computing.* Cambridge, MA: MIT Press.

Katz-Kimchi, M. (2015). "Singing the strong light works of [American] engineers": Popular histories of the Internet as mythopoetic literature. *Information & Culture, 50*(2), 160–80. doi:10.7560/IC50202

Krol, E., & Hoffman, E. (1993). RFC 1462: FYI on "What is the Internet? Retrieved from https://tools.ietf.org/html/rfc1462

Latour, B. (2005). *Reassembling the social: An introduction to actor-network-theory.* Oxford: Oxford UP.

Mackenzie, A. (2006). *Cutting code: Software and sociality.* Oxford: Peter Lang.

Mailland, J. (2016). 101 Online: History of the American minitel network and lessons from its failure. *IEEE Annals of the History of Computing, 38*(1), 6–22. doi:10.1109/MAHC.2015.54

Manovich, L. (2001). *The language of new media.* London: MIT Press.

Marino, M. C. (2006). Critical code studies. *Electronic Book Review.* Retrieved from http://www.electronicbookreview.com/thread/electropoetics/codology

McKee, H. A., & Porter, J. E. (2009). *The ethics of internet research: A rhetorical, case-based process.* New York, NY: Peter Lang.

Moe, H., & Van den Bulck, H. (Eds.). (2016). *Teletext in Europe: From the analog to the digital era.* Göteborg: Nordicom.

Negro, G., & Bori, P. (2016, October). *Global internet(s) histories, open issues.* Paper presented at the "History Not Found: Challenges in Internet History and Memory Studies" workshop – Association of Internet Researchers Conference, Berlin.

Nevejan, C., & Badenoch, A. (2014). How Amsterdam invented the internet: European networks of significance, 1980–1995. In G. Alberts & R. Oldenziel (Eds.), *Hacking Europe: From computer cultures to demoscenes* (pp. 189–217). London: Springer.

Paloque-Berges, C. (2011). *Entre trivialité et culture : Une histoire de l'Internet vernaculaire. Emergence et médiations d'un folklore de réseau* [Between triviality and culture: A history of the vernacular Internet] (dissertation). Université Paris VIII Vincennes-Saint-Denis, France.

Paloque-Berges, C. (2017). Usenet as a web archive: Multi-layered archives of computer-mediated-communication. In N. Brügger (Ed.), *Web 25: Histories from the first 25 years of the world wide web.* Oxford: Peter Lang.

Pew Research Center. (2017). Internet/broadband fact sheet [Web page]. Retrieved from: http://www.pewinternet.org/httfact-sheet/internet-broadband/

Quarterman, J. S. (1990). *The matrix: Computer networks and conferencing systems worldwide.* Bedford, MA: Digital Press.

Russell, A. (2014). *Open standards and the digital age. History, ideology and networks.* Cambridge, MA: Cambridge University Press.

Salus, P. (1994). *A quarter century of UNIX.* Boston, MA: Addison Wesley.

Schafer, V., & Thierry, B. (2012). *Le Minitel: L'enfance numérique de la France* [Minitel: France's digital childhood]. Paris: Nuvis.

Schulte, S. R. (2013). *Cached: Decoding the internet in global popular culture.* New York, NY: New York University Press.

Shirley, J. (2012). *A song called youth.* Gaithersburg, MD: Prime Books.

Stevenson, M. (2016a, October). *CPR for a CMS: On bringing the Everything Development Engine back to life.* Paper presented at the History Not Found: Challenges in Internet History and Memory Studies Preconference Workshop at AOIR 2016, the annual conference of the Association of Internet Researchers, Berlin.

Stevenson, M. (2016b). The cybercultural moment and the new media field. *New Media & Society, 18* (7), 1088–1102. doi:10.1177/1461444816643789

Streeter, T. (2011). *The net effect: Romanticism, capitalism, and the internet.* New York, NY: New York University Press.

Tréguer, F., Panayotis, A., & Söderberg, J. (2016). Alt. vs. Ctrl.: Editorial notes for the JoPP issue on alternative internets. *Journal of Peer Production,* (9). Retrieved from http://peerproduction.net/issues/issue-9-alternative-internets/editorial-notes/.

Turner, F. (2006). *From counterculture to cyberculture: Stewart Brand, the Whole Earth Network, and the rise of digital utopianism.* Chicago, IL: University of Chicago Press.

Out from the PLATO cave: uncovering the pre-Internet history of social computing

Steve Jones and Guillaume Latzko-Toth

ABSTRACT
PLATO was a pioneering educational computer platform developed at the Computer-based Education Research Laboratory at the University of Illinois at Urbana-Champaign in the 1960s and 1970s. It quickly evolved into a communication system used for educational purposes, and also for social interaction (message boards, real-time messaging), collaboration and online gaming. The PLATO system was one of several precursors to today's Internet, but it has been little studied. It illustrates the value of the study of Internet histories and pre-histories (insofar as PLATO and other computer-mediated communication infrastructures like it predated Advanced Research Projects Agency Network (ARPANET)), particularly as those histories entail rhetorical discursive elements regarding technical resources, social values and ethical norms that continue to shape the development of Internet technologies.

Introduction

Contrary to the "canon" of the history of Transmission Control Protocol/Internet Protocol (TCP/IP) and Advanced Research Projects Agency Network (ARPANET), there is no single, simple history of the Internet; instead, it should be seen as a set of multithreaded, parallel histories, most of which are still to be told. The purpose of this article is to shed light on an early digital, networked system that was the hothouse of several computer-mediated communication applications that would become standards of social computing. PLATO was a pioneering educational computer platform developed at the Computer-based Education Research Laboratory (CERL) at the University of Illinois at Urbana-Champaign (UIUC) in the 1960s and 1970s. It quickly evolved into a communication system used for educational purposes, and also for social interaction (message boards, real-time messaging), collaboration and online gaming.

The PLATO system was one of several precursors to today's Internet, but it has been little studied. Though widespread at the peak of its development,[1] that early precursor of what we call a digital platform today has received scant attention from scholars interested in computer-mediated communication, in part likely due to lack of availability of data about it and its users, and in part likely due to its primary stated targeting of educational markets rather than the broader market of information services for the larger public. However, early actors and witnesses of the system's uses noted its "social" features and its application to building and sustaining online communities (Lamont, 1975; Woolley, 1994). Recent work examined the values exhibited by PLATO users, and noted that while PLATO "was not originally conceived of as a computer-mediated communication (CMC) platform or device," it nevertheless "was reframed as a social platform used for educational purposes" (Latzko-Toth & Jones, 2014, p. 1).

Brügger wrote that, "technology is constantly formed and shaped in a continuous interplay between its socio-technical potentialities and its actual social use, marked by a number of defining moments at which hitherto unacknowledged potentialities are made visible" (2016, p. 1060). One aspect of these defining moments is their crystallisation into technological frames, socially shared structures of meaning that orient the ways various groups of actors relate to a specific technological artefact and make sense of it (Bijker, 1987; Orlikowski & Gash, 1994). Designers and various groups of users may use congruent or incongruent frames to interpret how and why a device should be used, resulting in a struggle between competing "frames of use" (Flichy, 2007). *Reframing the device* can then be defined as constructing an alternative frame of use that challenges the pre-existing dominant one, established in a user community or imposed by the leading designers (Latzko-Toth, Söderberg, Millerand, & Jones, in press). It is not just a matter of "repurposing" artefacts; beyond prescribed use (Akrich, 1992), a new normative frame of use comes with a whole set of norms, values and expectations that guide and underlie the subsequent development of a socio-technical device. The reframing of PLATO illustrates the value of the study of Internet histories and pre-histories (insofar as PLATO and other computer-mediated communication infrastructures like it, including Bulletin Board Systems predated the modern Internet), particularly as those histories entail rhetorical discursive elements regarding technical resources, social values and ethical norms that continue to shape the development of Internet technologies.

PLATO (an acronym for Programmed Logic for Automated Teaching Operations) was invented and developed at the CERL at the UIUC in the 1960s. It was conceived as a computer-based educational system using graphical touch-screen displays, emerging in large part from research by Dr Donald Bitzer on plasma display panels that reduced eyestrain and decreased the demand for computer processing power that had been associated with earlier graphical display systems. While PLATO networking technology did not directly inspire ARPANET (since it was still a mainframe-based, time-sharing system for education and not a networking protocol strictly speaking), many software concepts and applications of networked computing were indeed originally developed on PLATO and then ported to the Internet. As for our specific object of study – digital environments promoting social interactions, collaboration and online communities – it is worth noting that two sets of applications have been acknowledged as having had direct offsprings in today's social computing. First, *multiplayer games*, some of which have evolved into the "virtual worlds" that have become commonplace (e.g. *World of Warcraft* and *Second Life*). Second, *group communication tools*, synchronous and asynchronous, two of them having proved particularly influential: Notes (which inspired Lotus Notes and many threaded, topic-oriented message boards or "forums") and Talkomatic, which laid out the basic concept of the chatroom and inspired many chat applications including, indirectly, Internet Relay Chat.[2]

Research context and methods

First author began inquiries in the early 2000s concerning archival material that UIUC might have maintained. While no electronic files appeared to have been saved (little wonder, perhaps, given that most files would have been stored on magnetic tape and would likely have deteriorated over time and become almost impossible to read unless properly stored along with appropriate hardware), the university archives did contain three boxes with approximately three cubic feet of ledger-sized fanfold computer printouts of Notes files.[3] These documents contain discussions among users largely at higher system administration levels that illustrate key issues that arose during the period 1972–1976, an era of rapid PLATO development. In 2010–2011, the second author joined forces as a postdoctoral research fellow and funding was secured to digitise the files.[4] Using a qualitative data analysis software, we performed an inductive thematic and rhetoric analysis. It was aided by the fact that one of the authors had been a PLATO user and author in the 1970s and 1980s, and was familiar with some of the acronyms, terms and issues discussed. More insights were obtained by collecting testimonies from some key actors (including David Woolley, who was instrumental in the development of both Notes and Talkomatic). Combined together, these various methods make this study a (asynchronous) virtual ethnography (Hine, 2000) of this digital platform.

The historical and scientific value of the files archived by UIUC is immense and illustrates the value of the search for non-digital archival assets related to Internet history. While digital archives are increasingly available in relation to network technologies developed since the late 1990s, it is important to assay the varieties of non-digital materials that can provide historical insight. And while archives of online discourse can be fruitful data sources, analogue materials like memos, user manuals and oral histories are of great value, too. Perhaps of greatest importance at the present time is the collection and preservation of interviews and oral histories with the developers and users of the earliest networked computing systems.

Previous work has shown that much can be learned about the variety of uses to which computing resources were put and the social construction of norms that developed around those uses from PLATO's history (Latzko-Toth & Jones, 2014). That work notably documented how the proliferation of games and the rise of gaming as an unofficial use of PLATO sparked an acute controversy about what constituted "proper use" of digital resources. Similarly Jenny Korn examined the gendered discourse of early digital systems development (2015). Both of these works show the dynamic nature of and struggle over practical matters like system resources as well as political matters such as the purpose and future direction of the system vis-a-vis both its educational mission and its metamorphosis into a social computing platform. The next section offers an outline of this process by showing some aspects of the social dynamics that could be observed in the online exchanges.

PLATO as social computing platform and online community

One dimension of sociality, salient in current social media, is the state of "aimless connect-edness" (Jones, 1997) that can be achieved through computer-mediated communication and that emulates the casual small talk and chit-chat that occurs at the coffee machine or in a pub – a metaphor often used to designate the digital premises of early online com-munities (see for instance Kendall, 2002; Rheingold, 2000). This was epitomised on PLATO by Talkomatic, a synchronous text conferencing application developed by Doug Brown and David Woolley. Up to five active participants in a "channel" could type text each in a separate horizontal window and see other users' messages appear one character at a time while they were typing (Woolley, 1994). An unlimited number of silent readers could join the channel and follow the conversation. As noted by Woolley, this forerunner of Internet Relay Chat became extremely popular and even addictive for some PLATO users (referred to as "talkomaniacs" in a comment posted on Notes):

> Talkomatic was an instant hit. Soon it was logging over 40 hours of use per day. It was not offi-cially part of the PLATO system software, and in fact it was used mostly for what administra-tors would consider frivolous purposes. [...] People would hang out in a channel and chat or flirt with whoever dropped by. (1994)

Another aspect of online sociality is the formation of social relationships through the digital device, both at the individual and collective levels – the latter being arguably described as "online communities." As with most every computer system a hierarchy of user privileges was established from the outset. In the case of PLATO user categories included, in order from less access to most, student, teacher, author and system. The distri-bution of access, and therefore power, created boundaries across PLATO that essentially ensured the formation of social relations predicated on them. Such formation may be viewed as an indicator of the structuration of a community of practice (Wenger, 1998), and specifically, given the newness of PLATO, of the development of a "community of innovation" (Kelty, 2008; von Hippel, 2005). PLATO was designed to be an open system that invited users to become co-designers (Latzko-Toth, 2014; Latzko-Toth & Jones, 2014). However, this view alone is insufficient. The system designers, like those of many other systems, were keen to limit the access particular groups of users had, as illustrated by this passage from the PLATO programming manual from 1969:

> The user of a student station in AUTHOR MODE has a great deal of power. He can alter virtu-ally any lesson available as well as control student access to lessons. It is therefore necessary to limit use of AUTHOR MODE to responsible individuals. This point cannot be emphasized too strongly. Never let any student or other unauthorized individual see how you shift a sta-tion to AUTHOR MODE. Likewise you should never leave a station unattended while it is in AUTHOR MODE. It should go without saying that careless actions of an authorized person can also cause a great deal of damage. (Avner & Tenczar, 1969, p. 72)

While such precautions seem commonplace in software platforms (see for instance Gillespie, 2006), what is most intriguing about PLATO and the development of user com-munities therein is that, unlike rudimentary computer networks in the late 1960s and 1970s, PLATO was intended to be open to non-technical users. In other words, it was designed so as to invite users to take an active part in its evolution by providing ways for them to contribute additions to the initial set of features. The most obvious element of this openness was the provision of an advanced, user-friendly authoring language

(TUTOR) giving non-computer specialists the opportunity to develop a broad range of programs. Other aspects of PLATO openness included a technical design that (at least initially) did not discriminate between programs for resource allocation (notably memory), an organisational culture set by CERL's management (so-called "systems" people) encouraging suggestions from all user categories, as well as a literal "open door" policy regarding the physical premises were the terminals were located, which resulted in the enrolment of a very diverse population as users – including teenage students from a high school nearby.

That said, the matter of users, boundaries and protocols occupied considerable discussion within PLATO itself, through the Notes message board, another (asynchronous) conferencing tool developed by David Woolley but this time commissioned by PLATO administrators. The tension that developed between classes of users is illustrated in the following two examples of message posted by "authors" as replies to interventions by members of the "systems" group:

> [...] it is not the prerogative of systems people to propose (especially after the fact) programming methods at the TUTOR level that they prefer; rather they should either (1) conduct author training courses for everybody, or (2) make impossible those methods they don't like [...], or (3) develop a method of system development that accounts for the common idiosyncracies of the user community. (PLATO Lesson Notes 07_1973-02-06_TO_1973-03-01)

> Is this to say that non-systems people aren't allowed to attempt to answer questions posed in notes? Is there some law that says that only system responses are meaningful? I like to be helpful, and give my ideas on someone's problem. I certainly hope my efforts are not considered a waste of disc space. (PLATO Lesson Notes 19_1974-11-22_TO_1974-12-18)

The latter passage shows a familiar pattern of participative (contributive) behaviour typical of the current "social web." What is even more remarkable about the first passage written in February 1973 is not that it merely shows the aforementioned tension between classes of users but that it shows a remarkable degree of awareness of a "user community." By 1975, there are numerous references to "the PLATO community" as a homogenous group. But the tensions persisted, and in a later exchange in June 1973, one of the system programmers noted that, "For some time now hostilities between system programmers and the user community seem to have been growing" (PLATO Lesson Notes 07_1973-06-18_TO_1973-07-05).

Some of the hostility was related to increasing numbers of users and demands that growth placed on the computer system. Many of these involved conflicts between those using the system for games (often termed "unwanted behaviours") and those using it for education (deemed "legitimate" uses). For instance, in an exchange in April 1975, one "author" wrote:

> we are again [...] reaching the point where funded projects, which are required to deliver courseware at a high rate, can not work in the afternoon hours. unfortunately, and somewhat incomprehensibly, authors, even well paid ones, are extremely hard to reschedule. if the situation doesn't improve, the old specters of limiting game players and other relatively less productive members of the community (to be generous) will rise from their recent burials. (PLATO Lesson Notes 26_1975-04-05_TO_1975-04-14)

As noted in 2014 by Jones and Latzko-Toth, the community was often fractured in regard to the proper use of PLATO's limited computing and storage resources. Some would argue that gaming itself was educational, and others would note, as this "author" did, that inclusivity would be bred by keeping the community open and welcoming:

> "Kids" are an important part of the PLATO community whether they are playing games or doing authoring for some project. The experience they are gaining from this exposure to computation will be invaluable to them later on whether it is -dogfight- or -edit-. Keep in mind that the ones that are bothering people will benifit (sic) from learning that they have responsibilities to the other users. They will learn it more effectively with positive reenforcement (sic) of good behavior if you have the time to spare on it. (PLATO Lesson Notes 28_1975-04-26_TO_1975-05-08)

Often the proposed resolution to conflicts was to carve out separate Notes groups (i.e. forums) and channel the energies of the users toward what system programmers believed would be productive ends. This led to a discussion of appropriate and inappropriate messages (e.g. whether a request for help should go to the general Notes group or to one dedicated to programming) and in 1974, a discussion of the distribution and dissemination of knowledge more broadly, with one user noting that, "PLATO seems too much of a clique for a user system" (PLATO Lesson Note 09_1974-04-12_TO_1974-05-14) because it too often relies on users passing information to one another in private rather than making the information generally available as a user system, designed to be openly documented, would.

The observations above tend to show that, early in its development, the social affordances of PLATO as a networked digital environment were recognised by its users (see Figure 1) and leveraged, which was made possible by the openness of the socio-technical device. By "social affordances", we mean perceived features of the socio-technical device that allows and encourages social interactions, social bonding and community building. We draw here on recent works that mobilise Gibson's (1986) concept of "affordance" to analyse the specific features of social media (Bucher & Helmond, 2017; Leonardi & Vaast, 2017). As summarised by Leonardi and Vaast:

> technologies are constructed out of material features that have properties that transcend their context of use. Although social constructivist approaches to technology use rightly argue that

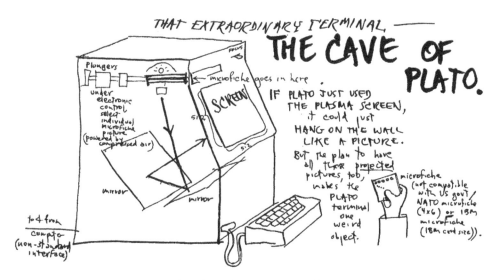

Figure 1. A drawing by Ted Nelson describing the PLATO terminal.
Source: Drawing reproduced with permission from Nelson (1974, p. 27).

individuals can exercise their human agency to make choices about how to use the features of new technologies in their work [...], those features are constructed out of materials that permit certain actions and limit others. When individuals perceive that those features allow them to perform certain actions, the technology can be said to provide an "affordance." (2017, p. 152)

Nagy and Neff (2015) revisited the concept of affordance, underlining the role of perceptions and affects by putting forward the notion of "imagined affordances," ones that evoke "the imagination of both users and designers – expectations for technology that are not fully realized in conscious, rational knowledge but are nonetheless concretized or materialized in socio-technical systems" (p. 1). In the case of PLATO, this imagination work around its social affordances is well illustrated by the use of Notes to discursively construct users, create and share knowledge, and explore material changes to the system. PLATO, as design project, formed an intertwined affective, material and mediated system within which actors struggled over the constituent parts of its formation and future.

Concluding remarks

PLATO's historical record shows us how affordances of system architecture and resources were contributing to the evolutionary dynamics of community development well before the Internet's debut. While there were other early digital platforms contemporaneous with PLATO (Kerr & Hiltz, 1982, provide a useful inventory) none were as open and dynamic as PLATO. Emergency Management Information Systems and Reference Index (EMISARI), created by Murray Turoff in 1971 at the Office of Emergency Preparedness to coordinate President Nixon administration's wage-price freeze policy, for instance, was based on Delphi, an online implementation of the multi-expert decision-making method, Electronic Information Exchange System (EIES, pronounced "eyes") was based on EMISARI and began development in 1974 at the New Jersey Institute of Technology by Turoff and Hiltz. EIES is seen by several historians of computing as the prototype of computer-mediated communication platforms developed since (Hiltz & Turoff, 1978, 1993). Developed by Jacques Vallee, Roy Amara, Robert Johansen and others at the Institute for the Future in the early 1970s, FORUM and PLANET (Planning Network) were basic conferencing platforms, specifically designed to reduce the need for in-person meetings, in a context of the 1970s energy crisis that led organisations and governments to turn to alternate options to physical travel. Another contemporary of PLATO, NLS (oN-Line System) was created by Douglas Engelbart in 1968 at Stanford Research Institute. Rheingold (1995) called it a "delicate coalition of people, electronic devices, software, and ideas" (p. 138). Designed as an intelligence "augmentation" technology, the system was, like PLATO, an attempt to use innovative human–computer interfaces (meshing together text, pictures and video) to transform the very nature of collaborative intellectual work.

However, none of these systems were designed to be used by lay people. They all required a long learning process before they could be used effectively. They were designed by computer people for computer people or, at least, highly trained professionals (Bardini, 2000). This is what makes PLATO unique among its kind in those days, as it was aimed at users with no particular technical skills: college students and teachers in all fields. That it was an open and dynamic system is well illustrated by its transformation from its original design as an educational platform into a social and gaming platform (albeit not abandoning education) fostering the development of thriving online communities at UIUC and on the other campuses where it was deployed. Insight into its evolution, then, gives insight into the social dynamics of the contexts within which it was operating and evolving. It offers clear evidence of the "continuous interplay" Brügger describes as critical to understanding the emergence of technological innovations (2016).

An analysis of rhetorical strategies that make claims about community can show, among other things, how PLATO users understood their community and can be especially useful when compared with similar analyses of other pre-Internet systems. But the value of such historical work is not merely in its comparative power, but also in its fruitful contribution to better understanding the socio-technical dynamics at play in the innovation process underlying digital media development. Networked technologies are examples of what Grossberg, borrowing from Stuart Hall, termed "conjunctures," namely "social formation[s] as fractured and conflictual, along multiple axes, planes and scales, constantly in search of temporary balances or structural stabilities through a variety of practices and processes of struggle and negotiation" (2006, p. 4). The Internet was not the beginning of networked communication. Without historical research that examines pre-Internet forms of network technology and delves into non-digital archival materials, we will lack not only history and context but, as or more importantly, understanding of the sometimes blatant, sometimes nuanced, social, political, economic and technical struggles that contributed to the uneven development and distribution of network technologies. Even more importantly, a history of digital media that would bound the analysis to a specific network, platform or artefact would fail to capture the long-hauled histories of Internet uses, which constitute dynamic sociocultural formations overlapping the many digital infrastructures that predated what we call "the Net."

Notes

1. In its heyday, PLATO implementations could be found at dozens of US universities and in several countries, including Canada, South Africa and France. In the 1970s, Control Data Corporation partnered with, and eventually purchased, PLATO to commercialise it.
2. For a more detailed account of this influence/lineage, see Latzko-Toth (2010).
3. Lessons 1–19 are printouts made in February 1975 from files that predate introduction of Group Notes, the actual message board application. Subsequent files have been printed in June 1976. They contain "General Interest" and "Public" Notes.
4. Funding was made available by the University of Illinois at Chicago Department of Communication and The Pew Internet & American Life Project. The files have since been made public by UIUC Library and are available at the following address: http://archives.library.illinois.edu/archon/?p=collections/controlcard&id=5145

Disclosure statement

No potential conflict of interest was reported by the authors.

References

Akrich, M. (1992). The de-scription of technical objects. In W. E. Bijker & J. Law (Eds.), *Shaping technology/building society: Studies in sociotechnical change* (pp. 205–224). Cambridge, MA: The MIT Press.

Avner, R. A., & Tenczar, P. (1969). *The tutor manual*. Urbana: University of Illinois.

Bardini, T. (2000). *Bootstrapping: Douglas Engelbart, coevolution, and the origins of personal computing*. Stanford, CA: Stanford University Press.

Bijker, W. E. (1987). The social construction of bakelite: Toward a theory of invention. In W. E. Bijker, T. P. Hughes, & T. Pinch (Eds.), *The social construction of technological systems: New directions in the sociology and history of technology* (pp. 159–187). Cambridge, MA: The MIT Press.

Brügger, N. (2016). Introduction: The Web's first 25 years. *New Media & Society, 18*(7), 1059–1065. doi:10.1177/1461444816643787

Bucher, T., & Helmond, A. (2017). The affordances of social media platforms. In J. Burgess, T. Poell, & A. Marwick (Eds.), *The SAGE handbook of social media*. London: Sage.

Flichy, P. (2007). *Understanding technological innovation: A socio-technical approach*. Northampton, MA: Edward Elgar.

Gibson, J. J. (1986). *The ecological approach to perception*. Hillsdale, NJ: Lawrence Erlbaum Associates.

Gillespie, T. (2006). Designed to 'effectively frustrate': Copyright, technology and the agency of users. *New Media & Society, 8*(4), 651–669. doi:10.1177/1461444806065662

Grossberg, L. (2006). Does cultural studies have futures? Should it? (Or what's the matter with New York?). *Cultural Studies, 20*(1), 1–32. doi:10.1080/09502380500492541

Hiltz, S. R., & Turoff, M. (1978). *The network nation: Human communication via computer*. Reading, MA: Addison-Wesley.

Hiltz, S. R., & Turoff, M. (1993). *The network nation: Human communication via computer* (Revised ed.). Cambridge, MA: The MIT Press.

Hine, C. (2000). *Virtual ethnography*. London: Sage.

Kelty, C. (2008). *Two bits: The cultural significance of freesoftware*. Durham, NC: Duke University Press.

Jones, S. (1997). The Internet and its social landscape. In S. Jones (Ed.), *Virtual culture : Identity and communication in cybersociety* (pp. 7–35). London: Sage.

Kendall, L. (2002). *Hanging out in the virtual pub: Masculinities and relationships online*. Berkeley: University of California Press.

Kerr, E. B., & Hiltz, S. R. (1982). *Computer-mediated communication systems: Status and evaluation*. New York, NY: Academic Press.

Korn, J. U. (2015). "Genderless" online discourse in the 1970s: Muted group theory in early social computing. In R. Hammerman & A. L. Russell (Eds.), *Ada's legacy* (pp. 213–229). Williston, VT: Association for Computing Machinery and Morgan & Claypool Publishers.

Lamont, V. C. (1975). Computer-based communications media and citizen participation. In H. D. Anthony & W. J. Cameron (Eds.), Perspectives in *information science* (pp. 553–561). Proceedings of the NATO Advanced Study Institute on Perspectives in Information Science, August 13–24, 1973. Aberystwyth, Wales, UK: Springer.

Latzko-Toth, G. (2010). Metaphors of synchrony: Emergence and differentiation of online chat devices. *Bulletin of Science, Technology & Society, 30*(5), 362–374.

Latzko-Toth, G. (2014). Users as co-designers of software-based media: The co-construction of Internet Relay Chat. *Canadian Journal of Communication, 39*(4), 577–595.

Latzko-Toth, G., & Jones, S. (2014, June). *Sharing digital resources: PLATO and the emerging ethics of social computing*. Paper presented at the *ETHICOMP 2014* Conference, Paris.

Latzko-Toth, G., Söderberg, J., Millerand, F., & Jones, S. (in press). Misuser innovations: The role of "misuses" and "misusers" in digital communication technologies. In D. Ribes & J. Vertesi et al. (Eds.), *digitalSTS: A handbook and fieldguide.*

Leonardi, P., & Vaast, E. (2017). Social media and their affordances for organizing: A review and agenda for research. *Academy of Management Annals, 11*(1), 150–188. doi:10.5465/annals.2015.0144

Nagy, P., & Neff, G. (2015). Imagined affordance: Reconstructing a keyword for communication theory. *Social Media + Society, 1*(2), 1–9.

Nelson, T. H. (1974). *Dream machines: New freedoms through computer screens – a minority report.* Chicago, IL: Self published.

Orlikowski, W. J., & Gash, D. C. (1994). Technological frames: Making sense of information technology in organizations. *ACM Transactions on Information Systems (TOIS), 12*(2), 174–207. doi:10.1145/196734.196745

Rheingold, H. (1995). Tools for thought: The history and future of mind-expanding technology. (Last accessed March 5, 2017). Retrieved from http://dlc.dlib.indiana.edu/dlc/bitstream/handle/10535/22/Tools_For_Thought.pdf.

Rheingold, H. (2000). *The virtual community: Homesteading on the electronic frontier* (Revised ed.). Cambridge, MA: MIT Press.

von Hippel, E. (2005). *Democratizing innovation.* Cambridge, MA: The MIT Press.

Wenger, E. (1998). *Communities of practice: Learning, meaning, and identity.* Cambridge: Cambridge University Press.

Woolley, D. R. (1994). *PLATO: The emergence of online community.* Retrieved from http://www.thinkofit.com/plato/dwplato.htm

Internet histories: the view from the design process

Sandra Braman (ID)

ABSTRACT
The electrical engineers and computer scientists who have designed the Internet are among those who have written Internet history. They have done so within the technical document series created to provide a medium for and record of the design process, the Internet Requests for Comments (RFCs) as well as in other venues. Internet designers have explicitly written the network's history in documents explicitly devoted to history as well as indirectly in documents focused on technical matters. The Internet RFCs also provide data for research on Internet history and on large-scale sociotechnical infrastructure written by outsiders to the design process. Incorporating the history of the Internet as understood by those responsible for its design, whether in their own words or by treating the design conversation as data, makes visible some elements of that history not otherwise available, corrects misperceptions of factors underlying some of its features, and provides fascinating details on the people and events involved that are of interest to those seeking to understand the Internet. Within the RFCs, history has served both technical and social functions.

Internet history is of course neither linear nor singular. This is in part because even in the first years of the design process, the US effort was not the only source of ideas ultimately used (Braman, 2012; Russell & Schafer, 2014); in part because early network designers took part in multiple other histories as well, such as that of the origins of computer science as a discipline (Malčić, 2015); and in part because of differences in the relationships to the Internet of those telling the tales. The launch of a new journal focused on histories of the Internet prompted the question of how history was referred to, used, and described during the course of the Internet design process by those involved with the process itself.

This essay explores answers to this question by adding another dimension to a body of work that examines how the computer scientists and electrical engineers involved in the Internet design process dealt with social policy and political issues in the course of their design work as documented within the Requests for Comments (RFCs) – the medium for and record of the technical design process – from 1969 to 2009. Investigation of the treatment of history within the RFCs and by RFC authors yields two very different types of uses. The first is *technical*, treating history as a concept, tool, and/or functional goal of value for design purposes themselves. The second is *social*, serving a variety of political, cultural, and personal uses of Internet history by designers both within and outside of the RFCs.

These two types of uses of history should be read in very different ways. On the technical side, history serves a variety of functions internal to the design process; uses of history could (and should) have been included in an analysis of the techniques used by Internet designers to sustain their process in the midst of unceasing instability in the technologies, concepts, and empirical realities involved (Braman, 2016). On the social side, reports from those involved in the Internet design process that are described in this essay as information sources should be read by those who do further analysis using all of the critical lenses provided by scholars such as Latour (1987), Latour and Woolgar (1979), and Shapin and Shaffer (1985). The work by Internet design insiders published outside of the RFCs appears to be motivated less by the claims of exceptionalist expertise that have sometimes been of concern (Merton, 1972) than by a variety of factors that range from sheer instrumentalism to the desire to memorialise key figures. Where exceptionalist expertise is claimed – "I was there and a part of it" – it is mentioned in support of the credibility of the report and the access to information upon which the report is based. Research on participants in the design process provides additional frames for understanding these documents. Network analysis of the RFCs, for example, reveals the social networks of those involved in development of specific standards (Gençer, Oba, Özel, & Tunahoğlu, 2006). As-yet-unanalysed data have been gathered on the employers of authors of RFCs that will provide the basis for a political economic analysis of the decision-making process; and numerous other methods can be used for this type of work as well.

The essay opens with a brief look at how documents in the series are used as historical primary and secondary data by outsider scholars. It then turns to the technical and social uses of history by design insiders that are the focus of this piece.

The RFCs as historical data

The Internet RFCs technical document series was launched just a few months after the first US government grant to develop a network linking computers at different sites in 1969, and is still in use. As of the time of writing in March of 2017, there were over 8100 documents in the series, which is hosted by the Internet Engineering Task Force (IETF) and is freely available at https://www.ietf.org/rfc.html. The RFCs are used regularly as primary sources by historians of the Internet, critics of historians of the Internet, those who study transformations of the nature of society as a result of informatisation, and those who study large-scale sociotechnical infrastructure in general.

Many historians of the Internet (e.g. Abbate, 1999; deNardis, 2009; Mueller, 2002) rely upon RFCs as secondary (Carpenter & Partridge, 2010) and primary sources that provide critically important information about the decisions and decision-making processes through which the network was developed, with particular documents marking significant turning points in that history. These documents are also useful to those seeking to understand how the network – its goals, uses, and users – was understood by designers. For example, it turns out that the computer scientists and electrical engineers involved distinguished among possible types of users not only by such characteristics as level of technical expertise, type of equipment relied upon, or geographic location, but also by whether the users were human or not. Designers were as much or more interested in solving problems for the software, operating systems, and levels of network architecture referred to "daemons" (see, e.g. RFC 114, 1971) as they were in designing for humans (Braman, 2011).

Critics of mainstream Internet histories, too, rely upon the Internet RFCs for evidence (e.g. Fidler & Currie, 2016). Internationalisation and language issues are examples of areas in which information in the RFCs counters common misperceptions of the history of the network. It is commonly assumed that the American designers of the network who dominated during its early years were uninterested in internationalisation and in serving non-English speakers (see, e.g. Danet & Herring, 2003), but the RFCs make clear that designers were committed to internationalisation of the network and accommodation of all languages from the earliest years of the design process. It was the complexity and difficulty of the technical problems involved, not will, that delayed network multilingualism for so long (Braman, 2012).

Reading the RFCs alters how we understand the history of ideas about the ways in which informatisation has affected society in sometimes surprising ways. Tensions between geopolitical citizenship and what we can usefully think of as "network political" citizenship began to ripen as a subject of interest for social scientists in the second decade of the 21st century, for example, but had been evident for decades within the RFCs (Braman, 2013). Similarly, Lessig's (1999) much-cited notion of "code is law" was very much on the minds of Internet designers several decades before the legal scholar's work was published ibid.

The RFCs as primary historical data have been fruitful for those doing conceptual and theoretical work on the nature of decision-making processes for large-scale sociotechnical infrastructure (e.g. Benoliel, 2003; Nickerson & zur Muehlen, 2006) as well. In one example of this type of use of the material, the concept of a "recursive public", meaning "a group constituted by a shared, profound concern for the technical and legal conditions of possibility for their own association" (Kelty, 2005, p. 185), has been developed for understanding Internet designers' "argument-by-technology" as well as their concern with rules for group conversation and decision-making processes. From this perspective, the network is not just as a technical structure but also a set of legal rules for discussing issues of common concern that values the ability to rewrite those rules. Kelty's notion of the Internet design community as a recursive public can be used to enrich the findings of those who have studied such matters as the resistance of that community to facilitating government surveillance (deNardis, 2015) and the combination of technical and social processes required to exercise leadership in open source environments (Fleming & Waguespack, 2007). The RFCs are also used as historical data by those for whom the technical history of the Internet is critical to other types of analyses, whether legal (e.g. Feigin, 2004), economic (e.g. Dell, 2010), or political (e.g. Crawford, 2004).

As an historical record of a decision-making process, the RFC conversation is considered a persuasively successful model for decision-makers working on other large-scale sociotechnical systems (RFC 2555, 1999) as well as for those working in purely social environments (Braman, 2016). Cailless (2007), for example, argues that "rough consensus and running code", a succinct and influential summary of the Internet design community approach to decision-making first introduced in RFC 2418 (1998), is an accurate way of understanding the essence of how transnational law is made. The US National Aeronautical and Space Administration (NASA) is one among a number of organisations that use the history documented in the RFCs as a model of how to diffuse technologies and practices developed by system insiders to the broader community (Ullman & Enloe, 2006).

Finally, as is further discussed below, knowledge of the history of the design process as documented in the RFCs is useful for Internet designers themselves. As key figure David Clark (2016) notes in his analysis of conceptualisations for possible futures of the Internet developed with support from the US National Science Foundation (NSF) Future Internet Architecture project, the network could have been quite other than what it is, so knowing just how the decisions were made that created what we now have can be invaluable going forward.

Technical uses of history within the Internet design process

The RFCs document a variety of ways in which Internet designers used history to serve technical functions. The fact that a term had been in use for a while, for example, was considered adequate justification for continuing to use it (RFC 1009, 1987). A "Guide for Internet Standards Writers" argued that including the history of decision-making for specific technical problems should be a writing principle for those contributing to the RFCs so that those involved in the design process in the future do not misunderstand – and thus potentially undermine, interfere with, or misuse – a technical feature because they don't know why something was done:

> In standards development, reaching consensus requires making difficult choices. These choices are made through working group discussions or from implementation experience. By including the basis for a contentious decision, the author can prevent future revisiting of these disagreements when the original parties have moved on. In addition, the knowledge of the 'why' is as useful to an implementer as the description of 'how.' For example, the alternative not taken may have been simpler to implement, so including the reasons behind the choice may prevent future implementers from taking nonstandard shortcuts (RFC 2360, 1998, p. 6).

The authors of RFC 2474 (1998) not only acted on this writing advice in their discussion of an IP header field, but additionally describe how history is recorded in network architecture itself because histories of flows of information are embedded in network codepoints. Such technical embodiments of network history have pragmatic utility. Thus, RFC 4244 (2005) suggested using a "histinfo" option that embeds the history of a call request in a session initiation protocol extension because doing so helps implement that call request should a repeated effort be required. This does require including additional information in the initial request but, as this RFC notes,

> [The] fundamental objective is to capture the target Request-URIs as a request is forwarded. This allows for the capturing of the history of a request that would be lost due to subsequent (re)targeting and forwarding (p. 12).

It was understood that having this kind of information available would be of great use to those pursuing cybersecurity and other issues involving the provenance and history of information and its transfers.

Appreciation of the need to support implementation and those involved in future technical decision-making for the network also underlay the choice to retain documents even after they were made technically obsolete by later decision-making and/or technological innovation. Genre distinctions were established to make explicit the level of agreement upon a particular approach and the extent to which the details had been formalised. "Historic" documents became one of three genre categories in the non-standards track. Amusingly, linguistic purists preferred the term "historical" as a label but series editors stayed with "historic" because doing so was itself historical (RFC 1310, 1992; RFC 2026, 1996). RFC 5000 (2008) reclassified a number of documents as historic.

Social uses of history by Internet designers

Reports by Internet designers on the history of the process, published both within and outside of the RFCs, served a variety of purposes. Full analysis of the functions these publications served for these authors is beyond the scope of this piece, with its focus on identifying the range of ways in which the RFCs and RFC authors provide historical data valuable for a wide variety of uses. However, it is clear that some documents served unabashedly celebratory or self-justificatory purposes, while others served positioning, pedagogical, and other functions. We can distinguish between documents presented as histories within the RFC series itself, and those by RFC authors published in other venues.

Within the RFCs

Although the purpose of the RFCs is to facilitate the technical conversation needed for the development of the technical standards for the Internet (protocols), many documents in the series present quite other types of material that are social in nature, including some texts wholly devoted to history. The best well-known among these is *Hobbes' Internet Timeline* by Robert H. Zakon, available online in full at www.zakon.org/robert/Internet/time line/, first published in 1993 and at the time of writing in March 2017 still being updated. In RFC 2235 (1997), Zakon excerpted some of this material so that it would appear within the RFCs and lead readers to the URL. Earlier, Ed Krol did much the same thing with his book on the history and nature of the network, *The Whole Internet User's Guide and Catalog* (1992/1994), publishing a portion of the text as RFC 1462 (1993).

Vint Cerf, a central figure in historical – and contemporary – politics of Internet design and governance, contributed RFC 3271 (2002) to mark the formation of the Internet Society (ISOC). The ISOC describes itself as a "cause-driven" organisation devoted to open development and use of the network, so it is not surprising that the history Cerf wrote to mark the launch of the organisation was titled "The Internet is for Everyone" and emphasised the goal of universal accessibility in its telling of the story in support of the organisation's goals. Cerf wrote a second historical document, RFC 2468 (1998) (as in "who do we appreciate"), to memorialise his friend and colleague Jon Postel, designer and long-time manager of the domain name system, upon Postel's death.

Just as the construction of history is crucial to formation of the identity of nations (Anderson, 1983/2006), so the way in which the history of the Internet is told has been important for the network's design vision. Much of the task of the design process, particularly during the early years, was conceptualising just what the network should be (Braman, 2011, 2016). This began with such basics as achieving a consensus on the size of a byte, a digital unit fundamental to the packet switching that is a key characteristic of the Internet (RFC 136, 1971) and other matters we now treat as givens.

Two RFCs already mentioned served this function particularly well and demonstrate how significantly the stories told can differ. *Hobbes' Internet Timeline* (RFC 2235, 1997) begins with the 1957 launch of Sputnik by the Soviet Union, framing the design process as part of the US Department of Defense Cold War response and fueling perceptions that the central thrust of the effort was to meet defense needs even though almost all of the development work for secure defense network systems took place outside of the RFCs. Cerf's emphasis on universal access to the network in RFC 3271 (2002), on the other hand, was a deliberate effort to provide a very different vision of the purpose of the Internet and the policy goals that vision implicates.

Other RFCs not explicitly devoted to the topic also provide insights into the history of network decision-making. RFCs 557 (1973) and 705 (1975), for example, descriptively discuss the development of subcultures within the design community. The first distinguishes between the East and West coast communities of Internet designers in ways that would be of interest to readers of Fred Turner's *From Counterculture to Cyberculture* (2006). The second treats cross-cultural concerns in a very different manner, identifying them as arising from differences in the technologies used at various sites. RFC 468 (1973) provides detail on the social activities that helped those involved in the design process cohere as a community.

The need to have a shared vision served as a primary motivator for a number of documents in the series. There was a concerted effort to ensure that all decision-making was community-based (Braman, 2011). RFC 5998 (2009) is an example of a specific text devoted to producing a shared story. This document introduces its narrative about email, which tries to provide a history upon which all can rely, by noting the difficulty of achieving a common perspective because the 35-year history of development of the pertinent protocols involved viewpoints that differed widely in terms of knowledge base, technical problem of focal interest, the nature of the stakeholder's interest in problem solution, and geopolitical relationship to the centre of Internet activity.

Even fake history contributed to the building of a vision for the Internet. For many years, it was a tradition within the Internet design community to publish joke RFCs on April 1 of each year, known as April Fool's Day in the US. A history of IPv9 published as a 1994 April Fool's joke (RFC 1606) – in the second decade of the twenty-first century, we are still working to implement the sixth version of the Internet protocol, IPv6, with any possible ninth version of the protocol far into an uncertain future – includes the assignation of a billion addresses to each house, a million for each room or floor, so that each light switch and appliance could be assigned one. The order of magnitude of IP addresses involved may not (yet) be accurate, but much of what is described in this joke document is now taking place as the Internet of Things.

Outside of the RFCs

Some participants in the Internet design process have published outside the RFCs on developments in which they had taken part. The first appeared before the network was commercialised: Gerich (1991), who was employed by host MERIT at the time, wrote about the development of the Internet registry during the period in which the registry was established by that organisation.

More of this work has been appearing in recent years. When a key document on cyber-security, RFC 1281 (1991), "Guidelines for the Secure Operation of the Internet", was identi-fied as of seminal importance, two of its three authors published an analysis of the social, institutional, and political context within which it was written (Fraser & Crocker, 2008). Similarly, work on the history of the Network Information Center (NIC) at Stanford Research International (SRI) has been published by someone who was an employee there when the NIC was formed (Feinler, 2010) and on the history of the International Packet Network Working Group (INWG) by an individual who was an active participant from the early 1970s on (McKenzie, 2011). Partridge's (2016) insider history of the relationship between the Internet Advisory Board (IAB) and the Internet Engineering Task Force (IETF) at the moment when it was first realised the network would run out of address space dif-fers significantly from the story as it has been told by design process outsiders.

Conclusions

The writing of Internet history is a burgeoning enterprise. The range of fields from which analyses are coming continues to expand, now including perspectives from disciplines such as anthropology and business as well as history and science and technology studies (STS). We are fortunate that the graduate students who participated in the launch of the process to design what we now call the Internet had the creativity and foresight to put in place the organisational innovation of using the Internet RFCs technical document series to provide a medium for the decision-making processes involved, as the series provides invaluable data on that history for use by those doing research on that history. The induc-tive analysis of the RFCs as a discourse undertaken by this author, discussed above, found the material enormously fecund; there is much more work of this kind to do.

Disclosure statement

No potential conflict of interest was reported by the author.

Funding

U.S. National Science Foundation [grant number 0823265].

ORCID

Sandra Braman (iD) http://orcid.org/0000-0002-5244-5680

References

Abbate, J. (1999). *Inventing the Internet*. Cambridge, MA: MIT Press.

Anderson, B. (1983/2006). *Imagined communities* (revised ed.). New York, NY: Penguin Random House.

Benoliel, D. (2003). Cyberspace technological standardization: An institutional theory retrospective. *Berkeley Technology Law Journal, 18*, 1259–1339.

Braman, S. (2011). The framing years: Policy fundamentals in the Internet design process, 1969–1979. *The Information Society, 27*(5), 295–310.

Braman, S. (2012). Internationalization of the internet by design: The first decade. *Global Media and Communication, 8*(1), 27–45.

Braman, S. (2013). Laying the path: Governance in early Internet design. *Info: The Journal of Policy, Regulation, and Strategy for Telecommunications, Information, and Media, 15*(6), 63–83.

Braman, S. (2016). Instability and Internet design. *Internet Policy Review, 5*(3), 1–18.

Calliess, G.-P. (2007). The making of transnational contract law. *Indiana Journal of Global Legal Studies, 14*(2), 469–483.

Carpenter, B. E., & Partridge, C. (2010). Internet requests for comments (RFCs) as scholarly publications. *Computer Communication Review, 40*(1), 31–33.

Clark, D. (2016). Designs for an Internet. Retrieved from https://groups.csail.mit.edu/ana/People/DDC/archbook

Crawford, S. P. (2004). The ICANN experiment. *Cardozo Journal of International and Comparative Law, 12*, 409–448.

Danet, B., & Herring, S. C. (2003). Introduction: The multilingual Internet. *Journal of Computer-Mediated Communication, 9*(1), 629–636. doi:10.1111/j.1083-6101.2003.tb00354.x

Dell, P. (2010). Two economic perspectives on the IPv6 transition. *Info: The Journal of Policy, Regulation, and Strategy for Telecommunications, Information, and Media, 10*(4), 3–14.

DeNardis, L. (2009). *Protocol politics: The globalization of Internet governance*. Cambridge, MA: MIT Press.

DeNardis, L. (2015). The Internet design tension between surveillance and security. *IEEE Annals of the History of Computing, 37*(2), 72–83.

Feigin, E. J. (2004). Architecture of consent: Internet protocols and their legal implications. *Stanford Law Review, 56*, 901–941.

Feinler, E. (2010). The Network Information Center and its archives. *IEEE Annals of the History of Computing, 32*(3), 83–89.

Fidler, B., & Currie, M. (2016, July–September). Infrastructure, representation, and historiography in BBN's Arpanet maps. *IEEE Annals of the History of Computing, 3*, 44–57.

Fleming, L., & Waguespack, D. M. (2007). Brokerage, boundary spanning, and leadership in open innovation communities. *Organization Science, 18*(2), 165–180.

Fraser, B., & Crocker, S. (2008). *Epilogue for RFC 1281, guidelines for the secure operation of the internet*. Presented to the 2008 Annual Computer Security Applications Conference, Turku, Finland.

Gençer, M., Oba, B., Özel, B., & Tunahoğlu, V. S. (2006). Organization of Internet standards. In E. Damiani, B. Fitzgerald, W. Scacchi, M. Scotto, & G. Succi (Eds.), *Open source systems* (pp. 267–272). Boston, MA: Springer.

Gerich, E. (1991). Expanding the Internet to a global environment but . . . how to get connected? *Computer Networks and ISDN Systems, 23*(1–3), 43–46.

Kelty, C. (2005). Geeks, social imaginaries, and recursive publics. *Cultural Anthropology, 20*(2), 185–214.

Krol, E. (1994). *The whole Internet user's guide and catalog* (2nd ed.). Sebastopol, CA: O'Reilly Publishing.

Latour, B. (1987). *Science in action: How to follow scientists and engineers through society*. Cambridge, MA: Harvard University Press.

Latour, B., & Woolgar, S. (1979). *Laboratory life: The social construction of scientific facts*. Beverly Hills, CA: Sage.

Lessig, L. (1999). *Code and other laws of cyberspace*. New York, NY: Basic Books.

Malčić, S. (2015). Interentity communication: The ontological imaginary of early network design. *The Velvet Light Trap, 76*(Fall), 19–36.

McKenzie, A. (2011). INWG and the conception of the Internet: An eyewitness account. *IEEE Annals of the History of Computing, 33*(1), 66–71.

Merton, R. K. (1972). Insiders and outsiders: A chapter in the sociology of knowledge. *American Journal of Sociology, 78*(1), 9–47.

Mueller, M. L. (2002). *Ruling the root: Internet governance and the taming of cyberspace*. Cambridge, MA: MIT Press.

Nickerson, J. V., & zur Muehlen, M. (2006, August). The ecology of standards processes: Insights from Internet standard making. *MIS Quarterly, 30*, 467–488.

Partridge, C. (2016). The restructuring of Internet standards governance: 1987–1992. *IEEE Annals of the History of Computing, 38*(3), 25–43. doi:10.1353/ahc.2016.0032

Russell, A. L., & Schafer, V. (2014). In the shadow of ARPANET and Internet: Louis Pouzin and the Cyclades network in the 1970s. *Technology and Culture, 55*(4), 880–907.

Shapin, S., & Schaffer, S. (1985). *Leviathan and the air-pump: Hobbes, Boyle, and the experimental life*. Princeton, NJ: Princeton University Press.

Turner, F. (2006). *From counterculture to cyberculture: Stewart Brand, the Whole Earth network, and the rise of digital utopianism*. Chicago, IL: University of Chicago Press.

Ullman, R. E., & Enloe, Y. (2006). *Accelerating technology adoption through community endorsement* . In Standard-based data and information systems for earth observation (pp. 227–248). Berlin/Heidelberg: Springer.

RFCs cited

RFC 114, File Transfer Protocol, A.K. Bhushan, April 1971.

RFC 136, Host Accounting and Administrative Procedures, R.E. Kahn, April 1971.

RFC 468, FTP Data Compression, R.T, Braden, March 1973.

RFC 557, Revelations in Network Host Measurements, B.D. Wessler, August1973.

RFC 613, Network Connectivity: A Response to RFC 603, A.M. McKenzie, January1974.

RFC 705, Front-End Protocol B6700 Version, R.F. Bryan, November 1975

RFC 1009, Requirements for Internet Gateways, R.T. Braden, J. Postel, June 1987.

RFC 1281, Guidelines for the Secure Operation of the Internet, R. Pethia, S. Crocker, B. Fraser, November 1991.

RFC 1310, The Internet Standards Process, L. Chapin, March 1992.

RFC 1462, FYI on "What is the Internet?", E. Krol, E. Hoffman, May 1993.

RFC 1606, A Historical Perspective on the Usage of IP Version 9, J. Onions, April 1 1994.

RFC 2026, The Internet Standards Process – Revision 3, S. Bradner, October1996.

RFC 2235, Hobbes' Internet Timeline, R. Zakon, November 1997.

RFC 2360, Scalable Support for Multi-homed Multi-provider Connectivity, T. Bates, Y. Rekhter, January 1998.

RFC 2418, IETF Working Group Guidelines and Procedures, S. Bradner, September1998.

RFC 2468, I Remember IANA, V. Cerf, October 1998.

RFC 2474, Definition of the Differentiated Services Field (DS Field) in the IPv4 and IPv6 Headers, K. Nichols, S. Blake, F. Baker, D. Black, December 1998.

RFC 2555, 30 Years of RFCs, RFC Editor, et al., April 1999.

RFC 3271, The Internet is for Everyone, V. Cerf, April 2002.

RFC 4244, An Extension fo the Session Initiation Protocol (SIP) for Request History Information, M. Barnes, Ed., November 2005.

RFC 5000, Internet Official Protocol Standards, RFC Editor, May 2008.

RFC 5998, An Extension for EAP-Only Authentication in IKEv2, Y. Sheffer, September2010.

The Internet as a structure of feeling: 1992–1996

Thomas Streeter (ID)

ABSTRACT
Between 1992 and 1996, the Internet went from being an experiment in connecting computers to being the inevitable next step in delivering the digital "revolution." This change in perception was not just a recognition. It was an act of social construction, setting the stage for the major reorganisation of global communications over the next two decades. The Internet as we know it was constructed with a species of elite cultural imagination. Building on earlier work, this essay elaborates the causes and character of the particular "structure of feeling" that emerged during this period. The resulting habits of thought can be seen in a number of subsequent developments, from the rapid build out of Internet infrastructure in the late 1990s, to the net neutrality debates and to design choices favouring intense, always-connected interaction. The essay concludes by suggesting that technologies are best understood, not so much as agents in their own right, but as thought-objects for the collective enactment and exploration of hopes, desires and political visions.

1. Introduction: a policy wonk turns Byronic

In the summer of 1998, Clinton administration official Ira Magaziner flew to Geneva to attend an international meeting on the newly emerged problem of "Internet governance," centred on the coordination of domain names and numbers. Because at the time whatever legal control existed for the Internet technically laid with the US government, Magaziner, a senior advisor to the President for Policy Development, had become the administration's point man on this issue. He got off the plane and launched the Geneva meeting by saying:

> I'm going to welcome you, and then I'm going to leave. Not to insult you by withdrawing my attention, but to symbolize just how the United States government conceives of this process. Our job is to begin these discussions, and then get out of the room.

These comments met with enthusiastic applause, and as soon as his 10-minute talk was over, he left the stage and, still "jet-lagged and a bit rumpled," went back to the airport (Lessig, 1998; Mueller, 2004, pp. 159–162).

This was a neoliberal moment: privatisation of the Internet seemed so obvious that it need not be even discussed. But it was also a cultural moment, reflecting style and attitude as much as ideology or policy positions. Both Magaziner and his audience knew that as a government bureaucrat, he was acting against type. We do not expect government officials to so willingly "get out of the room," and generally when an official does not keep an eye on things, it is interpreted as an abdication of responsibility, not a heroic move. Magaziner, furthermore, was no principled opponent of government, known as one of the more wonkish officials in a wonkish administration. Long a proponent of "industrial policy" involving government–business partnerships, a few years prior he had led the Clinton administration's failed effort to create a US national health care system.

Yet, here he was cheerfully ceding any role for government. At that moment, he knew that this gesture of turning power over to the private sector would be so automatically accepted by this audience that it would need no defending. He seemed to enjoy making it. Not long after, a news article appeared titled "Ira Magaziner's legacy: doing nothing well" (McCullagh & McKay, 1998). Perhaps not fully consciously, he was picking up on something that was in the air. His action in 1998 only made sense to an audience that had spent the past few years immersed in a style evident in places like *Wired* magazine, in business press coverage of stock-bubble darlings like Mark Andreessen and more generally from other bits of libertarian cyberculture[1] that had been seeping into the worlds of business and policy-making.

Over the past quarter century, we have become accustomed to expecting digital novelty at our fingertips. We are habituated to stories of people using computers to throw established authorities into disarray; of surprising computer-related business start-ups, from Apple and Microsoft around 1980 through Facebook in the last decade; of peculiar digital inventions taking the world by storm; of Internet use by political rebels from the Tea Party to the Arab Spring to Bernie Sanders; of disruptive events that throw entire industries into confusion, like college students downloading music or uploading videos. Novelty in the digital does not surprise us; over the last 30 years, it has become an expectation.

In 2017, to be sure, the belief that all this novelty and openness is inherent in Internet technology itself may not seem nearly as irrefutable as it did a few years ago. Beginning with the failures of the Arab Spring movements and concluding with the 2016 elections in the USA, the world has watched as what at first seemed to be Internet-fuelled democracy efforts have collapsed into rising authoritarianism, on a scale that has not been seen since the 1930s. As painful as this historical moment is, we can now look back and ask the question: if the Internet technology is not the guarantor of democratic openness, why, from the mid-1990s on, were so many convinced that it was?

The rise of cyberculture has been widely examined in many different ways from many different perspectives. This essay will sketch a framework intended to provide more precision to understanding the specific relations between culture and the Internet, and argue that Raymond Williams' old but still useful notion of a "structure of feeling" not only helps account for actions like Magaziner's, but also helps explain what we mean when we talk about the Internet itself. The goal, given the limited space, is to be illustrative rather than comprehensive. Building on earlier work (2011, 2016), I focus on the 1992–1996 period, which established a structure of feeling for the Internet in the USA which persisted in various ways for the subsequent two decades, shaping policy-making and thus the Internet itself. Beginning with a discussion of Williams' concept and its potential value to discussion of Internet history, the essay goes on to outline an historical understanding of the peculiar emergence of the Internet-associated structure of feeling in the 1990s. It argues that the structure of feeling in question was not only associated with the Internet, but had a causal effect on the development of the Internet itself, and in came to be embedded in what we mean when we talk about the "Internet." The essay concludes with some suggestions about how to understand the relationship of culture to technology in history.

2. Structures of feeling

Early in his career, Raymond Williams described a "structure of feeling" as something that "is as firm and definite as 'structure' suggests, yet it operates in the most delicate and least tangible parts of our activity" (Williams, 2012, p. 69). Always wary of analyses that read events in a Hegelian manner – in terms of grand abstractions like a central "spirit" or *Zeitgeist* which is then assumed to be expressed everywhere in a given society – Williams used the term "feeling" to help distinguish the concept from more formal, rigid concepts like world view or ideology. Structures of feeling, he wrote, concern "meanings and values as they are actively lived and felt ... characteristic elements of impulse, restraint, and tone; specifically affective elements of consciousness and relationships: not feeling against thought, but thought as felt and feeling as thought" (Williams, 1978, p. 132). This framework can help explain how something like Byronic cybercultural gestures might, at certain points in time, come to seem desirable and effective to a government official such as Ira Magaziner.[2]

The existing literature about trends like the rush to remove government from Internet governance in the 1990s is highly varied in its explanatory frameworks. One common approach is to suggest the existence of "chaos" associated with an unusual level of conflicts between groups, so the story becomes one of "conflicts, trade-offs, and unexpected events" or perhaps "innovation from the edges" by upstarts against entrenched firms (e.g. Abbate, 2010; Greenstein, 2015). Another is to illustrate how many widespread small actions and statements fit a broad pattern, say, of economic conservativism and myopic individualism; the significant force is an ideology that explains why people came to believe in and act on dubious propositions (e.g. Barbrook & Cameron, 1996; Borsook, 2000; McChesney, 2013). While one approach sees chaos where the other sees nefarious order, they both assume the existence of a baseline of rational policy-making behaviour that is interfered with by external forces.

Another approach is to apply an anthropological sense of culture, where human behaviour is understood as driven less by rational calculation and more by lived habits, traditions and impulses, by "thought as felt and feeling as thought." The myth and symbol school, first applied to technology by Leo Marx and then by Carey and Quirk, operated by identifying broad cultural patterns that underlie talk and actions of the present, and identify their connections with larger, or older, patterns of thought. So, for example, myth and symbol school scholars looked at literary and popular texts in American history and identified recurrent themes such as "the machine in the garden" and the "city on the hill" which could then be shown to be operating in contemporary talk about new technology (Carey & Quirk, 1970; Marx, 1967).[3] In the early 1970s, the claim that new electronic technologies could lead us to a cleaner, more peaceful, integrated and prosperous society, Carey and Quirk showed in "The Mythos of the Electronic Revolution," was shaped as much by patterns of thought inherited from the US's puritan past as by new technological discoveries. The new was actually old.

This type of analysis functions largely as a form of demystification: what people say about new technology is actually neither new nor just about technology. Classic Marxist scholars make similar moves: they argue (sometimes quite elegantly) that various symbolic themes function as justifications for or distractions from unequal social relations (e.g. Mosco, 1989, 2005). The danger here, as Williams pointed out, is that this basically base/superstructure-driven view of events rests on an idealist abstraction of both culture and the economy; in material life, one never occurs without the other (1978). These approaches leave difficult questions of causality and function to the level of narrative description, and offer little guidance on how to explain why some themes emerge at a given time and others do not, and how particular discourses function in (rather than merely reflect) society.

The difficulty of the problem in the context of the Internet was laid out by historian Roy Rosenzweig (1998), in an important early overview article. Rosenzweig noted the many competing narratives and visions in writing about Internet history, ranging from counter-cultural utopianism to cold war visions of command and control. "[S]uch a profound development" as the Internet, Rosenzweig concludes, cannot be:

> divorced from the idiosyncratic and personal visions of some scientists and bureaucrats whose sweat and dedication got the project up and running, from the social history of the field of computer science, from the Cold Warriors who provided massive government funding of computers and networking as tools for fighting nuclear and conventional war, and from the countercultural radicalism that sought to redirect technology toward a more decentral-ized and non-hierarchical vision of society. (p. 1551)

Since Rosenzweig's essay, works have appeared that address some of the complexities and internal dynamics of the emergence of cyberculture, works that explain the emer-gence of Internet-associated habits of thought and action in terms of their historical com-plexities and cultural forms (Flichy, 2007; Streeter, 1999; Turner, 2008). In contrast with forms of technological determinism which remain popular in discussions of the Internet (e.g. Shirky, 2009), these works instead to various degrees emphasise the role of cultural imagination in the *construction* of the Internet; culture shapes technology as much as the other way around.[4] The remainder of this essay sketches out an example of how to make specific causal connections between a structure of feeling and the Internet as we under-stand it, and suggests that those connections point to ways to understand the Internet in history.

3. The Internet surprise: 1992–1996 and beyond

Central to Williams' thought is an interest in cultural and social change. In the opening paragraphs of *Keywords*, Williams recalled the experience he had, upon returning to Cam-bridge University after service in WWII. "I had been away only four and a half years," he wrote, but as he reflected on the "strange world around" him, he concluded, "the fact is, they just don't speak the same language" (Williams, 2014, p. 11). Changes in style, shades of meaning and unstated assumptions are an indicator of the presence of structures of feeling. In some circles, the mid-1990s felt like a "strange world" in a similar way post-war Cambridge was for Raymond Williams; the policy conversations associated with computer communication had a remarkably different feel in 1996 than they had a few years earlier.

The style, the attitude and language had changed, leading to perplexing events such as normally liberal policy-makers embracing a rush to privatise the Internet in the 1990s.

Before 1992, the Internet was a colloquial term for an experiment, and by 1996, it had become *the* global network of networks. Between 1992 and 1996, the meaning of "Internet" was transformed from being a quiet testbed known mostly to experts, to a global institution whose name seemed to be on everyone's lips and whose existence and importance was taken for granted (2011, pp. 93–137). By late 1995, the remaining consumer computer communication systems from the 1980s (e.g. AOL and Compuserve) were all selling themselves as means of access to the Internet rather than the other way around, the U.S. Congress was revising the structure of its communications law for the first time in more than half a century, major corporations from the phone companies to Microsoft to the television networks were radically revamping core strategies, television ads for consumer products routinely displayed URLs and the Internet stock bubble was starting to inflate.

With that in mind, this essay revisits the changes of the essential 1992–1996 period, during which the Internet emerged from relative obscurity to broad public attention, and the pattern for much subsequent thinking about the Internet was set.[5] *The Net Effect* (2011) reviewed the cultural history of Internet policy, emphasising the rise and functioning of, among other discourses, a discourse of romantic individualism in shaping the embrace and construction of the Internet from the 1950s to the 2000s.[6] But it made its case, not just by identifying examples of texts or actions that fit a romantic pattern. It (1) identifies specific shared feelings – the compulsive draw of computer use most generally, but also specific experiences like discovering something surprising on a network unknown to the powers that be, or unboxing and assembling a microcomputer for the first time; (2) explores ways that groups drew on existing discourses like romanticism to make meaning of those experiences and (3) looked at ways in which those trends might have influenced policy-making involving the Internet. The argument, then, is that the conviction that Internet technology was inherently democratising, unpredictable and a vehicle for unique expression was not simply the triumph of a world view or a vision, but grew out of a set of specific historical accidents, a conjuncture of institutional blindspots, cultural traditions and political pressures, all pivoting around particular interplays of thought and feeling. What I add here, besides the example of Magaziner, is a more explicit analytical framework, the sharper focus on the core 1992–1996 period and more explicit use of Williams' notion of structure of feeling as a way of analysing historical process.

None of the change in this period was inevitable or necessary to the technology. Alternative ways of imagining computer networks – e.g. the "information superhighway," Minitel – were available at the time. In 1990, what existed of the Internet was understood as a research-oriented prototype that, according to legislation, would "be phased out when commercial networks can meet the networking needs of American researchers" (2011, p. 108). At the beginning of the 1990s, the language was that of the "information superhighway" which was presented in official documents and press reports as something that would develop on a national basis, neatly coordinated by orderly consortia of established corporations like IBM and AT&T, perhaps eventually linking up with equally orderly systems developing in other nations around the world. It was all very high-minded. What was then officially called the National Science Foundation Network (NSFNET) would be used by scientists for sophisticated research and perhaps as a kind of electronic library where thoughtful patrons would quietly and studiously gather useful information. While Steve Jobs and Bill Gates were celebrated like rock stars in the late 1980s and early 1990s, the Internet itself garnered very little attention in comparison. A widely reported 1992 public dispute about the funding of computer networking between incoming Vice President Al Gore, Jr. and the head of AT&T had no reference to the Internet. A news report interviewing technology leaders about the future of networked computing in May of 1993 quoted government leaders promoting information superhighways and corporate leadership like Bill Gates predicting PCs connected with home appliances, yet it contained no mention of the Internet (Impoco, 1993). The first issue of *Wired* released that month mentioned the Internet only briefly in passing, as one example of many networking test-beds, not as the system that would become the network of networks. A major *Scientific American* article on computer networking released later that summer similarly had little to say about the Internet (Stix, 1993).

By 1996, all that had changed, and the Internet was transformed in the elite imagination from an experiment to an inevitable force. But it is important that, at that point, the Internet had yet to have much real social or economic impact. Looking back, the technologies and market structures of the Internet were hardly less experimental and unsettled in 1996 than they were in 1992; the practical use of the Internet had yet to come. In 1996, there was no appreciable non-metaphorical market, no substantial population of individuals competitively buying and selling things over the Internet. There were, by and large, only experimenters, speculators and enthusiasts, people who expected a market to emerge where one did not yet exist. Much was made of how fast the Internet was growing at the time, but in 1995, Internet access remained below half a percentage point of worldwide population (Global Policy Forum).

What happened in the 1992-1996 period was not so much a revolution in internetworking technology as a revolution in the way internetworking technology was imagined by American leadership. And it was imagined in very particular ways (Streeter, 2016). First, it was imagined as uniquely interactive rather than transmissive. Unlike, say, phone networks or technologically similar X.25 networks used by banks, the Internet was expected to provide individual users instant, constant interactive feedback; it was supposed to be surprising, not a means to a predetermined end, not a data storage and retrieval system. Second, it became imagined through a spatial metaphor, as a forum rather than a conduit, a cyberspace rather than an information highway. Third, it was imagined to embody a telos of inevitable change and progression, a kind of agency attributable to the technology without human agency or design; the recurring question about the future became "what will happen on the internet next?" instead of, say, "what will we as a society choose to do with computer communication?"

So how did this transformation happen if it cannot be attributed to the technology itself? A romantic construction of the emerging Internet as an unpredictable space for adventure was certainly more alluring than, say, the information retrieval or shopping mall visions being proffered by corporate and government leadership at the time. But more specifically, several structures or historical contingencies helped set the stage. One was that in the early 1990s, mid-level white collar workers who in the early 1990s did their own word processing – including, significantly, journalists – were able to experiment with the online world via modems, most centrally with the PC and Mac versions of Mosaic that were released in the summer of 1993. They thus were able to see, experience and share online practices and visions that their superiors were unaware of. The feeling of having knowledge of surprising events while one's superiors were oblivious lent itself to a romantic narrative of pleasure and rebellion; it was a case of feeling as thought and thought as feeling. And the direct experience of rapid development of new spaces online lent itself to a narrative in which the Internet had a telos.[7] It seemed to grow with a force of its own, beyond reach even of, say, Bill Gates.

Of course, there were more contingencies at play: the collapse of the Soviet Union and the return of the stock market to pre-1987 levels in the early 1990s, for example, gave new energy to individualist, pro-market, anti-government sentiments. The point is that all these structural forces in context set the stage for romantic individualist interpretations of what the Internet could be, at the expense of other possible narratives, such as a communitarian, social democratic or corporate liberal frames, which might have emphasised the role of public investment and perhaps allow for a more accurate, gradualist understanding of Internet development.

As a result, while the Internet did not emerge overnight from nowhere, in the American white collar imagination, it seemed to. What changed was less technology than public perception, but because that change in perception in the 1992–1996 period emerged more from the middle ranks than the top, it took the dominant institutions in the USA by surprise, a fact which just reinforced the romantic narrative. Historians like Abbate (2000) have made it clear that the 1980s was a rich period in the development of computer communication technology. Because that happened out of the limelight, however, the Internet seemed to burst forth on the scene in a way that made it seem like it was coming from nowhere. Business and mainstream journalists devoted sudden, adoring and uncritical attention to Internet technologies. Investors simultaneously flocked to the space, setting off the dotcom stock bubble, where the narrative that the Internet was revolutionary and an unstoppable force generated massive investments that we now know to have been mistaken.

The Internet's success, therefore, did not turn it in to the global network of networks that was subsequently recognised by an astonished society. Rather, it was largely the other way around: the culture's enthusiastic embrace of a romantic vision of the Internet as an agent of change is what generated a flood of engagement and investment in the technology, and then shaped its character. The structure of feeling thus had a causal effect on subsequent developments. The 1990s stock bubble not only reflected that vision, but also funded it. Stock-bubble funds created a massive build out in backbone fibre optic infrastructure, and directed investment in the computer industries towards graphically oriented, always-on compulsive interaction with computers; colour screens, fast connections and instant response time became more important than, say, long battery life or usefulness in education.[8] The visions of the time, furthermore, encouraged the sense of the Internet as a forum rather than a conduit, which in turn influenced both platform design and law, such as the 1998 U.S. Supreme Court case creating free speech rights on the Internet (Streeter, 2016, p. 188).

The larger point is that, in this case, the structure of feeling that swirled around the Internet in the mid-1990s, the structure of feeling that shaped Ira Magaziner's out-of-character approach to Internet governance, not only reflected the emergence of the Internet but also helped cause and shape it. That Magaziner's actions helped set the stage for the formation of Internet Corporation for Assigned Names and Numbers (ICANN), i.e. today's structures of Internet governance, is emblematic.

4. Conclusion: towards a theory of culture's relation to technology

The Internet is not a thing, it is not an object. While at given moments in time there have existed discrete sets of artefacts, technical forms of knowledge and practices that have made global digital communication possible, "the Internet" is both more and less than those discrete sets. Magaziner's peculiar action in 1998 cannot be explained without putting something called the Internet front and centre, but that something encompassed much more than gadgetry; it involved culture, political movements and social structure. The word Internet functions as a non-neutral metonymy for an historically embedded set of institutions and practices; in a sense it has more in common with the term "Hollywood" than, say, "moving image" (Streeter, 2016).

One could argue that we therefore might be better off abandoning the word "Internet" altogether as imprecise and potentially obfuscating. But another approach would emphasise that cultural expectations of the Internet *shaped the development of and thus are part of the artefact itself*. Cultural expectations and technological artefacts exist in an inextricably intertwined way. Technologies are perhaps best understood, not so much as agents in their own right, but as thought-objects for the collective enactment and exploration of hopes, desires and political visions.

Scholarly discussions of the role of technologies in social life seem to follow a pattern. If you press on the details of what look like clear instances of technology-caused change, you often find instances where the technologies themselves are less determinate, and matters of expectations and cultural habits more so. Eisenstein (1980) made an eloquent case that the printing press was an agent of change because typographic fixity created the conditions for the spread of science and other key features of modernity; Adrian Johns (2000) followed up with examples where print was more fluid and less reliably fixed than we imagined, and institutional and social relations played a larger role in the early formation of science than Eisenstein's work would suggest. James Aho (1985) showed how double entry bookkeeping, that other key "cause" of modernity, worked less mathematically and more rhetorically than traditional histories of capitalism assume. (Such patterns of argument sometimes seem endemic to the field of science and technology studies.)

The repeated discovery of culture inside what we have assumed to be the technological is not merely a cautionary tale about overgeneralising. Rather, it points to a general understanding of how what we call "technologies" work. Technologies in the first instance perhaps work as ways for people to enact hopes and expectations more than realities; *that* is core to their social impact. The effects of technologies, their affordances, are to a large degree not in some concrete, isolatable causal social change, but in the expectations that technologies become intertwined with from early on in their conception. Technologies cannot be understood apart from what they are imagined to be, unintended consequences included.

What that would suggest is that a field of "Internet history" should neither imagine itself in terms of the study of a technology, as the study of the technological thing called "the Internet" and its impact on culture and society, nor should it focus only on critiques of various technological determinisms, on ways in which we imagine the Internet to be a thing when it is not, when really we are looking at cultural forms and social relations, on things outside the technological. Rather, the point is to investigate what has happened since people began to talk about the Internet, to look at the cultural and social factors, not as independent from but as in certain ways constituent of, all that goes with the emergence of "the Internet" on the world stage.

Notes

1. I use the term "cyberculture" here loosely, to refer to a general sense that there exist style or styles associated with digital technology. Turner (2008) is an example of such a use of the term.
2. Williams here anticipated the concerns later associated with both affect theory and Bourdieu's notions of habitus: the goal is an understanding of the connections between habits of the heart and social processes, in a way that neither explains actions simply in terms of a grand abstraction (such as economic self-interest, bourgeois ideology or neoliberalism) nor denies the historically and socially embedded character of strategic actions. The hope is to get at the force field between the individual and society, at the very complicated and crucial interplay between subjective experiences and social structures, without reducing one to the other. It is no accident that Williams played a key role in introducing Bourdieu's theories to English-speaking scholars of media and culture (Garnham & Williams, 1980). Williams and Garnham approvingly quote Bourdieu as seeking a way to escape the "crude reduction of ideological products to the interests of the classes they serve (a short-circuit effect common in 'Marxist' critiques), without falling into the idealist illusion of treating ideological productions as self-sufficient and self-generating totalitietass amenable to pure, purely internal analysis (semiology)" (Garnham & Williams, 1980, p. 210).
3. While fond of lived experience and irony, the myth and symbol school, with its tendency to identify persistent themes across time shared by the society as a whole, could still be said to have some Hegelian tendencies.
4. While often in the literature about cyberculture the exact relationship of cultural trends to technological development is left more implied than explicit, there exist models of work that are explicit in their ambition to identify specific moments where culture shaped technical and policy choices (Flichy, 2007; Sewell, 2014; Sterne, 2012; Streeter, 1996).
5. Works that set out to explain how a set of computer communication technologies become associated with narratives of appealing unpredictability and rebellion are numerous and highly varied. They are typically based on interpretations of popular texts such as Levy's *Hackers* (2001), and writings on and about various early online systems such as The Well and outlets such as *Wired*. A thorough review of these works would require a separate essay. Flichy (2007) is exemplary, but also exemplifies some of the difficulties of making sense of such a sprawling range of sources: when reviewing diverse statements, white papers, news coverage and popular texts which do not all agree with each other, it becomes difficult to say exactly why some texts might be significant in what way, and others may turn out to be cultural curiosities. It becomes difficult to specify the *imaginaire* in question without falling back towards a kind of Hegelian *Zeitgeist*. That is why this essay offers the theory of the structure of feeling and an emphasis on experience and historical contingencies as a way to sharpen our understanding.
6. *Net Effect* defines romantic individualism less as a philosophy than an enduring discourse, what Swidler (1986) might call a cultural tool kit, that constructs the self as a process and source of unique truths rather than a want-satisfying calculator, celebrates authenticity over measurable facts, rebel heroes over rational managers and unpredictability over efforts to fit social life into a measurable grid (Streeter, 2011, pp. 45–46).
7. This experience was already familiar to the small groups who had been online in the 1980s, but new for the much larger group outside of research labs just entering the online world for the first time.
8. An example of a technological possibility that was not pursued because of this vision might be Apple's emate 300, which had a battery life of up to a week, was rugged and inexpensive, had a monochrome screen and was optimised for educational use, but not for web surfing. It was only released on a limited basis, and never manufactured on a scale that could have led to widespread adoption (Edwards, 2012).

Acknowledgments

I would like to thank the editors and anonymous reviewers of *Internet Histories* for their insightful and helpful criticisms and suggestions on drafts of this essay.

Disclosure statement

No potential conflict of interest was reported by the author.

ORCID

Thomas Streeter (iD) http://orcid.org/0000-0002-5274-981X

References

Abbate, J. (2000). *Inventing the internet*. Cambridge, MA: The MIT Press.

Abbate, J. (2010). Privatizing the internet: Competing visions and chaotic events, 1987–1995. *IEEE Annals of the History of Computing, 32*(1), 10–22. doi:https://doi.org/10.1109/MAHC.2010.24

Aho, J. A. (1985). Rhetoric and the invention of double entry bookkeeping. *Rhetorica: A Journal of the History of Rhetoric, 3*(1), 21–43. doi:https://doi.org/10.1525/rh.1985.3.1.21

Barbrook, R., & Cameron, A. (1996). The Californian ideology. *Science as Culture, 6*(1), 44–72. doi: https://doi.org/10.1080/09505439609526455

Borsook, P. (2000). *Cyberselfish: A critical romp through the world of high-tech*. London: Little, Brown & Company.

Carey, J. W., & Quirk, J. J. (1970). The mythos of the electronic revolution. *American Scholar, 39*(1–2), 219–241; 395–424.

Edwards, B. (2012, December 21). The Forgotten eMate 300– 15 years later. *Macworld*. Retrieved from http://www.macworld.com/article/2020270/the-forgotten-emate-300-15-years-later.html

Eisenstein, E. L. (1980). *The printing press as an agent of change*. Cambridge: Cambridge University Press.

Flichy, P. (2007). *The internet imaginaire*. (L. Carey-Libbrecht Trans.). Cambridge, MA: MIT Press.

Garnham, N., & Williams, R. (1980). Pierre Bourdieu and the sociology of culture: An introduction. *Media, Culture & Society, 2*(3), 209–223. doi:https://doi.org/10.1177/016344378000200302

Greenstein, S. (2015). *How the internet became commercial: Innovation, privatization, and the birth of a new network*. Princeton, NJ: Princeton University Press.

Global Policy Forum. Retrieved March 9, 2017, from https://www.globalpolicy.org/tables-and-charts-ql/27519-internet-users.html

Impoco, J. (1993). Technology titans sound off on the digital future. *U.S. News and World Report*, 114 (17), 62.

Johns, A. (2000). *The nature of the book: Print and knowledge in the making* (1st ed.). Chicago, IL: University of Chicago Press.

Lessig, L. (1998, October). *Governance*. Paper presented at the meeting of Computer Professionals for Social Responsibility on Internet Governance, Oct. 10, 1998.

Levy, S. (2001). *Hackers: Heroes of the computer revolution* (Updated (original 1984)). New York, NY: Penguin (Non-Classics).

Marx, L. (1967). *The machine in the garden: Technology and the pastoral ideal in America*. New York, NY: Oxford University Press.

McChesney, R. W. (2013). *Digital disconnect: How capitalism is turning the internet against democracy*. New York, NY: The New Press.

McCullagh, D., & McKay, N. (1998, November 12). Clinton net guru's legacy: Doing nothing well. *Los Angeles Times*.

Mosco, V. (1989). *The pay-per society: Computers and communication in the information age*. Aurora, Canada: Garamond Press.

Mosco, V. (2005). *The digital sublime: Myth, power, and cyberspace*. Cambridge, MA: The MIT Press.

Mueller, M. (2004). *Ruling the root: Internet governance and the taming of cyberspace*. Cambridge, MA: MIT Press.

Rosenzweig, R. (1998). Wizards, bureaucrats, warriors, and hackers: Writing the history of the internet. *The American Historical Review, 103*(5), 1530–1552. doi:https://doi.org/10.2307/2649970

Sewell, P. W. (2014). *Television in the age of radio*. New Brunswick, NJ: Rutgers University Press.

Shirky, C. (2009). *Here comes everybody: The power of organizing without organizations* (Reprint ed.). New York, NY: Penguin Books.

Sterne, J. (2012). *MP3: The meaning of a format* (1st ed.). Durham, NC: Duke University Press Books.

Stix, G. (1993). Domesticating cyberspace. *Scientific American, 269*(2), 84–92.

Streeter, T. (1996). *Selling the air: A critique of the policy of commercial broadcasting in the United States*. Chicago, IL: University of Chicago Press.

Streeter, T. (1999). "That deep romantic chasm": Libertarianism, neoliberalism, and the computer culture. In A. Calabrese & J. C. Burgelman (Eds.), *Communication, citizenship, and social policy: Rethinking the limits of the welfare state* (pp. 49–64). Lanham, MD: Rowman & Littlefield.

Streeter, T. (2011). *The net effect: Romanticism, capitalism, and the internet*. New York, NY: NYU Press.

Streeter, T. (2016). Internet. In B. Peters (Ed.), *Digital keywords: A vocabulary of information society and culture* (pp. 184–196). Princeton, NY: Princeton University Press.

Swidler, A. (1986). Culture in action: Symbols and strategies. *American Sociological Review, 51*(2), 273–286. doi:https://doi.org/10.2307/2095521

Turner, F. (2008). *From counterculture to cyberculture: Stewart brand, the whole earth network, and the rise of digital Utopianism*. Chicago, IL: University Of Chicago Press.

Williams, R. (1973). Base and superstructure in Marxist cultural theory. *New Left Review*, (82), 3.

Williams, R. (1978). *Marxism and literature*. New York, NY: Oxford University Press.

Williams, R. (2012). *The long revolution* (Reprint ed.). Cordigan: Parthian Books.

Williams, R. (2014). *Keywords: A vocabulary of culture and society* (New ed.). New York, NY: Oxford University Press.

Precorporation: or what financialisation can tell us about the histories of the Internet

Greg Elmer

ABSTRACT

This paper outlines a framework for a financialised history of social media companies, focusing on Facebook. Developing the concept of "precorporation", the paper argues that the years immediately preceding the company's initial public offering offer a micro-history of the forces that produce and constrain the core business model of Facebook.

Introduction

One of the more common promises and conclusions of historical studies of media is that media use, practices, formats and controversies reappear over long periods of time with a surprising degree of commonality (Bolter & Grusin, 1998). Decades-old media histories thus remind us of such continuities, and provide lessons to be learned from them. In this paper, I make a similar historical appeal to appreciate and study early Internet histories, yet one that is focused on a distinct period of time in the life of social media companies. This paper argues for a *financialised* history of social media, that is when a social media company's user policies, services, interfaces and, ultimately, business models are developed with an eye to large-scale financial investment (from both institutional and "public" investors).

The study of "micro-histories" of companies, typically anywhere from two to four years in length, are not without precedent in the field of Internet and social media studies. The constant updating of worldwide web browsers from Netscape, then later Microsoft explorer and Google Chrome, likewise can be broken down into distinct and short historical periods where the prominence of various functions such as indexes, customised search tools, and add-on apps are date stamped as "versions" (1.0, 1.2 and so forth).[1] This "periodisation" of internet histories, for example, has been conducted on web search engines.[2] We could also reimagine and moreover rewrite the early years of the web through the micro-histories of mass consumer Internet service providers (ISPs) such as American Online & CompuServe, services that constantly redesigned their interfaces to grow fee-paying users. More recently, Niels Brügger (2015) outlined a comprehensive history of the Facebook platform, broken down into four distinct periods beginning with 2004–2006, providing "…an outline of a history of one single element of Facebook, namely the textual and interactive media environment that users can see and interact with on the web site and on mobile media" Brügger (2015). Such micro-histories thus provide insight into how the Facebook platform redefined its core services visible on its user interface.

Following Brügger's Facebook case study, this paper similarly posits a slice of the Facebook company's history, but it is argued one far more distinct and instrumental than the rest – the years immediately preceding the company's listing on the NASDAQ stock exchange on 18 May 2012. It is my contention that the years immediately preceding a company's listing on stock exchange markets such as the technology heavy NASDAQ and others offer a condensed view on the development of commercially driven Internet enterprises. Political economists would typically define this period in time as a process of corporate financialisation, which at its most basic level aims to provide vast amounts of capital to Internet companies.[3] Such pre-marketised histories offers tremendous insight into how Internet companies, and in this instance, the Facebook company, are fundamentally restructured in advance of "going public". Such periods witness structural changes in the business models of companies as a signal to markets about their future sustainability and moreover prospective profits. In short, a historical study of Facebook helps to understand in both broad and increasingly granular terms the business model of Internet and particularly social media companies today,[4] and by extension, the associated concerns with the economic value and sustainability of companies (stemming from the dot com bubble of 2000), the ethical transgressions of companies (privacy and data discrimination), and the social impact of Internet-based communications and networking on various communities and demographics.

From incorporation to precorporation

Mark Fisher (2009) notes that the term "incorporation" is typically used to highlight the early transformation of businesses into legally recognised institutions such as limited companies, partnerships or corporations. The history of negotiations, funding and, in some instances, the actors involved in establishing the terms of incorporation is fundamental to understanding the goals, mission and structure of corporations, and their core business model. But Fisher goes one step further, preferring the term *precorporation*, to describe the periods in time where a set of legal, political and economic conventions establish the *prospects* (the "future-look") of a company. Moreover, the precorporate view of Internet company histories emphasises the moments where businesses must be "sold" – perhaps "pitched" is a better term – to investors. As a result, in addition to the years preceding stock market listing – the period of "going public" – *precorporate histories* might also include the early years of a company's formation, where partners, angel investors or other technology companies often make important initial investments in a company to allow it to explore business models. In this respect, the company prospectus often serves as the penultimate precorporate document, where at various stages in the capitalisation of a firm, the business model, philosophy and source of financial value, going forward, are articulated to prospective partners and investors (Dror, 2015; Elmer, 2016).

The *precorporate* view of Internet histories thus argues that the process of financialisation serves a unique motivating factor in the early history of social media companies – that there are common processes established in the process of financialisation of companies such as

Facebook. In what follows, I detail albeit briefly a set of common and intersecting political and economic processes and trajectories that inform the precorporate years of the Facebook company. It is my contention that the sum of these trajectories, ultimately condensed into the most intense years of precorporate financialisation, provides fundamental answers to a host of questions concerning the historical change in practices, interfaces, platforms and ultimately business models of new web and increasingly mobile/app-focused social media companies.

These intersecting trajectories can be summarised into three categories. First, by focusing on the financialisation of Facebook, I am explicitly calling attention to the core value proposition of social media, specifically asking what will lead to the generation of profits and/or value for stock holders? During moments of precorporation, in other words, investors of all stripes are often invited to imagine the future possibilities of unproven and untested technologies. In short, where is the financial value proposition in social media?

The second trajectory closely follows this process of imagining financial value. As the dotcom gold rush cascaded forwarded, leading to the dot-bomb market crash of 1999–2000, precorporate histories of the Internet, and then social media also become governmental stories, highlighting the rules that dictate the conditions of financial promotions, offers, "pitches" and IPOs. Indeed while much has been written about the collaborative genesis of the Arpanet, the precursor to the Internet (Abbate, 1999). But Brian Murphy (2002) reminds us that since the late 1990s the Internet has been governed as a for-profit commercial sphere. Murphy traces the work of Vice President Al Gore, as he shepherded a series of government bills that would place control of the Internet in the hands of the private sector. Murphy writes:

> The final link in the chain of enabling legislation came with the Communications Act of 1996. The new law governing the operations of all media in the United States affirmed that "the Market will drive both the internet and information highway. (p. 31)

Finally, precorporation helps us to understand the shaping of the Internet itself through the projections and properties of its leading companies as we have entered the social media era, the scarce interface of the Google search engine, Facebook's prompting social network site and Twitter's endless vertical ticker, to name just three of the more successful properties. That is to say, precorporation reshapes and reforms not only the corporate structure of Internet companies, and where it sets up its head offices and houses its workers, it also reshapes the relationships with users and non-users.

Facebook's precorporate era

On the question of economic value, a fundamental component that communications and Internet-based companies often face during the years of precorporation is the process of convincing investors to part with their money.[5] For companies like *Facebook*, the question of value remains immaterial and elusive for most critics and market watchers. Indeed, the company's prospectus, again the key document that was used to sell the company's future financial viability and worth to investors and the market, was revised six times to answer this very question (Blodget, 2012). In each instance, revisions were sought by market regulators and financial underwriters (Morgan Stanley, JP Morgan and Goldman Sachs), so as to sharpen the case for how the company was going to make money. While most recognised that ad sales would lead the way for Facebook, revisions to the prospectus also noted the role of the company's recently developed "social graph" algorithm[6] – in conjunction with the roll out of a mobile platform – would enhance the company's future financial prospects.[7]

Earlier rounds of capitalisation of Facebook similarly invoked the process of imagining and rewriting the core value of the company. This moment in the history of Facebook was dramatically represented in director David Fincher's cinematic story of the rise of Mark Zuckerberg's Facebook, *The Social Network*. In one of the key scenes in the film, Zuckerberg and Facebook co-founder Eduardo Savarin discuss strategies with former Napster co-founder Sean Parker, to sell their vision of Facebook to angel investors, financing that would effectively launch the company and provide much needed resources to develop the company's platform.

While the process of seeking investment is mostly clearly associated with the process of financialisation (seeking investment through the stock market), almost all Internet companies share a precorporate period of external capitalisation and investment, often by these so-called "angel investors", or by other larger digital media and software companies like Google and Microsoft, who take a small stake or ownership in the emerging firm. Such histories are often hidden from the public's view, and only revealed years later. But such moments of precorporation place an important emphasis on visions and visionaries (leaders) within the emerging company, and conversely potential constraints and pressures exerted upon the company by early investors.

Next, with regards to the process of economic regulation, the years of precorporation are closely attuned to market regulations of the day, the rules that define the responsibilities and processes that incorporated and so-called "public" companies must follow. The precorporate view of Internet histories, in other words, must also be viewed as a history of corporate governance, both in terms of what pressures have produced market regulations and company law (banking crises, market crashes, widespread fraud, etc.), and conversely how companies themselves actively play a role in co-producing (interpreting) pre-existing and evolving laws and regulations.

For Facebook, the writing and rewriting of the company's prospectus was chiefly governed by the US Securities Act, and overseen by the Securities and Exchange Commission.[8] This moment of precorporation, however, proved to be a major embarrassment for Facebook as it was later revealed that while the publicly available prospectus was shared with investors and the public, warnings about future growth being stifled by the as-yet unproven mobile platform was only shared with institutional investors.[9]

In addition to questions of immaterial value, IPO sales and market regulation, this last section highlights how Facebook used its precorporate years, specifically 2008–2012, leading up to the NASDAQ IPO, to reconfigure its relationship with its user base to intensify efforts to collect social networking data. The first thing to note about Facebook as an employer is that unlike tech firms like Apple and some Internet-based firms like Amazon and Google, leading up to the IPO Facebook employed a startlingly low number of staff in relationship to its corporate value, roughly 3000. This made Facebook's per worker company valuation – meaning the ratio of staff per value of the company – nearly five times greater than Apple or Google. Derek Thompson (2012), however, argues that this figure is somewhat misleading. In *The Atlantic*, Thompson writes that "…Facebook's workforce isn't just 3,000 employees, but also 835 million users, who create information that is valuable to advertisers, and therefore valuable to Facebook..." What's more, in 2011, it was revealed that Facebook also data mines *non*-Facebook users, that is, those individuals who have not expressly opened an account on the platform.[10] Such "ghost or shadow profiles" thus highlight how the intensification of data collection by Facebook was not restricted to its user base.

This is not to suggest, however, that a precorporate Facebook was turning away from collecting ever more granular information and data points on its users. Returning to the work of Brügger above, the process of precorporation in social media companies is commonly synonymous with rapid changes in interfaces and user services that in the case of Facebook represent a more intensified period of user surveillance and data mining. That is to say, Facebook intensified their search for economic value in immaterial communications and networking in this precorporate period, particularly immediately preceding their stock flotation.[11]

Quantitatively speaking, the years 2004 and 2005 saw very little changes to Facebook's interface and core user services. There were only seven changes to the social networking site over these 24 months.[12] By 2008, however, at the start of the precorporate period, Facebook made 24 substantial changes to their platform, including adding a "wall" on users pages where friend could leave messages and comments. By 2010, 12 months prior to the company IPO, the platform witnessed 48 changes, many focused on promoting more networking with other users – tagging friends in updates, uploading photos, friend anniversaries and so forth. Most importantly, for the future prospectus of Facebook was the introduction of the open graph protocol in April of 2010, where all objects, users, nonusers, media and text were integrated into Facebook's back-end algorithms and data mining technologies. Taken as a whole, during the period of precorporation (2008–2012), changes to the Facebook platform sought to reaffirm its core business model of social data mining, by proliferating the opportunities it developed for its user interface, and in many cases, the changes were experienced by users as "prompts'" encouraging them to post more, upload more, and engage with their friend networks through ever more granular means.

Conclusion

In this paper, I have sought to briefly outline a precorporate view of the Facebook company, one that placed emphasis on structural decisions that produced long-lasting and ever-increasing possibilities for capital accumulation for investors. This is not an exercise in tinkering, nor is it one that is easily changed in a matter of years. Rather precorporate histories serve as a structural forecasting for social media companies, the end goal being to communicate and "pitch" the core value proposition in the context of growth opportunities.

In this forward-looking financial context, we have seen in the first instance that due to the immaterial nature of much Internet business and the elusive value of social media data, the precorporate years of companies are driven by imaginations, symbolic gestures and, as Dror noted (2015), broad "manifestos" of friendly corporate values. Not surprisingly, many new media, technology, and Internet and particularly social companies have been led by charismatic and visionary leaders who, while lacking in specifics on the development of core business models and profits, are rich in ideas that should be seeded, by other tech firms or by institutional and individual investors during the IPO process.

This is not to suggest, however, that ideas and personalities run amok during periods of precorporation, for we have seen that such years must recognize and adhere to – or for some contribute and rewrite—the regulatory environment of the day. It would be hard to argue that no other sector has not had more of a "free hand" in the market place than US-based tech and Internet companies. That said, Facebook still managed to run afoul of market regulators and prove to all market watchers that there are clear hierarchies of market knowledge, especially during the IPO process.

This leaves us with the question of how *precorporation*, as a concept for understanding particular historical periods of the Internet has impacted individual users and society in general. Much ink has been spilt on the privacy transgressions of Facebook, yet this brief precorporate view of the years preceding the company's IPO has also revealed that the company's social networking algorithm, the "social graph", combined with various new services and interface prompts to post or otherwise interact more with the platform, are not entirely directed at the new user-worker of Facebook. Rather this would be only one part of the precorporate picture. Looking forward, Facebook's prospects would lie in the production of an infinite field of data points.

Notes

1. My previous study of web browser cookies follows this exact method (Elmer, 2003).
2. The Digital Methods team at the University of Amsterdam designed a short video to highlight just such a history of Google: https://movies.digitalmethods.net/google.htm>
3. Cf Winseck (1998) on an earlier view of financialisation and corporations in the 1850s.
4. Especially those social media companies/platform, as we shall see, that has developed user-data-based income models.
5. And as I have previously detailed in an early study of the Marconi company, this is not a contemporary phenomenon (Elmer 2016). Like Marconi's wireless business, Internet and social media companies like Facebook face unique questions concerning the *immateriality* of their core business – what is it that they are proposing to sell? To make a profit from? Marconi's "apparatus" as it was initially dubbed, for instance, was commonly pitched as a "magical" or otherworldly advance in science, making communications in essence not only disappear but travel vast distances. But concrete applications of the invention took years to establish and thrive (Elmer 2016).
6. Former Facebook designer Matt Hicks summarises the importance of the social graph algorithm here: <https://www.facebook.com/notes/facebook/building-the-social-web-together/383404517130>
7. < https://www.sec.gov/Archives/edgar/data/1326801/000119312512034517/d287954ds1.htm>
8. cf. < https://www.sec.gov/divisions/corpfin/guidance/securitiesactrules-interps.htm>
9. < https://www.ft.com/content/403077b8-af28-11e5-993b-c425a3d2b65a>
10. < http://www.zdnet.com/article/anger-mounts-after-facebooks-shadow-profiles-leak-in-bug/>
11. We can see the exact same trend in the precorporate years at the micro-blogging social media company Twitter in advance of their November 2013 IPO where wholesale changes are made to the company's privacy and data use policies.
12. < http://www.jonloomer.com/2012/05/06/history-of-facebook-changes/>

Disclosure statement

No potential conflict of interest was reported by the author.

Funding

Social Sciences and Humanities Research Council of Canada

References

Abbate, J. (1999). *Inventing the Internet*. Cambridge: MIT Press.
Blodget, H. (2012, December 20). Revealed: The full story of how Facebook IPO buyers got screwed. *Business Insider*. Retrieved from http://www.businessinsider.com/how-facebook-ipo-investors-got-screwed-2012-12.
Bolter, J., & Grusin, R. (1998). *Remediation: Understanding new media*. Cambridge: MIT Press.
Brügger, N. (2015). A brief history of Facebook as a media text: The development of an empty structure. *First Monday, 20*(5).
Dror, Y. (2015). We are not here for the money: Founders Manifestos. *New Media & Society, 17*(4), 540–555.
Elmer, G. (2003). *Profiling machines*. Cambridge: MIT Press.
Elmer, G. (2016). *A new medium goes public:* The financialization of Marconi's Wireless Telegraph & Signal Company. *New Media and Society*. Retrieved from https://doi.org/10.1177/1461444816643505
Fisher, M. (2009). *Capitalist realism: Is there no alternative?* London: Zero Books.
Murphy, B. M. (2002). A critical history of the Internet. In G. Elmer (Ed.), *Critical perspectives on the internet* (pp. 27–45). Boulder, MO: Rowman & Littlefield.
Thompson, D. (2012, February 2). The profit network: Facebook and its 835 million-man workforce. *The Atlantic*. Retrieved from http://www.theatlantic.com/business/archive/2012/02/the-profit-network-facebook-and-its-835-million-man-workforce/252473/
Winseck, D. (1998). *Reconvergence: A political economy of telecommunications in Canada*. New York, NY: Hampton Press.

Internet in the Middle East: an asymmetrical model of development

Ilhem Allagui ⓘ

ABSTRACT
The paper adopts an interdisciplinary approach to examine Internet history in the Middle East and fill a gap in the subfield of regional Internet histories studies. It is a narrative of Internet development in a complex area and era. It draws on influential key events to question the role of Internet development in current debates about regulation and change and to highlight its asymmetry throughout the region. The paper uses a critical analysis as well as a historical analysis of policies and usages to map Arab countries' Internet development and suggests a political and cultural framework to help understand the tensions and contentions around this development.

Introduction

This paper attempts to bring up to the fore one of the stories of the Internet in the Middle East; it stresses out the evolving dialogic conversations occurring in the political, cultural and economic realms. It aims to give pointers to think about the history of the Internet given its specificities in the region. It does not give a full account of its histories. Writing such a history of the Internet with limited material and within limited space cannot be exhaustive. This history is an attempt to capture some specificity, particularly in light of post-Arab uprisings tour de force that gave new media in the Arab world new dynamism and some significance.

The paper starts with a conceptual frame that posits the tensions and contentions around which Internet grew and developed in the Arab region. Then, it moves with a discussion and empirical evidence around the model.

Participation in the digital society has been subject to factor apparatus that includes access, infrastructure, education, equipment, talent, demographics, geography and freedom. Since the early adoption of the Internet, scholars attempted to understand the disparity of its growth within and between countries, within and between regions. For instance, social inequalities, have and have not computer ownership and Internet link service were among the first access determinants discussed by van Dijk (2005, 2006). DiMaggio, Hargittai, Celeste, and Shafer (2004) associated inequality with not taking advantage of benefits of the Internet while Jenkins (2006) spoke about participation gap and Hargittai and Hinnant (2008) linked lack of access to bad digital skills. The term "digital gap" moved from a literal meaning of owning and using a computer to the quality of Internet connection, fast or slow and intermittent and then to the "integration with the many ubiquitous networked technologies embedded into daily life" (Graham, 2011, p. 213).

In the Middle East, Shirazi, Gholami, and Higón (2009) argue that the growth of information and communication technologies (ICT) in the region is conditional to its economic freedom. Farris (2013) adds that access to the Internet across the Arab region depends on income and country; he also argues that the digital inequality empowered youth and revived their sense of activism during the Arab uprisings. Kaba and Said (2014) compared the digital divide among and across three groups of countries, GCC countries (Gulf Cooperation Council countries include the United Arab Emirates, Saudi Arabia, Qatar, Kuwait, Bahrain and Oman), ASEAN countries (Association of Southeast Asian Nations) and other Arab countries. They found a better ICT infrastructure and usage in GCC countries but noted no significant difference in regards to governments' support to and usage of ICT.

With this paper, my aim is to provide a narrative of historical development of the Internet across the region, prompted by major factors that influenced the way this evolution has happened. To illustrate this historical development, I suggest a schema that points to variables that emerge from this history. These variables are politics, culture and economics.

Conceptual implications for Internet development

The Internet evolved under the triangular taut relations between politics, culture and economics. While political and cultural influence kept inhibiting technological innovation and hampering development (concerns for political stability, traditions and religion inhibited the access to technology and investment in innovation), the economic urge and aspirations played the opposite effect amidst the conjectural model of a growing Internet society.

Entangled at the foundation of this pyramid (Figure 1), the political and cultural factors are not mutually exclusive as they use each other in the dynamics of Internet development such as when political agency uses cultural factors to justify protectionism. In this case, and from a Western model of development, they gradually limit the growth of the Internet and the prospect of any consequential economic outcome. However, the opposite occurs when both political and cultural factors intersect to propel Internet development, which eventually leads to improvement of the overall economic ecosystem.

The political, cultural and economic spheres that will be discussed in the following, tie into each other in several ways. At times, they support each other and Internet growth; they may also interconnect but end up limiting the benefits of their cohesiveness. Following is three fitting examples to this model. The first example can be found in the uneven adoption stage of the technology when global liberalisation agreements as well as domestic pressure from the private sector (UNESCWA, 2015) weighed in the political decision to embrace the Internet despite hostility and protectionism expressed by Arab political agents. Then, these agents adopted a narrative on the verge of technological determinism and that contrasted with what they had really enacted in the majority of the countries.

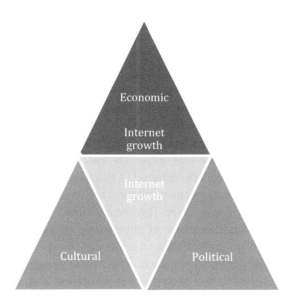

Figure 1. Framework for an asymmetrical model of Internet development.

Arab governments' responses to the promise of the public space were common about reinforcing policies and regulations, but poles apart on the grounds of developing infrastructure that supports the new economy.

A second fitting example can be found in the cultural sphere. Culture has been the primary reason for Arab users to visit the Web in the first place, especially in its early days. The desire to speak about the self, one's culture and identity is what first attracted Arab youth and the Arab diaspora to the Internet (Anderson, 2000; Antaki, 2000; Wheeler, 2005), enabled to build an Arab audience and drive traffic to the Arab cyberspace. This was consistent with the political agenda and economically promising, until concerns about protectionism took over and regulations tightened.

Another example that illustrates the tensions of Arab Internet development from a combined cultural and political perspective can be found in the short development of Arabic digital content, especially in the pre-social media times, that led Arab politicians to adopt a top–bottom strategy for content production (UNESCWA, 2015). Such government initiatives proved once again the entanglement of the political and cultural in the development of the cyberspace and the Internet. While this interconnectedness is not unique to the Arab world, it is indicative of an upper level of complexity when it comes to the Arab sphere. Building on the tradition of media content and censorship in the region, one can expect that this content would also be crafted carefully and in line with old practices.

The asymmetrical trajectories of the Internet across the region inform about three pillars, culture, politics and economy, decisive to Internet development.

Politics in relation to Internet development

Initially, politicians welcomed the Internet with great apprehension. This is illustrated in a number of ways: first, its adoption came to the region under negotiation of free trade agreements with the World Trade Organization and pressure by international telecommunication and development agencies (Abdullah, 2008; Murphy, 2009). Second, the restrictive and protected environment that the Internet ushered within inhibited its development. Regulations and policies infringed a fair experience. Arab leaders' negative attitudes towards this new technology that promises freedom of expression, open environment and democracy encrusted them with hostility towards its adoption and increased concern with political movements offline and online (Human Rights Watch, 1999). Consequently, governments intensified surveillance, which translated into limitation to access to the technology and a preference for a substandard digital infrastructure.

In the 1990s, Internet diffusion was extremely low and Web content in Arabic was undeveloped. A number of factors contributed to this lack, chief among these are a weak digital infrastructure, unequal connectivity through the region, challenges of literacy and problems of Arabic language adaptation (The Arab Human Development Report, 2002, 2003). Literacy policy was another cause of discrepancy. While Morocco failed to put in place a plan to educate its population about the Internet (Human Rights Watch, 1999), the UAE was heavily investing in digital literacy in schools and universities (UNESCWA, 2015). Similar trends can be noted in the Levant where education and knowledge influenced Internet adoption (Anderson, 2000). Within the GCC countries, socio-economic factors, income and education were major factors in setting apart adoption patterns.

This is not to suggest that the Arab world was not receptive to the potential of the Internet, but only to point out that the development of the Internet throughout the region has not been consistent or even. While the technology evolved, Arab government's approach to "new" media did not evolve due to their protective approach as well as a set of rules and regulations that kept lagging behind. Arab governments' Web content was a projection of traditional state media practices that include distribution of official information, at times making available some useful communications to the public, but also offering propaganda material (Human Rights Watch, 1999). Alongside the government's promulgated information sphere developed a semi private sphere where populations sought and accessed material of a different nature. For instance, in early days of the Arab cyberspace, advocates of cyber-Islamism were very active reaching out to new audiences and spreading messages and information about virtues and image of Islam while pledging for a more conservative Islamic society (Eickelman & Anderson, 2003).

Arab governments were not concerned with such a socio-cultural development; it is only when Arab users migrated to the Web that the governments realised the perils of this migration and started censorship. With Web 2.0, Arab users discovered the participatory culture and experienced the rise of blogging with prominence of Salam Pax blog during the 2003 Iraq invasion. For the following years, blogging trends picked up enabling users, well-organised groups as well as citizens who individually or collectively organised in networks, to further engage online creating discussions about topics including human rights and national and international political stories that would be non-existent or censored offline. This drew governments' attention to the perils of open access and hindered users' conversations in an environment that has been averse to free speech.

Arab governments have controlled the ICT market since the inception, with a narrative framing the Internet as a tool for institutional development, mainly in the economic domain. The fear of losing political control led governments to opt for a monopoly or duopoly and the economic development has been tied with this control until recent years prior to the uprisings, when the liberalisation of the public sphere and the calls for political restructures threatened the development of the economy-driven ICT sector (Al-Qudsi-Ghabra, AlBannai, & Al-Bahrani, 2011).

The tension within the steer of Internet growth in the Arab world has a historical precedent, namely the development of the telecommunication sector's infrastructure. The adoption of the technological innovation in the 1980s led to the development of a new communication era in the Arab world. Driven by regional dynamisms, political rivalries, security concerns as well as economic opportunities, this started regional inception of the satellite revolution in the Arab world, which led to the emergence of hundreds of satellite channels and a vibrant broadcasting media sphere.

Thus, the evolution of the Arab telecommunications sector happened in the shadow of a political component that is much stronger than anywhere else in the world (Sborowski & Sourbes-Verger, 2009). Eventually, the satellites forced in a commercial and economic perspective, along with a global informational perspective. With the Internet, there is a similar strong economic component to the telecom infrastructure development. Both telecommunication companies and Internet service providers capitalised on business opportunities with the Internet offering; the monopolies or duopolies of the telecom markets in several of the countries of the Arab region are commercial opportunities for the states as much as it is about their need to exert control (Anderson, 2013).

Culture in relation to Internet development

A different history of the Internet in the Arab region started with blogs and social media use for activism, combined with the occurrence of the Arab uprisings. Despite governments' attempts to censor and control, social media equipped people with space for self- and group-expression and ultimately, with increased and broadband penetration, forced in greater usage of the technology.

Adopting neither a utopian nor dystopian approach about media's role in the Tunisian uprisings, Zayani (2016) uses the concept of "contentious digital culture" to make sense of the events. By looking at the everyday life, as well as the social and cultural practices, he argues that mundane interactions have constructed a contentious cyberspace, which could no longer hold with keeping users politically disconnected. The contention is born from the incongruity of connecting people with ICT while at the same time forcing a political silence. Along these lines, Al-Qudsi-Ghabra et al. (2011) note inconsistencies and contradictions among controlling governments, who want to be modern, global and local, while also authoritarian, in a cyberspace that is occupied by a "new generation of educated, well equipped technologically and differently acculturated" youth (2011, p. 62). Howard and Parks (2012, p. 360) think about the Arab uprisings as a complex "connection between technology diffusion, the use of digital media and political change." Howard (2011) notes that social media is the tools of social movements and will continue to play a role in catching dictators; similarly, Lynch (2012) highlights that Arab youth have been experiencing blogging and social media before the "events", and both broadcast and digital media played crucial role in the uprisings, and he also referred to historical deeper roots found in social struggles, ideological conflicts and prior wars and popular riots.

With social media, we witnessed the development of various kinds of digital content, activist and militant at times, but also mundane and cultural at others. While initially concerns were raised about proliferation of Westernised digital content in local cultures (for instance, the critical perspective adopted by Albirini (2008) who points to an Internet cultural bias as it developed under a Western design and content), the uprisings proved cultural content appropriation and congruence with the local culture, customs and values. Further to their relation to the everyday life as described by Zayani (2016), activists and users alike used political humour, jokes, satires, their bodies (Kraidy, 2016) and other kinds of creativity offline and online that speak to the locale and energise their individual and group mobilisation (Allagui, 2014).

Although historically the evolution of the Internet in the Arab region has been one "of filters and checkpoints" (Deibert, 2009, p. 324), social media and mobile technology propelled the use of the Internet in the region. The ease-of-use of social media has enabled Arab users, especially those who did not encounter technological education in schools or work environments, to get online, in their preferred language, and on a relatively not expensive device. Mobiles have been preeminent in the uprisings and mobile broadband connectivity continues to be much higher than fixed broadband penetration[1] serving as a primary apparatus for social or business interactions and leading one to believe that development is within reach.

Economy in relation to Internet development

Development studies have celebrated the advent of the "technological revolution" also called "information revolution" or "network revolution" (Benkler, 2006; Castells, 1996; Toffler, 1980) for what it is supposed to drive, whether it is employment, economic growth, democracy or the overall betterment of the society. For developing countries, in general, and the MENA region, in particular, there was considerable faith in the ability of the information revolution to bring by a technological "leap frog" (Antonelli, 1991) that would enable these societies to catch up with the progress developed societies have achieved and that the developing region has "missed" in the pre-information society time. With the post-uprisings, and while there is barely any economic improvement achieved in the Arab uprising countries where unemployment rates are still significantly high, there is a dominant discourse that suggests technology and digital media would puzzle out youth unemployment. Government agents, capitalising on better access to ICT and improved broadband infrastructure, push an optimistic-led discourse suggesting enthusiastically that a shift from conventional economies to start-ups and online entrepreneurship would help resolve unemployment and address youth economic struggles.

The oil-rich Arabian Gulf countries succeeded implementing an advanced Internet infrastructure early on that enabled achieving better connectivity, but mainly enabled a passage into the new economy. For instance, the UAE has betted on the new economy early on and has been leading the region in developing ecommerce ventures. In 2015, its market size is $10.25 billion,[2] the highest in the region (OMD Arabnet report, 2016). Other Arab countries are still challenged with poor or moderate infrastructure, high connectivity costs, low penetration rates and low access, archaic banking facilities including very low credit card penetration, and slow agents to effectively promote the new economy. Experts agree that today, the main factors that still inhibit the transition to digital economy are "Infrastructure, Industry, Individual (education, skills), and Information (information available online from commerce, e-gov and freedom of information etc.)" (Hfaiedh, 2016, online).

Evidently, the coming of the digital age and the promise of the digital economy have not benefitted the region equally. The region is still marked by flagrant discrepancy between lowest gross domestic product (GDP) countries tied with conflicts and setbacks and those so far tied with technological development. While the Arab uprisings aggravated the economy of some Arab countries and their populations who still suffer increasing unemployment, the GCC countries responded to the Arab uprisings with increasing job opportunities, financial supports and aids to their populations.

The asymmetrical model of Internet development laid in this paper discusses the ways the entanglement of politics, culture and economics has factored in the rise or stagnation of Internet adoption and usage. Digital opportunities may have eased off the economic sphere in some cases (i.e. The UAE), yet, other experiences show that although culture and politics may work in synergy towards Internet growth, the improvement of the digital economy is not an unequivocal outcome. The Tunisian case proved to be the only democracy of the region where culture and politics are allies, yet Tunisia has been struggling economically since the uprisings; the development of its Internet infrastructure combined with the growth of digital media usage has had little or no significant improvement on the economy (TAP, 2017).

This paper adds to the body of research interested in understanding the histories of non-Western Internet development. Obviously, the schema discussed is only a prototype of a model; the model would be much more complex, but it provides a conceptual framework to understand the development of the Internet in the region and enable to point to key aspects such as interventionism and regulation. The overall aim is to give the reader an overview of the ways Internet has initially developed unequally through the region, because of economic, political and cultural choices that countries and agents of the region made. Further in-depth history that looks at specific actors and at specific points in time should follow this work.

Notes

1. In 2012, the mobile broadband connectivity in the Arab region is six times the fixed broadband connectivity (ESCWA, 2013).
2. For comparison basis, some Nordic countries like the Netherlands or Austria have achieved an ecommerce market size nearing $10 billion in 2014 (http://www.adigital.org/media/2014/06/european-b2c-ecommerce-report-2014.pdf).

Acknowledgments

I am thankful to the editors for the opportunity to be part of this inaugural issue and grateful to the anonymous referees and editors for their comments and suggestions.

Disclosure statement

No potential conflict of interest was reported by the author.

ORCID

Ilhem Allagui (iD) http://orcid.org/0000-0002-3379-6442

References

Abdullah, R. (2008). *The Internet in the Arab world. Egypt and beyond.* New York, NY: Peter Lang.

Albirini, A. (2008). The Internet in developing countries: A medium of economic, cultural and political domination. *International Journal of Education and Development Using ICT, 4*(1), 49–65.

Allagui, I. (2014). Waiting for spring: Arab resistance and change. Editorial Introduction. *International Journal of Communication, 8*, 983–1007.

Al-Qudsi-Ghabra, M., AlBannai, T., & Al-Bahrani, M. (2011). The Internet in the Arab Gulf cooperation council (AGCC): Vehicle of change. *International Journal of Internet Science, 6*(1), 44–67.

Anderson, J. (2000). Producers and Middle East internet technology: Getting beyond "impacts". *The Middle East Journal. The Information Revolution, 54*(3), 419–431. Retrieved from http://www.jstor.org/stable/4329509

Anderson, J. (2013). Is informationalization good for the Middle East? *Arab Media & Society,* (18). Retrieved from http://www.arabmediasociety.com/?article=836

Antaki, G. (2000). Internet development in Lebanon. *Journal Electronic Markets, 10*(2), 147–147.

Antonelli, C. (1991). *The diffusion of advanced telecommunications in developing countries.* Paris: OECD.

Arab Human Development Report. (2002). *Creating opportunities for future generations.* New York, NY: UNDP.

Arab Human Development Report. (2003). *Building a knowledge society.* New York, NY: UNDP.

Benkler, Y. (2006). *The wealth of networks.* New Haven, CT: Yale University Press.

Castells, M. (1996). *The rise of the network society.* Oxford: Basil Blackwell.

Deibert, R. (2009). The geopolitics of internet control. Censorship, sovereignty, and cyberspace. In A. Chadwick & P. N. Howard (Eds.), *The Routledge handbook of internet politics* (pp. 323–336). Oxon: Routledge.

DiMaggio, P., Hargittai, E., Celeste, C., & Shafer, S. (2004). Digital in-equality: From unequal access to differentiated use. In K. Neckerman (Ed.), *Social inequality* (pp. 355–400). New York, NY: Russell Sage Foundation.

Economic and Social Commission for Western Asia (ESCWA). (2013). *Regional profile of the information society in the Arab region.* New York, NY: United Nations. Retrieved from https://www.unescwa.org/publications/profile-information-society-arab-region-2015.

Eickelman, D., & Anderson, J. (2003). *New media in the Muslim world.* Bloomington: Indiana University Press.

Farris, D. M. (2013). Digitally divided we stand: The contribution of digital media to the Arab spring. In M. Ragnedda & G. W. Muschert (Eds.), *The digital divide: The Internet and social inequality in international perspective* (pp. 209–221). New York, NY: Routledge.

Graham, M. (2011). Time machines and virtual portals: The spatialities of the digital divide. *Progress in Development Studies, 11*(3), 211–227. doi:10.1177/146499341001100303

Hargittai, E., & Hinnant, A. (2008). Digital inequality. Differences in young adult's use of the internet. *Communication Research, 35*(5), 602–621. doi:10.1177/0093650208321782

Hfaiedh, I. (2016, May 19). Middle East DNS forum Tunis 2016: Exposing reality and possible prospects. *Non Commercial Users Constituency*. Retrieved from http://www.ncuc.org/middle-east-dns-
forum-tunis-2016-exposing-reality-and-possible-prospects/

Howard, P. N. (2011). *The digital origins of dictatorship and democracy: Information technology and
political Islam*. Oxford: Oxford University Press.

Howard, P. N., & Park, M. R. (2012). Social media and political change: Capacity, constraint, and consequences. *Journal of Communication, 62*(2), 359–362. doi:10.1111/j.1460-2466.2012.01626.x

Human Rights Watch. (1999). *The internet in the Mideast and North Africa: Free expression and censorship*. Retrieved from https://www.hrw.org/legacy/advocacy/internet/mena/int-mena.htm.

Jenkins, H. (2006). *Convergence culture: Where old and new media collide*. New York, NY: New York
University Press.

Kaba, A., & Said, R. (2014). Bridging the digital divide through ICT: A comparative study of the countries of the Gulf Cooperation council, ASEAN and other Arab countries. *Information Development,
30*(4), 358–365. doi:10.1177/0266666913489987

Kraidy, M. (2016). *The naked blogger of Cairo: Creative insurgency in the Arab world*. Cambridge, MA:
Harvard University Press.

Lynch, M. (2012). *The Arab uprisings: The unfinished revolutions of the Middle East*. New York, NY:
Public Affairs.

Murphy, E. C. (2009). Theorizing ICTs in the Arab world: Informational capitalism and the public
sphere. *International Studies Quarterly, 53*(4), 1131–1153. doi:10.1111/j.1468-2478.2009.00571.x

OMD Arabnet report. (2016). Ecommerce insights and best practices. Retrieved from http://intelli
gence.arabnet.me.

Sborowski, F., & Sourbes-Verger, I. (2009). Vu d'en haut: Les pays Arabes et la Communication Spa-
tiale [Seen from above: Arab countries and spatial communication]. In Y. Gonzalez-Quijano &
T. Guaaybess (Eds.), *Les Arabes parlent aux Arabes. La revolution de l'information dans le monde
arabe* [Arabs talk to Arabs: Information revolution in the Arab world] (pp. 53–67). Arles: Editions
Sindbad.

Shirazi, F., Gholami, R., & Higón, D. A. (2009). The impact of information and communication technology (ICT), education and regulation on economic freedom in Islamic Middle Eastern countries.
Information & Management, 46, 426–433.

Tunis Afrique Press (TAP). (2017). Tunisia digital 2020. New structure to carry out projects. Retrieved
from https://www.tap.info.tn/en/Portal-Top-Slide-EN/8676764-tunisia-digital

Toffler, A. (1980). *The third Wave*. New York, NY: Bantam.

UNESCWA. (2015). *Cultural diversity and identity, linguistic diversity and local content*. New York, NY:
United Nations. Retrieved from https://www.unescwa.org/sites/www.unescwa.org/files/publica
tions/files/profile-information-society-arab-region-2015-english_0.pdf

van Dijk, J. (2005). *The deepening divide: Inequality in the information society*. Thousand Oaks, CA:
Sage.

van Dijk, J. (2006). *The network society. Social aspects of new media* (2nd ed.). London: Sage.

Wheeler, D. L. (2005). *The Internet in the Middle East. Global expectations and local imaginations in
Kuwait*. Albany, NY: SUNY publisher.

Zayani, M. (2016). *Networked publics and digital contention: The politics of everyday life in Tunisia*.
Oxford: Oxford University Press.

The unexplored history of operationalising digital divides: a pilot study

Bianca C. Reisdorf ⓘD, William H. Dutton, Whisnu Triwibowo ⓘD and Michael E. Nelson ⓘD

Since the early years of the personal computer, when computing began to diffuse to the general public, social researchers have focused on the (non)use of information and communication technologies in the household and the impact of the resulting digital divides on social and economic inequalities. The Internet's diffusion led this work to become an increasingly central focus of research, but not following a sustained trajectory of attention. This study tracks the questions used to operationalise digital divides as a heretofore unexplored history that throws light on the course of social research – illuminating problems that are masked by traditional studies that follow the responses to these questions, but not the questions. By focusing on surveys of Internet use, analysing questionnaires from the USA, Britain, Hungary and South Africa reaching back to 1997, we examine how survey research questions on Internet (non)use have evolved. Study of the changing operational definitions of Internet use across time and space provides a formerly unexamined perspective on the ebb and flow of academic interest in digital divides, the changing meaning of that term and the relationship of social research to technology and policy change.

Introduction

The rise of personal computing in the early 1980s led to the first studies of the diffusion of computer-based information technologies across households, and the factors shaping their adoption and implications, building on earlier studies of the use of telephones, television and cable technologies (Dutton, Rogers, & Jun, 1987). This work initiated a focus on digital divides and inequalities across households that became a much larger focus of research since the Internet became available to the general public in the early 1990s, particularly with the advent of the web browser. Several different methodologies, such as surveys, qualitative interviews, participant observation and experiments, have been applied to research how and why people are (not) using the Internet and related information and communication technologies in households, and increasingly on the move.

The diffusion of the Internet has been tracked in many nations and globally overtime through graphs that illustrate the smooth S-curve of the Internet as an innovation. But in the background of such curves are the specific operational definitions that define how access to the Internet was defined by survey research. By looking at these changing operational definitions, it is possible to see reflections of the changing nature of the Internet and related digital divides and how they map into changes in technology and policy. This article reports on these changing operational definitions by focusing on several key surveys done over the major periods of Internet diffusion. This enables a comparison between survey research in the social sciences and the technology and policy context of the Internet's history, identifying shortcomings in research that could be addressed as Internet studies continue to develop.

Internet diffusion

Since the invention of Internet protocol suite (TCP/IP) in 1973, the Internet has continually and rapidly evolved. While personal computers began to diffuse across households in the early 1980s, few households used the Advanced Research Projects Agency Network (ARPANET) or National Science Foundation Network (NSFNET), preferring to link to local bulletin board systems (BBS), until the web, and later the web browser in 1993, made the Internet more easily accessible to households through modems linked to phone lines. It was not until the late 1990s that the Internet was perceived to be a potentially major innovation for the public, albeit set back by the dotcom crash of 2000, when some researchers incorrectly wrote the Internet off as a fad (Wyatt, Thomas, & Terranova, 2002).

It was in the late 1990s, when survey research on the diffusion of the Internet began, as distinct from research on personal computer use in the household, such as with the launch of the World Internet Project (WIP) in 1999 (Cardoso, Liang, & Lapa, 2013). By 2016, the Internet had changed in dramatic ways to reach half of the world's population (World Bank, 2015a). The USA has nearly 80% of the public online and the UK has over 90% online (World Bank, 2015a). In following the diffusion of the Internet in these countries, how was access to and use of the Internet operationalised in survey research? How did they differ from the questions asked in nations at earlier stages of diffusion, such as South Africa?

Approach

The questions asked over time, and cross-nationally are likely to differ. Questions asked in countries where Internet technologies diffused rapidly and are now perceived as a tool of everyday life for most people should be different from the questions asked in countries at earlier stages of Internet diffusion. However, there has been little systematic investigation of how digital divides have been measured overtime, and how they have changed with shifts in the technological and policy context. One important exception is a systematic review of digital divide definitions and statistical approaches used to measure digital divides by Vehovar, Sicherl, Hüsing, and Dolnicar (2006). They discuss not only the operationalisation of digital divides in access, but also the inclusion of skill levels, reasons for non-use, types of access, speed of access, services used and frequency of use (Vehovar et al., 2006, pp. 280–281).

The idea for this study of changing operational definitions arose from a longitudinal study of digital divides in the US state of Michigan based on an archive of State of the State Surveys (SOSS) conducted by Michigan State University. Based on preliminary review of the SOSS surveys, we conducted a wider review of previous literature as well as survey questionnaires in multiple contexts from the mid-1990s until 2016. This led to a focus on four national surveys, developed and revised over several years of data collections, as part of the WIP, in addition to the surveys of Michigan (1997–2016). These included the USA (2000–2015), Britain (2003–2013), Hungary (2009) and South Africa (2012).

These national surveys were selected on the basis of several criteria: First, access to the original instruments was a necessary condition. It was difficult to obtain original questionnaires from many Internet researchers across the world, despite multiple requests. Many studies simply fail to keep strong documentation, and could not locate original questionnaires, especially for older surveys. Second, we focused on questionnaires used in the WIP, such as the Oxford Internet Survey (OxIS) of Britain, since it has been one of the most coordinated international data collection efforts, with a cross-national focus on the development of questionnaires. While this process resulted in a limited number of instruments, these surveys are representative of a larger set of WIP surveys, and enable cross-national comparison over time. Together, they identify clear patterns and demonstrate the potential for further research.

The evolution of digital divide research

In each nation, research tended to reflect changes in national policy. For example, in the USA, the use of the digital divide concept tied to the Internet emerged in the 1990s when the US National Telecommunications and Information Administration (NTIA) released a report entitled *Falling through the Net*, which identified a division among Americans in access to the Internet, with advantages for the "haves" who were predominantly male, white, urban and highly educated (NTIA, 1995). In 1996, the US government launched programmes to address this problem, such as the E-rate programme to provide Internet connections to schools and public libraries (Mossberger, Tolbert, & Franko, 2012). Government efforts to provide more universal Internet access did not resolve this issue, with studies indicating that the divide had increased rather than decreased by the late 1990s (NTIA, 1999).

The persistence of divides led to research in the early 2000s that focused on factors that could reduce inequalities, which examined patterns of Internet uses and skills (Mossberger et al., 2012; Mossberger, Tolbert, & Stansbury, 2003; Van Dijk, 2005; Warschauer, 2004; Witte & Mannon, 2010). The report *A Nation Online* (NTIA, 2004) identified variations in the kinds of online activities across users, and discrepancies among users between regular and non-regular users – so-called second-level divides beyond mere access. Research demonstrated the continued relevance of key demographic factors, such as age, income and education in explaining usage inequalities (DiMaggio & Hargittai, 2001; Hargittai, 2001). The international OECD (2001) study "Understanding the Digital Divide" showed that other factors, such as pricing, were associated with time spent online, and pricing was linked to the number of available Internet providers, suggesting that competition had a positive impact on uptake.

However, between the early to mid-2000s and 2009, interest in digital divide and digital inequality research seemed to diminish with only a few studies conducted in the area (e.g. Chen & Wellman, 2004; Fuchs & Horak, 2008; Livingstone & Helsper, 2007; Selwyn, 2004; Van Dijk, 2005). This coincided with a gap in new digital divide policies in the USA, which had been focusing on providing greater uptake of Internet services in the 1990s and early 2000s (see Table 1). The digital divide as a topic of government concern was only picked up again by the Obama administration in 2009 with the State Broadband Initiatives Program (NTIA, n.d.) and other initiatives aimed at increasing rural access, broadband access, digital skills and tackling the so-called "homework gap" (Horrigan, 2015). By 2015, with most individuals and households online, the concept of universal access to broadband

Table 1. Technology, digital divide policy and research timeline.

Year(s)	Technology	Policy (USA)	Research
1980–	PC adoption, and local dial-up BBS	Lifeline and Link Up Program to assist with phone lines	Early research into computer/digital divides, a personal computer in the home
1991–	World Wide Web and Internet browsers	Distance Learning and Telemedicine Program (rural)	
1995	Commercialisation of Internet (Netscape; Amazon; eBay)	First NTIA Falling Through the Net report; focus on access	
1996–	Google starts as research project	Telecommunications Act of 1996 (Internet); from innovation to service; Universal Service Fund (service in high-cost areas)	SOSS asks about Internet access for the first time (1997)
1999–2000	Craigslist; BlackBerry; Internet of Things coined	Rural Broadband Access Loan and Loan Guarantee Program; Last NTIA Falling Through the Net Report	World Internet Project (WIP) founded, studies of public access, e.g. cyber cafes vs. libraries
2001–	Wikipedia; LinkedIn; Voice over the Internet; Skype	Community Connect Grant Program	Academic surveys; focus on broadband, digital inequalities/differentiated use
2004–	Facebook; Youtube; Twitter; Google Maps	No new Internet policies since 2002	Lull in digital divide research; research on applications, such as Wikipedia
2007	iPhone; Netflix starts streaming online		
2008–	iPad; WhatsApp	State Broadband Initiatives; Broadband Technology Opportunities Program (rural)	Increase in research with focus on gradations of use/inequalities
2011–	Snapchat; Siri; Apple Maps	FCC Transformation Order (modernise broadband rollout); Connect America Fund (rural)	Skill and participatory divides; next generation users
2013–	Smart watches	Rural Broadband Experiments Order	Cultures of the Internet
2015–	Amazon Echo; Google Home; Periscope	Lifeline Revision to include Internet	

Internet becoming prominent in the USA and many other nations, research in this area saw renewed interest. The latest studies have focused on differentiated patterns of use (e. g. Dutton & Blank, 2011; Van Deursen & Helsper, 2015; Zillien & Hargittai, 2009), typologies of Internet users (Brandtzæg, Heim, & Karahasanović, 2011) as well as factors other than socio-economic background, for example, attitudes (e.g. Reisdorf & Groselj, 2015), skills (e. g. Helsper & Eynon, 2013) and cultures of the Internet (Dutton & Blank, 2013, 2015).

As a pilot study, this paper has focused on questions pertaining to the first-level divide, which is basic access and use. Further research should extend to examine questions on second- and third-level divides, such as skills, usage and the benefits and outcomes of using the Internet, which have received increased attention over the history of the Internet, as research moved from mere access to patterns of use.

The changing character of the Internet

Over these decades of research, the technical and social aspects of the Internet have changed dramatically. Living without the Internet in 1996 is not the same as living without access to Internet in 2016. Due to changes in the possibilities afforded by the Internet, the costs and benefits of access, and expectations surrounding access to the technology, this technology has become increasingly essential to larger proportions of the public (Dutton & Blank, 2013).

Shifts in the way users experience the Internet have been shaped by such innovations as the graphical web browser in the mid-1990s, the social web in the mid-2000s and the present ever-increasing ubiquity of the Internet in mobile and embedded devices. Performing a content analysis of newspaper articles in order to study the changing image of the Internet, Oggolder (2015) found a trajectory from the early 1990s Internet as a foreign, often intimidating space that required expertise to navigate safely, to the early 2000s Internet as a tool for firms and entrepreneurs (Rössler, 2001). The mid- to late-2000s marked the shift to the social web (Ankerson, 2015). Today, the Internet is embedded in an increasing number of devices, such as the Internet of Things and smartphones, that individuals may not even realise that their device is online. At the same time, with half the world not online, challenges remain in how to measure Internet use overtime and across different social contexts.

Digital divide survey instruments over time

Patterns emerged from tracking operational definitions of the digital divide from surveys in the USA, the UK, Hungary and South Africa. The following sections describe the evolution of questions and highlight key patterns linked to changing technical, policy and social contexts of the questions.

Personal computing, pre-Internet diffusion

Digital inequality research began prior to the diffusion of the Internet that was spurred by the World Wide Web and the browser, which made the Internet a trigger for households acquiring a personal computer. But early research began tracking households with a personal computer, with access to networks being viewed as one rationale for using a PC (Dutton et al., 1987).

The 1990s

When the Internet began to diffuse in the mid-1990s, researchers were slow to respond. Digital divide research was led mainly by government agencies, such as NTIA, which published *Falling through the Net* in 1995. Among the survey instruments in our sample, only the SOSS asked questions about the Internet prior to 1999, with the launch of WIP, albeit not as part of a survey specifically designed to study the Internet. However, questions on Internet access and use were included regularly in early SOSS waves. Table 2 shows that in the 1990s, questions on Internet use contained explanations of what the Internet is considered to be; for example, visiting a "site on the World Wide Web" that begins with http or www. This reflects the early notion that the Internet was something new and complicated and still quite rare in the late 1990s across the USA, although it was one of the first countries to adopt the Internet more widely.

The early 2000s

Developments in the early 2000s included innovations that made the Internet more useful to the public, such as through the use of Skype and Wikipedia. SOSS questions in the early

Table 2. Michigan State of the State Survey Internet questions over time (1997–2016); answer italicised in parentheses.

Year	Internet	Computer	Frequency	Non-use
1997	Do you own or regularly use a computer that has access to the Internet or World Wide Web? (yes/no)			
1998	Have you ever accessed the Internet, either at home, work, school or somewhere else? (yes/no) Have you ever visited any site on the World Wide Web, that is a site with http or www in its address (this does not include just sending or receiving email)? (yes/no)		Have you accessed the World Wide Web in the past three months? (yes/no)	
1999	Do you access the Internet mostly from home, work, school, the library or somewhere else? (multiple answers) –		How often, if at all, do you access the Internet, either for the purposes of sending email or visiting or browsing the "world wide web"? Would you say daily, 3–4 times a week, once a week, a couple of times a month, once a month, a few times a year or never? (one answer)	What is the main reason why you have not used the Internet? (no computer; too complicated; not worth time/hassle; no trust; no interest; physically unable; other; one answer)
2001 2002 2003 2004	What form of Internet access do you have from home? Do you have a dial-up modem, ISDN, cable, DSL or some other form of access? (2004 only)			Why have you not used the Internet? (no computer; do not know how to use; too much junk online; do not trust; too expensive; no interest/ need; no access; other; one answer)
2005 2008		Next, I have some questions about computer and Internet usage. Do you have a computer in your home? (yes/no)		What is the main reason that you do not access the Internet from home? (no access/computer; not worth time/hassle; security; too complicated; too expensive; access elsewhere; do not want children online; other; one answer)
	When accessing the Internet, do you most often use a personal desktop computer, a laptop, a PDA such as a Black-berry or Pocket PC, a cell phone or something else? (multiple)			
	Do you access the Internet at home through a traditional telephone modem (dial-up), through a high-speed service such as DSL or a cable modem? (multiple) Do you use the Internet? (yes/no)			
2009	Either at home, at work or somewhere else, do you have regular access to email and the Internet (the World Wide Web)? (yes/no)			

Table 2. (Continued)

Year	Internet	Computer	Frequency	Non-use
2013	Do you access the Internet at home using a personal computer? (yes/no) There are many different ways a person can access the Internet. These include dial-up modems or ISDN, DSL, broadband or cable, satellite and mobile broadband on a mobile phone. What type of Internet access do you have in your home? (multiple)	First of all, do you have a computer in your home? (yes/no)		Would you say that you are simply not interested in using the Internet under any circumstances? (yes/no) Is it impossible to have Internet service in your home because of a problem with technology or wiring? (yes/no) Would you say that you do not have Internet service at home because you are able to meet your Internet needs at other locations? (yes/no)
2016	Do you ever go online, whether using the Internet on a computer or on a mobile device, such as a smartphone or tablet? (yes/no)			There are a number of reasons that people give for not using the Internet. Please tell me whether each of the following is a reason why you do not use it. (not interested; no access; difficult; expensive; do not know how; yes/no for each question)

2000s asked about location of use, such as at work or home, and the frequency of use. In 2001, the SOSS first asked people why they did *not* use the Internet, which reflects that Internet access was becoming more common – the USA was well over 50% of Internet users at this point, and Michigan was leading the way with 67% Internet users at this point. Researchers at this time expected most households to have Internet access. From 1999 until 2005, the SOSS also asked about patterns of use, such as the frequency of using the Internet.

Similar questions were asked in the US Digital Futures questionnaires and the OxIS (2016) of Britain – both part of the WIP. In the earliest US WIP survey, questionnaires explained what the Internet was, but this was dropped in later versions. Even in 2003, in Britain, it was necessary to clarify the difference between using the Internet and using a computer that was not online. Hours and locations of use were asked throughout earlier and later questionnaires (see Table 3).

The mid- to late-2000s

Following a 2002 NTIA report, entitled *Connected Nation*, declaring the divide closed, no further US government initiatives were taken to increase Internet or broadband penetration until 2009. This coincided with the development of more participatory websites, such as social media, with Facebook launching in 2004, and the release of the first iPhone in 2007. Research in Internet studies focused on particular applications, such as Facebook, leaving digital divide research out of focus. For example, the SOSS did not ask about Internet use from 2006 until 2008. However, the WIP continued to gather relevant data on digital divides and started differentiating use across various devices, specifically mobile use.

From 2009 to 2016

During the later 2000s, there was a renewed interest in digital divide research at the same time as the US government started developing new policy initiatives to address digital divides in rural and low-income areas. Definitions continued to change, with surveys like the OxIS more often asking if you "go online," rather than "use the Internet." Later waves of the US and UK WIP questionnaires continue to differentiate use on different devices. This is also true for the 2009 questionnaire from Hungary and the 2012 questionnaire from South Africa – both part of the WIP – sharing core questions with other countries. All four countries ask about why people do not use the Internet across all observed waves.

However, there are some stark differences between the South African questionnaire and the other WIP questionnaires. In South Africa, Internet use was lower (41% in 2012) than in the other three countries (World Bank, 2015b), and Internet use and access existed in a different context. For example, the South African survey asks who in the household is using the Internet; a question that is missing from other current WIP questionnaires. The survey also gives examples of Internet use, i.e. Gmail, Google, Facebook, MXit, email, similar to earlier waves of the SOSS and US WIP questionnaires. In addition to questions on reasons for non-use – in line with the other questionnaires – the South African questionnaire also asks about what constrains Internet use, given that power outages and other constraints were more common. The South African survey also asks about the language of Internet use due to its multilingual background, whereas other countries did not.

Table 3. OxIS Internet questions over time (2003–2013); answers italicised in parentheses.

Year	Internet	Computer	Frequency	Non-use
2003	Does this household have access to the Internet? (*yes, at present; no, but in the past; no, never*) Do you yourself use the Internet at home, work, school, college or elsewhere or have you used the Internet anywhere in the past? (*yes, at present; no, but in the past; no, never*)	In this household, how many computers are available for people to use? (*numerical*)	During a typical week, about how many minutes or hours altogether, at home, work and elsewhere, do you use the Internet for… (various activities; *numerical*)	I will read a number of reasons that some people give to explain why they do not use the Internet. Tell me if any apply to you. (*no interest; no connection; no computer; difficult; not useful; expensive; privacy; viruses; time; nothing of interest; not know how to use; time consuming; not for me; not for my age; no/yes; multiple answers*)
2005			On average, how often do you check your email? (*hourly to less than once a week*)	
2007	Now, could I ask about all of the places where you access the Internet? (*at home; on the move; other person's home; work; school/university; internet café; library; no/yes*)	How many working computers are available for people to use in this household? (*None–three or more*) Do you yourself use a computer whether or not it is connected to the Internet? (*no/yes*)	During a typical week, on average how many hours do you use the Internet? How often do you use the Internet for the following purposes? (various activities; *several times a day to never*)	
2009				
2011		Leaving the Internet aside for a moment, how frequently do you use a computer? (*several times a day to never*)	During a typical week, on average about how many hours do you use the Internet at home? (*numerical*)	
2013	Overall, when you go online, do you mostly use your mobile phone or mostly use some other device like a desktop, laptop or tablet computer? (*mostly mobile; mostly other; both equal; don't use mobile Internet*)	How many working computers are available for people to use in this household? (*numerical*) Do you yourself use a computer whether or not it is connected to the Internet? (*no/yes*)	During a typical week, on average about how many hours do you use the Internet at work and/or at school? (*numerical*) How often do you use the Internet for the following purposes? (various activities; *several times a day to never*) During a typical week, including weekdays and weekends, about how many hours do you usually spend using the Internet … (at home, at school, at work, while you are on the move/while traveling; *numerical*) How often do you use the Internet for the following purposes? (various activities; *several times a day to never*)	I will read a number of reasons that some people give to explain why they do not use the Internet. Tell me if any apply to you. (*no interest; no connection; no computer; difficult; not useful; expensive; privacy; viruses; time; nothing of interest; not know how to use; time consuming; not for me; not for my age; no/yes; multiple answers*) And which of these reasons was the most important? (*same answers; one answer*)

Patterns in operationalising digital divide research

Several patterns emerged from this examination of operationalising digital divides. First, the operational definitions have changed overtime, both with regards to the questions asked and the answer options given. Behind the smooth S-curve of Internet diffusion is a shifting operational definition of what researchers are measuring. More appropriately, operational definitions need to constantly change in order to capture a changing phenomenon such as the Internet. Since these definitions reflect change in the technology, policy and public expression, it is important to communicate these shifts explicitly, rather than push them behind the data. For example, with increasing Internet use, reasons for non-use became more complex, which was exemplified in the OxIS asking about *all* reasons for being offline – and providing various answer options – rather than asking only for the most important one.

Second, the attention of research tends to be driven by the latest technical innovations, such as when the Internet was new, but then with the rise of such innovations as search, social media and mobile use. Questions on older – still pervasive – technologies, such as the PC, and even the Internet, were dropped from questionnaires and research to align with innovations and public understanding of being online. Likewise, survey research on divides tended to follow public policy and regulatory shifts, such as initiatives to close divides, and to move toward universal broadband. In the USA, digital divide research diminished rapidly in the aftermath of the NTIA determining that this issue was no longer a problem. The degree research follows behind technology and policy is not surprising, given the degree grants and publications are geared to innovation, but it is very transparent when seeing the fall-off in asking questions about Internet use, for example, in the SOSS case.

Third, at the same time that social research is driven by the latest technical innovations, it is simultaneously lagging behind technological innovation. Digital divide research is in a constant state of playing "catch-up" with the latest technological developments and seems to be one or more steps behind at all times. This is inevitable given that surveys are less useful for study of early innovations, which a large proportion of the public are not aware of, but this is also the case with policy, where social research cannot chase policy if it seeks to inform policy and practice. Arguably, social research requires a continuity overtime that is not overly susceptible to changes in public policy or regulation, as was the case with digital divide research – at least in the US context.

Finally, the comparison of questionnaires also showed that the Western digital divide research can gain from engaging with researchers and research instruments from non-Western contexts. Digital divide research in any context can benefit from broadening the scope of research by taking cross-national and global developments into account in designing research and operationalising digital divides.

This pilot study illustrates the potential for operational definitions to complement the answers to surveys overtime and contribute to understanding histories of the Internet. This research would be enhanced by the examination of more questionnaires from a wider range of countries and on a wider range of issues, such as higher levels of divide. However, even this limited pilot supports the analysis of trends reported here, which demonstrate that operational indicators have been a lost element of the study of the Internet's histories. More effort needs to be placed on documenting these survey instruments and bringing them into Internet studies.

Acknowledgements

We would like to express our gratitude to the members of the World Internet Project for kindly providing their questionnaires to us for this pilot study. We would also like to thank the editors and reviewers for their excellent comments and suggestions on this paper. Finally, we are very grateful for the funding and support provided by the Institute for Public Policy and Social Research at Michigan State University.

Disclosure statement

No potential conflict of interest was reported by the authors.

Funding

Michigan Applied Public Policy Research (MAPPR) Funding provided through the Institute for Public Policy and Social Research (IPPSR) at Michigan State University.

ORCID

Bianca C. Reisdorf (iD) http://orcid.org/0000-0002-0690-1956
Whisnu Triwibowo (iD) http://orcid.org/0000-0003-3429-5970
Michael E. Nelson (iD) http://orcid.org/0000-0002-5153-8674

References

Ankerson, M. S. (2015). Social media and the "read-only" web: Reconfiguring social logics and historical boundaries. *Social Media & Society, 1*(2), 1–12.
Brandtzæg, P. B., Heim, J., & Karahasanović, A. (2011). Understanding the new digital divide – a typology of Internet users in Europe. *International Journal of Human-Computer Studies, 69*(3), 123–138.

Cardoso, G., Liang, G., & Lapa, T. (2013). Cross-national comparative perspectives from the world internet project. In: W. H. Dutton (Ed.), *The oxford handbook of internet studies* (pp. 216–236). Oxford: Oxford University Press.

Chen, W., & Wellman, B. (2004). The global digital divide–within and between countries. *IT & Society, 1*(7), 39–45.

DiMaggio, P., & Hargittai, E. (2001). *From the 'digital divide' to 'digital inequality': Studying Internet use as penetration increases.* Princeton, NJ: Sociology Department, Princeton University.

Dutton, W. H., & Blank, G. (2011). *Next generation users: The internet in Britain. OxIS survey: 2011.* Oxford: Oxford Internet Institute, University of Oxford.

Dutton, W. H., & Blank, G. (2013). *Cultures of the internet: The internet in Britain. Oxford internet survey 2013 report.* Oxford: Oxford Internet Institute.

Dutton, W. H., & Blank, G. (2015). Cultures on the Internet. *InterMedia, 42*(4/5), 55–57.

Dutton, W. H., Rogers, E. M., & Jun, S-H. (1987). Diffusion and social impacts of personal computers. *Communication Research, 14*(2), 219–250.

Fuchs, C., & Horak, E. (2008). Africa and the digital divide. *Telematics and Informatics, 25*(2), 99–116.

Hargittai, E. (2001). *Second-level digital divide: Mapping differences in people's online skills.* Ithaca, NY: Cornell University Library. Retrieved from arXiv preprint cs/0109068.

Helsper, E., & Eynon, R. (2013). Distinct skill pathways to digital engagement. *European Journal of Communication, 28*(6), 696–713.

Horrigan, J. B. (2015). *The numbers behind the broadband 'homework gap'.* Washington, DC: Pew Research Center. Retrieved from http://www.pewresearch.org/fact-tank/2015/04/20/the-numbers-behind-the-broadband-homework-gap/

Livingstone, S., & Helsper, E. (2007). Gradations in digital inclusion: Children, young people and the digital divide. *New Media & Society, 9*(4), 671–696.

Mossberger, K., Tolbert, C. J., & Stansbury, M. (2003). *Virtual inequality: Beyond the digital divide.* Washington, DC: Georgetown University Press.

Mossberger, K., Tolbert, C. J., & Franko, W. W. (2012). *Digital cities: The internet and the geography of opportunity.* Oxford: Oxford University Press.

National Telecommunications and Information Administration (NTIA). (n.d.). State broadband initiative. Retrieved from https://www2.ntia.doc.gov/SBDD

National Telecommunications and Information Administration. (1995). *Falling through the net: The "have nots" in rural and urban America.* Washington, DC: U.S. Department of Commerce. Retrieved from http://www.ntia.doc.gov/ntiahome/fallingthru.html

National Telecommunications and Information Administration (NTIA). (1999). *Falling through the net: Defining the digital divide.* Washington, DC: U.S. Department of Commerce. Retrieved from https://www.ntia.doc.gov/report/1999/falling-through-net-defining-digital-divide

National Telecommunications and Information Administration (NTIA). (2004). A nation online: Entering the broadband age. Washington, DC: U.S. Department of Commerce. Retrieved from https://www.ntia.doc.gov/report/2004/nation-online-entering-broadband-age

Oggolder, C. (2015). From virtual to social: Transforming concepts and images of the internet. *Information & Culture, 50*(2), 181–196.

Organization for Economic Co-Operation and Development (OECD). (2001). *Understanding the digital divide* Paris: OECD Publications. Retrieved from https://www.oecd.org/sti/1888451.pdf

OxIS. (2016). *Oxford internet survey methodology, 2003–2013.* Oxford: Oxford Internet Institute. Retrieved from http://oxis.oii.ox.ac.uk/research/methodology/

Reisdorf, B. C., & Groselj, D. (2015). Internet (non-) use types and motivational access: Implications for digital inequalities research. *New Media & Society.* Advanced online publication. doi:10.1177/1461444815621539

Rössler, P. (2001). Between online heaven and Cyberhell the framing of 'The Internet' by traditional media coverage in Germany. *New Media & Society, 3*(1), 49–66.

Selwyn, N. (2004). Reconsidering political and popular understandings of the digital divide. *New Media & Society, 6*(3), 341–362.

Van Deursen, A. J., & Helsper, E. J. (2015). The third-level digital divide: Who benefits most from being online? *Communication and Information Technologies Annual, 10*, 29–52.

Van Dijk, J. A. (2005). *The deepening divide: Inequality in the information society.* London: Sage Publications.

Vehovar, V., Sicherl, P., Hüsing, T., & Dolnicar, V. (2006). Methodological challenges of digital divide measurements. *The Information Society, 22*(5), 279–290.

Warschauer, M. (2004). *Technology and social inclusion: Rethinking the digital divide.* Cambridge, MA: MIT Press.

Witte, J. C., & Mannon, S. E. (2010). *The Internet and social inequalities.* London: Routledge.

World Bank. (2015a). *Internet users (per 100 people).* Retrieved from http://data.worldbank.org/indicator/IT.NET.USER.P2

World Bank. (2015b). *Internet users (per 100 people).* Retrieved from http://data.worldbank.org/indicator/IT.NET.USER.P2?locations=ZA

Wyatt, S., Thomas, G., & Terranova, T. (2002). They came, they surfed, they went back to the beach. In S. Woolgar (Ed.), *Virtual reality?* (pp. 23–40). Oxford: Oxford University Press.

Zillien, N., & Hargittai, E. (2009). Digital distinction: Status—specific types of internet usage. *Social Science Quarterly, 90*(2), 274–291.

Early challenges to multilingualism on the Internet: the case of Han character-based scripts

Mark McLelland

ABSTRACT

In today's hyper-mediated world where computer software can deal seamlessly with a variety of the world's languages and scripts, it is difficult to recall the seemingly insurmountable computing problems raised by "Han" character-based scripts such as Chinese, Japanese (and to a lesser extent, Korean). In the early days of networked computing, some commentators even argued that the continued use of Han characters was a lost cause, and could only result in "intolerable inefficiencies" when used to communicate digital information. In this paper, I consider the orthographic factors that delayed the implementation of cross-platform protocols allowing for the input, display and transmission of character-based scripts across early computer networks (mid-1980s to mid-1990s). I note how Anglophone Internet histories have been largely oblivious to the inherent biases of Internet infrastructure that were built by programmers using ASCII (based on the limited range of characters provided by the Roman alphabet) who also assumed the QWERTY keyboard to be the obvious human–machine interface. Instead of stressing the deficiencies of character-based scripts, I invite the reader to consider how the Internet might look today had it not been founded upon assumptions based on Anglophone usage, and consider the potentialities of a non-phonetic character-based writing system.

Introduction

In today's hyper-mediated world where computer software can deal seamlessly with a variety of the world's languages and scripts across a range of applications, young people may find it difficult to imagine the seemingly insurmountable problems raised by the variety of scripts used to write the world's languages in the early days of networked computing. As Internet applications expanded in the 1980s, some commentators even argued that millennia-old native scripts such as Chinese (henceforth "Han") characters were a lost cause and would need to be replaced by Roman script if computerisation were to advance in the region (Unger, 1987, p. 8). I recall this situation very well myself though, due to my particular circumstances. From 1997 to 2000, I was a graduate student undertaking a PhD degree in Japanese Studies at the University of Hong Kong and so, despite being a native

English speaker, I have first-hand experience of the frustrations of trying to get software to work across three different languages. As Nishigaki noted at the time, "Any country that does not have English as the mother tongue will likely find the conditions of the Internet to be deeply unsatisfying" (1997, p. 6), and this was indeed my experience. Nothing about the Internet was straightforward at the time, including issues such as writing (and printing!) text that included both English and Japanese, sending (and receiving in an intelligible format) emails in Japanese or even displaying a Japanese website.

In this short overview, I consider the linguistic and orthographic factors that delayed the implementation of cross-platform protocols allowing for the input, display and transmission of character-based scripts across early computer networks (mid-1980s to mid-1990s) in North-East Asia. It is useful for the project of Internet histories to draw attention to how English speakers have been largely oblivious to the "invisible infrastructure of the Internet" (Pargman & Palme, 2009, p. 177) – since this helps us understand the bias that existed in early accounts of computer communication that saw languages and scripts other than English/Roman, particularly Han character-based scripts, as problems to be overcome. It is worth recalling that the foundation of today's networked computing was established by programmers using American Standard Code for Information Interchange (ASCII) that was based on the limited range of characters provided by the Roman alphabet. These programmers also adopted the QWERTY keyboard as the main human–machine interface, despite its inefficiency as an input system. Now that Internet histories is a developing field with more attention being paid to regional histories (Goggin & McLelland, 2007, 2017) as well as pre-Internet developments in computer-mediated communication (CMC) (McLelland, 2017), it is useful to recall the hidden and persistent biases in early computer communication and to at least imagine how things might have turned out differently had English speakers not played such a key role in internet development.

ASCII imperialism?

The dominance of English-speaking countries in the development of computing in the middle of the last century led to a situation where the Roman alphabet and the English language were the default script and language used both for the construction of computer code and commands and for discussion concerning research and development (Breen & Tokita, 2004, p. 1; UNESCO, 2005). The 7-bit code that was established by the US standards agency in the early 1970s, generally known as ASCII, was originally developed from telegraph code. It was a 7-bit code that allowed for 128 basic characters including lower and uppercase letters from a to z, numerals 0 to 9, and punctuation marks. With the extension to 8-bits, a further 128 characters were made available that included accented letters and additional punctuation marks (Breen & Tokita, 2004, p. 1; UNESCO, 2005, pp. 71–73). Most countries using European languages were thus able to deploy the standard ASCII set while using the extra character capacity to configure diacritic, punctuation and other marks to suit the local writing system. Non-Roman alphabets such as Greek or Cyrillic were able to use the extended code space to configure their own alphabets. However, languages such as Chinese, Japanese and, to a lesser extent, Korean, which use several thousand distinct Han ideographs that are not phonetic (in that the character itself contains only general indicators of how it might be pronounced) could not be written by such a restricted number of character options.

In 1983, ASCII became embedded in Internet architecture via the Domain Name System (DNS) which maps the names of hosts or websites to their Internet Protocol (IP) addresses (Torsen, 2005). Until 2003, it was not possible to link to addresses written with scripts that could not be accommodated by the limited ASCII code space. Another key feature that allowed networked communication via computers was the development in 1978 (and release onto ARPANET in 1983) of the TCP/IP set of protocols based on ASCII that allowed computers with different operating systems to communicate with each other via telephone lines (Carey & Martin, 2010, p. 217). The establishment of protocols enabled a range of text-based networks such as Fidonet, Compuserve and later America on Line to offer services outside of North America. However, language options on these networks were limited by the software. Internet expansion across the Arab world, for instance, was delayed by the technical difficulties of employing the traditional script, an issue not resolved until the release in 1997 of Microsoft's Arabic Office 97 (Daoudi, 2017, p. 229). Similarly, encoding issues across Chinese, Japanese and Korean limited the use of these scripts online until the roll-out of UNICODE in 1995.

Subsequent to the implementation of TCP/IP, the next development that increased the capacity for information to be sent and received via the Internet was the World Wide Web (henceforth the Web), made available to the public in 1993. The Web had numerous advantages when compared with earlier applications, especially its capacity for handling formatted text, embedded graphics, and sound and visual media. However, Web programming and Hyper Text Markup language (HTML) carried over existing biases in terms of their reliance on Roman script. For instance, the lack of Arabic script HTML and browsers capable of displaying the script meant that "text had to be rendered as graphics, making it extremely slow to load" (Houissa, 2000, p. 59). This was also a problem for other languages using scripts other than Roman that initially needed to upload their Web pages as image files, resulting in slow download speeds and lack of searchability. Hence, as Pargman and Palme, in their analysis of "ASCII imperialism" conclude, "there does exist a bias among the organisations, institutions, and individuals" involved in setting the standards for computer communication "that works in favour of English-speaking Internet users and to the disadvantage of (in varying degrees) speakers of all other languages" (2009, p. 197). These concerns about the language bias written into Internet infrastructures led authors of a 2005 UNESCO report to comment that "If digital literacy requires literacy in another language as a prerequisite, openness and universal access cannot be assured" (2005, p. 71).

Language problems on the early Internet

Revisiting newspaper and magazine reports, academic papers and BBS discussions about the Internet from the late 1980s and early 1990s reminds us just how novel and exciting the roll-out of networked computer technologies seemed at the time. The assumptions made remind us that the implications and applications of new technologies are not always clearly understood, nor are the ways in which they will be adopted and modified easily predicted. One key issue which has not so far been explored in detail in histories of the Internet is the impact of language, specifically orthographic (that is, script) differences and the challenges posed to CMC by character-based scripts.

In Euro-American societies, the roll-out of public Internet access, which was accelerated by the introduction of the Web and the first Web browsers in 1994, took place in a context where large segments of the population already had some prior experience of personal computing (Fouser, 2001, p. 274). The fact that most high-school graduates already had a familiarity with the QWERTY keyboard, originally popularised by the Remington typewriter in 1873, meant that prior to the development of the mouse and the graphic interface, the use of the keyboard to interface with a computer screen was easily intelligible. Despite the fact that the QWERTY layout, originally devised to slow down typing and prevent the jamming of commonly occurring letters in English words, is not the most efficient for computer input, the widespread familiarity established by the typewriter has made the keyboard difficult to change (Castillo, 2011, p. 613; Choi, 2013, p. 37; Zhang, 2016). Due to resistance from users, little adaptation of the original typewriter layout has taken place (Zhang, 2016), other than the addition of function and arrow keys necessary for navigating a screen and for computer commands.

An existing familiarity with typewriters was not, however, the case for many non-European language users, particularly those in North-East Asia whose written languages were not alphabet-based but depended to some extent upon the reproduction of complex Han characters – specifically Chinese, Japanese, and, to a lesser extent, Korean (in Korea since the end of the Second World War emphasis has been place on the use of the native Hangul alphabet over Chinese characters). China and Japan did not see the widespread office automation characteristic of Western societies in the early post-war period. Korea, however, did develop numerous prototypes for a Hangul typewriter but standardisation was always a problem with "up to eleven competing keyboard designs" by the 1960s (Choi, 2013, p. 42). Although typewriters for Chinese and Japanese scripts did exist, they were cumbersome and could only be used by highly trained operatives, making it impossible to reproduce the typing pools that had developed across western businesses and government departments. Hence, the possibilities for easier text input, display and retrieval afforded by computers were of interest to East Asian governments, and from the 1970s onwards, various schemes and protocols were explored by both government and commercial agencies across the region, including engagement with agencies such as the Internet Engineering Taskforce, but not in any unified manner (Contreras, 2014; Seo, 2013, p. 186).

One major problem was the restricted memory available in early personal computers making it difficult to develop code to deal with characters beyond the 26 letters of the Roman alphabet, Arabic numerals and a small number of key punctuation symbols associated with written English. The fact that the Internet and CMC more generally were pioneered in the United States, a largely English-speaking jurisdiction, meant that there was little inclination to invest in technology to expand this character range. Hence, as Breen (2005, p. 1) points out, at the time of these early developments in computing, it made little sense to speak of "computing in English" – since the use of the English language was embedded in the very architecture of computer programs and English was the default language for international communication on the early Internet (Breen & Tokita, 2004, p. 1; Parman & Palme, 2009, p. 184). However "computing in Japanese" (or Chinese or Korean) raised a whole set of issues particular to these languages and there have been a number of studies dedicated to the specific computing problems raised by the use of East Asian scripts (see, for example, Gottlieb, 2000; Lunde, 1999; Unger, 1987; W3C, 2012). As late as 1987, Unger was arguing that continued commitment to the use of Han characters as a major component of Japan's hybrid writing system would create "intolerable inefficiencies" (1987, p. 8) and that computerisation thus required script reform, including enhanced use of *romaji* or Romanized Japanese "in the majority of [data processing] applications" (1987, p. 171).

Unger, and others arguing for the Romanisation of East-Asian languages, viewed character-based scripts as fundamentally "irrational" and ill-suited to modern communications systems. As Nishigaki points out, Chinese characters "have always been criticized and attacked in the name of an *obsolete writing system* which prevents modernization" (1999, p. 17; emphasis in the original). Yet, it is pertinent to remember at this point that there is nothing "rational" about English spelling or the QWERTY keyboard which is, in fact, a rather inefficient input system that was standardised by a confluence of historical circumstances rather than deliberate policy based on efficiency (Choi, 2013, p. 38; Zhang, 2016). The view that character-based scripts are less optimal is also dependent on a bias in Western linguistics that assumes written language should be made up of phonemes, that is, a restricted number of letters laid out horizontally to make up separate words (Nishigaki, 1999, p. 18). Han characters represent language differently. A single character is constructed as if to fill a square-shaped block of space from up to 30 different strokes that are written in a distinct order (top to bottom, left to right, character spanning or enclosing strokes last, etc.). These strokes are organised according to 214 "radicals" that signify objects and abstract nouns – from basic elements like fire, earth, wind and water, through to more abstract ideas such as big and small, movement and speech, such that their combination gives a metaphorical sense of the character's overall meaning. For instance the radicals for "rice field" 田 and "strength" 力, when combined produce the character "man" 男 (that is, metaphorically, a person who provides strength in the fields). Given their condensed construction, a proficient reader can process the information in Han characters very quickly.

For Han characters, since meaning and pronunciation are separate issues, once a character's meaning is memorised it can be recognised and understood by anyone irrespective of the pronunciation assigned to it in different languages, just as a smiley face emoticon can be comprehended as signifying "happiness" despite the fact that the word happiness is different for speakers of different languages. For example, spoken Chinese is made up of numerous mutually unintelligible dialects – but the written characters can be understood by any literate person, irrespective of the pronunciation assigned in their specific region (Nishigaki, 1999, p. 18). Han characters can also be understood by readers across languages, such as those in Japan and Korea in a similar manner to how speakers of different languages can all use and comprehend emoticons. In the case of Japanese and also Korean, the large number of homophones (words with the same sound but different meanings) would make a Romanised version of a text difficult to comprehend – it is the Han characters, known, respectively, as *kanji/hanja,* that indicate the specific and unambiguous meaning, making *kanji* "indispensable for the reading of Japanese" (Shibamoto Smith, 1996, p. 210). In addition, since Japanese is written without word breaks, the *kanji* are critical "visual cues to morphological segmentation" that help the reader parse the lexemes essential to comprehension (Shibamoto Smith, 1996, p. 210). Although the transcription of Japanese via Roman letters or the local *hiragana* syllabary might seem more "logical" than the use of 2000 plus *kanji*, when written without *kanji* the language is extremely difficult to comprehend. Hence "language reform" that would have required the use of Roman or a similar alphabetic script, was never a viable option.

From monolingual to multilingual character coding

During the 1970s, separate attempts were made in countries of the North-East Asian region by computer manufacturing companies and other bodies to develop "double-byte character sets" that could cope with a non-phonetic ideograph-style writing system, but unlike in North America and Europe where the American system had become standard, there was no unifying system in place for the input and conversion of Han characters (which are used across all three languages). It was not until the 1980s that the needs for texts to move across national boundaries as well as the use of multiple scripts in the same document were clearly comprehended (Breen & Tokita, 2004, p. 2). Similarly, lack of agreement on how to handle the local *hiragana* and *katakana* syllabaries used in Japan and the Hangul alphabet in Korea also caused problems across different computer platforms. As Jo points out, attempts at standardization of the native Hangul script in Korea "repeatedly failed" and it was not until the roll-out of UNICODE in 1995 that there was broad agreement on its adoption as a national standard (2017, p. 199).

Further problems that delayed the development of a unified code were the facts that although Han characters originating in China are closely related across the region, they are not identical. Japan adapted existing characters and invented some new ones, as did Korea. Japanese usage of these characters also differs from the Chinese in that "[t]he same character may stand, as a homograph, for several different morphemes (each with its specific meanings and … pronunciation" (Shibamoto Smith, 1996, p. 209). In addition, other differences exist between Chinese-speaking territories. For instance, the People's Republic of China rolled out a simplified set of characters in 1956 (known as Simplified Characters). These forms are also used in Singapore but not in Japan, Korea, Hong Kong or Taiwan (where Traditional Characters are used). It was not until 1993 when the Unicode/ISO 10646 code, a 16-bit system allowing a potential 65,536 characters was developed, that a system of inputting and displaying "unified CJK ideographs" across platforms and applications was made available. Previous locally developed systems for the input and display of Han characters were not interoperable. Unicode's innovation was to give similar characters across the three languages the same code space meaning that any computer loaded with the required fonts was able to recognise and display them. Unicode has, however, been justly criticised for homogenising the characters and failing to provide code space for character variants (Auh, 1998) that are important for the writing of personal and place names, as well as characters that are seldom used in today's texts but are important in historical documents.

Moreover, the roll-out of Unicode did not address some fundamental biases concerning script built into the architecture of the Internet itself. Given the very large number of Han characters in circulation (some estimates exceed 50,000), the pronunciation and meaning of unfamiliar characters is often indicated by an interlineal annotation known as ruby (or *furigana* in Japanese). However, Web browsers are inconsistent in their ability to recognise and display this important information. In addition, Japanese and Chinese texts are traditionally written from right to left in a vertical manner from top to bottom of the page (Shibamoto Smith, 1996, p. 214) and, unlike European languages which separate words on the page and screen, other than paragraph spaces, they are written without word breaks (Unger, 1987, pp. 29–31). This distinctive writing style means there is no hyphenation for word breaks across lines, and consequently "word wrap" software must know where to break lexemes so as to maintain legibility. Similarly, the input and conversion software used to display text on the screen must recognise not just individual words but also lexemes since basic lexical components are not separated by spaces during input (W3C, 2012). Another fundamental bias concerning English is the reliance on the Roman alphabet plus numerals and common punctuation devices in the coding of Internet protocols and Web domain addresses, "the technical legacy of the DNS's development and initial implementation in the United States" (National Research Council 2005, p. 197). An International Domain Name task force was established to address this issue in 2000 and in 2003 a standard conversion algorithm was developed supported by the Internet Corporation for Assigned Names and Numbers (ICAN, n.d.; Torsen, 2005). This allowed for a domain name to be written in a local script familiar to end users (deploying Unicode) and then converted into the international format familiar to Web browsers that utilised the limited ASCII character set (Breen & Tokita, 2004, p. 3). It thus took a decade after the introduction of the Web before users in Japan and China were able to use their character-based scripts for the designation of local Web addresses.

The characteristics of written Chinese and Japanese also had implications for Web search engines. The development of search engines that enabled users to quickly locate a large amount of material, including image and sound files, by the use of key words or phrases was an important step. Yet, early pioneers in Web search technology such as Google and Yahoo deployed a standard framework for searching across all languages which served Japanese and Chinese rather poorly. As mentioned above, both languages are written without inter-word spaces or markers requiring a search engine to parse sections of text rather than pick up on isolated terms. Also, in Unicode, the Han characters used in Chinese, Japanese (and to a lesser extent, Korean) share the same code space, so when searched for using a global search engine, results can show up in each language despite the search terms having different connotations in the different languages (Auh, 1998). A further issue with Japanese is that there is flexibility in the orthography for writing some terms (often depending on personal style and preference). This is a particular issue with the use of *katakana* for the transliteration of foreign loan words, for which several variants may exist. In a trial of Google and Yahoo's capacity to search in Japanese and Chinese, Breen (2005, p. 6) noted that these issues could be mostly overcome by the use of the "exact phrase" option but that their effective use depended upon "being aware of the nature of the parsing and indexing in order to make full use of the engines". This of course required an extended period of acculturation prior to the efficient adoption of Web use by native speakers of these languages.

Conclusion

This brief discussion has looked at the influence of language on the early Internet, particularly script input and retrieval methods. Given the complex input and display issues associated with non-Roman scripts such as Chinese, Japanese (and to a lesser extent, Korean), the introduction of CMC in North-East Asia was less straightforward than in North America and Europe (Gottlieb, 2000; McLelland, 2017; Unger, 1987). Computer users in these societies had first to become familiar with Roman script, the QWERTY keyboard and the non-intuitive "conversion" input style required for local language display. Furthermore, the Roman script is part of the very architecture of the internet and early Web browsers were not configured to support domain names in non-Roman scripts or search for or display text in East Asian scripts as accurately as they could in European languages.

I have argued that these problems largely arose due to the fact that advances in computer communication and the establishment of the Internet took place in an English-speaking environment. However the calumny heaped upon North-East Asian scripts, particularly the continued use of Han characters, is due to a cultural bias that assumes the primacy of English and views other languages as problematic to the extent that they present challenges for software built with the use of English in mind. In particular, as Shibamoto Smith points out, "no writing system has been written about so pejoratively as Japanese" despite the fact that Japan is among the world's most literate societies (1996, p. 214) and was throughout the 1970s and 1980s seen as an economic powerhouse and model for Western economies (Vogel, 1979). Nishigaki also points out, with some irony, that the increasing use of "icons", that is, non-phonetic pictograms (such as the "trash" bucket) that are used to negotiate today's graphic interfaces, have much in common with how Chinese characters function, stating "No visual symbols on earth have higher ability of representing abstract concepts than Han characters" (1999, p. 19). Indeed the very condensed nature of Han characters and the fact that they are not tied to specific pronunciations promote speed reading and the efficient processing of information that makes them better for communication in a multilingual environment than a phonetic system like English (Nishigaki, 1999, p. 19). It has even been argued that given advances in predictive software, it is now faster to input Chinese on a computer using the stoke-order method than it is to input English text and that the continued reliance on the QWERTY keyboard is a liability for users of European languages (Zhang, 2016).

An interesting alternative history of language on the internet, rather than looking at the "problematic" nature of non-Roman, particularly character-based scripts, would instead problematize the manner in which one particular script became so embedded in computer software and Internet infrastructure. What might the history of the Internet have looked like had it been pioneered in China? Would we today be scoffing at the deficiencies of the QWERTY keyboard and discussing the inefficiencies of "computing in English"? Indeed "challenging the West as default" (Zhang, 2016) and imagining Internet histories outside of Anglophone paradigms can be a productive process, one that we should all look forward to in future issues of this journal.

Disclosure statement

No potential conflict of interest was reported by the author.

Funding

This work was supported by the Australian Research Council [DP1092878].

References

Auh, T. S. (1998). *Promoting multiculturalism on the internet: Korean experience*. Paper presented at the Graduate School of Journalism and Mass Communication. Retrieved from http://www.unesco.org/webworld/infoethics_2/eng/papers/paper_8.htm

Breen, J. (2005). *WWW search engines and Japanese text*. Paper presented at the Sixth Symposium on Natural Language Processing, Chiang Rai. Retrieved from http://www.edrdg.org/~jwb/paperdir/wwwjsrch.html

Breen, J., & Tokita, A. (2004). *The WWW in Japan: A threat to cultural identity or a domesticated system?* Paper presented at the First International Conference on Cultures and Technologies in Asia, Mumbai. Retrieved from http://www.edrdg.org/~jwb/paperdir/jwww.html

Carey, J., & Martin, E. (2010). *When media are new: Understanding the dynamics of new media adoption and use*. Ann Arbor, MI: MIT Press.

Castillo, M. (2011). QWERTY, @, &, #. *American Journal of Neuroradiology, 32*, 613–614.

Choi, Y. B. (2013). Path dependence on the Korean keyboard. *Journal of Economic Behaviour and Organization, 88*, 37–46.

Contreras, J. (2014). Divergent patterns of engagement in internet standardization: Japan, Korea and China. *Telecommunications Policy, 38*, 914–932.

Daoudi, A. (2017). Rethinking Arabic linguistics: The history of the internet in the Arabic-speaking region and the rise of e-Arabic. In G. Goggin & M. McLelland (Eds.), *The Routledge companion to global internet histories* (pp. 227–243). New York, NY: Routledge.

Fouser, R. (2001). "Culture", computer literacy and the media in creating public attitudes to CMC in Japan and Korea. In C. Ess (Ed.), *Culture, technology, communication: towards an intercultural global village* (pp. 261–278). Albany, NY: SUNY Press.

Goggin, G., & McLelland, M. (2007). *Internationalizing Internet histories: Beyond Anglophone paradigms*. Abingdon: Routledge.

Goggin, G., & McLelland, M. (2017). Global coordinates of internet histories. In G. Goggin & M. McLelland (Eds.), *The Routledge handbook to global Internet histories* (pp. 1–19). New York, NY: Routledge.

Gottleib, N. (2000). *Word processing technology in Japan: Kanji and the keyboard*. Richmond, VA: Curzon.

Houissa, A. (2000). The internet predicament in the Middle East and North Africa: Connectivity, access and censorship. *Journal of Librarianship and Information Science, 32*(2), 56–63.

ICAN. (n.d.). Guidelines for the implementation of internationalized domain names/ Version 1.0. Retrieved from https://www.icann.org/resources/pages/idn-guidelines-2003-06-20-en

Jo, D. (2017). H-mail and the early configuration of online user culture in Korea. In G. Goggin & M. McLelland (Eds.), *The Routledge handbook of global internet histories* (pp. 197–208). New York, NY: Routledge.

Lunde, K. (1999). *CJKV information processing*. Sebastapol, CA: O'Reilly & Associates.

McLelland, M. (2017). Early computer networks in Japan 1984–1994. In G. Goggin & M. McLelland (Eds.), *The Routledge handbook of global internet histories* (pp. 171–181). New York, NY: Routledge.

National Research Council. (2005). *Signposts in cyberspace: The domain name system and internet navigation*. Washington, DC: National Academies Press.

Nishigaki, T. (1997). A multilingual information environment for a multicultural world. *Social Science Japan, 10*, 6–8.

Nishigaki, T. (1998). *Multilingualism on the Net*. Paper presented at UNESCO INFOethics '98. Retrieved from http://www.unesco.org/webworld/infoethics_2/eng/papers/paper_5.htm

Nishigaki, T. (1999). *What can MT do for multilingualism on the Net?* Proceedings of Machine Translation Summit VII. Retrieved from http://citeseerx.ist.psu.edu/viewdoc/download?doi=10.1.1.493.1099&rep=rep1&type=pdf

Pargman, D., & Palme, J. (2009). ASCII imperialism. In M. Lampland & S. L. Star (Eds.), *Standards and their stories: How quantifying, classifying and formalizing practices shape everyday life* (pp. 177–199). Ithaca, NY: Cornell University Press.

Seo, D. B. (2013). *Evolution and standardization of mobile communications technology*. Hershey, PA: Information Science Reference.

Shibamoto Smith, J. (1996). Japanese writing. In P. Daniels & W. Bright (Eds.), *The world's writing systems* (pp. 209–214). Oxford: Oxford University Press.

Torsen, M. (2005). The domination of the English language in the global village: Efforts to further develop the internet by populating it with non-Latin-based languages. *Richmond Journal of Law & Technology, XII*(I), 1–23.

UNESCO. (2005). *Measuring linguistic diversity on the internet*. Paris: UNESCO.

Unger, J. M. (1987). *The fifth generation fallacy: Why Japan is betting its future on artificial intelligence*. New York, NY: Oxford University Press.

Vogel, E. (1979). *Japan and number one: Lessons for America*. Cambridge: Harvard University Press.

W3C Working Group. (2012). *Requirements for Japanese text layout*. Retrieved from https://www.w3. org/TR/2012/NOTE-jlreq-20120403/

Zhang, S. (2016). Chinese characters are futuristic and the alphabet is old news. *The Atlantic*. November 1. Retrieved from http://www.theatlantic.com/technology/archive/2016/11/chinese-com puters/504851/

African histories of the Internet

Herman Wasserman

ABSTRACT
This article explores the notion of Internet histories and associated digital cultures from an African point of view. It argues that histories of the Internet in Africa would need to be heterogeneous, multi-level and flexible, especially given the various platforms and applications through which the Internet is accessed and used on the continent. The article provides an overview of the major areas of research into the Internet in the Global South and Africa in particular, and makes suggestions for how these areas could inform a historiography of the Internet in Africa.

Introduction

Historical narratives about the Internet have tended to foreground the development of technology itself rather than the experiences of its users – hence the popular discourse of using the language of software development such as versions (e.g. "2.0") to mark key moments in Internet history (Allen, 2012, p. 261). Some accounts have used social behaviours as an indicator for change, but these approaches have been dominated by a technologically determinist approach to Internet histories (p. 265). The result has often been that "simple dichotomies of new and old are presented hand in glove with the assertion of a contrary developmental path from earlier times" (p. 265). When the development of technology and its spread around the world, rather than its applications or usage, forms the historiographical premise, it becomes possible and unproblematic to refer to the history, singular, of the Internet (see e.g. Cohen-Almagor, 2013). Critiques of this dominant approach have therefore called for plurality rather than linearity in Internet histories so as to "destabilize the American-centric, triumphalist, and teleological narrative of linear success—from Arpanet to Internet to global information society" that often mark popular accounts of Internet history (Russell, 2012, p. 1). Problems attendant upon a singular approach to Internet history include that it leads to a teleological/Whiggish view of history, fails to include the diversity and hybridity of convergent technologies and that it occludes less positive aspects of the development of the Internet as a result of being too close to the historical sources (Russell, 2012, p. 6).

If these tendencies have been noted in Internet histories generally, the predominance of technological, teleological narratives over social and cultural ones becomes even starker when considering Internet histories in the Global South. In those settings, the technologically determinist approach to studies of the Internet and digital media more generally has tended to be articulated in the form of an emphasis on development and access, premised on an assumed universal teleology of progress, rather than Internet use within multifarious digital cultures.

Attempts to broaden Internet research beyond the media-saturated Global North have often included case studies from Africa. These case studies frequently adopt one of several positions: a celebratory view of Internet adoption and adaptation in African settings intended to avoid technologically determinist approaches; transmission models aimed at assessing the impact of ICT for Development (ICT4D) initiatives or political economic critiques that focus on the economic, gendered, social and political obstacles to Internet access. The result of these theoretical and methodological differences is that histories of the Internet in Africa – both in terms of looking at the Internet's past and its contemporary use on the continent – often succumb to a teleological narrative of progress and development, and assessments of where different African countries are located on this linear track take the form of a "glass half full or half empty" perspective, depending on whether one chooses to foreground structure or agency.

A theoretical and methodological approach to African histories of the Internet is needed, that moves beyond singular questions of access, adoption or development. Such an approach would also apply to other communication and networking platforms that do not form part of the Internet per se (for instance the uses and applications of SMS technologies). Also, these historiographical approaches would have relevance not only for the tracing the development and use of these digital and networking technologies in the past, but also for contemporary understandings of how these technologies feature within digital cultures on the continent in the present. Instead, histories of the Internet in Africa that take as its foundational premise the dynamic interaction between technology and society, will require a multi-levelled historiographical approach that incorporates all these indicators, and acknowledges not only the differences between the Global South and the Global North, but also the differences within and between different African localities.

Such a multi-levelled approach to how the Internet has evolved in African societies, the roles that it is playing in economic and political relations as well as everyday life, and comparisons between applications of the Internet in African settings and those in other international contexts – whether in more media-saturated regions where access and use are mostly taken for granted, or those in other parts of the Global South where similar challenges and appropriations of the Internet may prove instructive – is important to contribute to Internet histories that are genuinely international in character. The imperative for such histories to be truly international is especially strong given the association between Information and Communication Technologies (ICTs) and globalisation (Mansell, 2015, p. 1). Since globalisation also spans a range of interlinked technologies and practices, such historiographical approaches would also involve paying attention to platforms such as mobile phones, even when they are not used as smartphones to connect to the Internet but perform networking functions that at certain points converge with it. The mobile phone in Africa is central to access of various media, including radio, television and newspapers, and the Internet (Willems & Mano, 2017, p. 1).

The development of such rich, textured histories would of necessity have to take place across different areas of inquiry. Especially important is taking note of the historical development of Internet use in African societies in heterogeneous ways – that is, guarding against the desire for unifying, homogenous, grand narratives of the Internet in Africa. This need for heterogeneity is as much an empirical as a theoretical consideration. Empirical, as a failure to recognise the different ways in which the Internet have developed in various African societies will lead to inaccurate conclusions, misdirected policy initiatives and unsubstantiated claim-making. Theoretical, as the tendency to homogenise "Africa" and use it as a case study to either confirm or contrast theories developed in the Global North is a recurring feature of global media studies and illustrates the persistence of colonial frames of analysis. In such approaches, one or two studies from the Global South are often made to stand in for whole regions, and used to illustrate theoretical discourses developed elsewhere. Global scholarship around the Internet and related ICTs such as the mobile phone have consistently provided good examples of what Comaroff and Comaroff (2012) and Mamdani (2011) have critiqued as a-historical and a-contextual knowledge production about the Global South that serve Northern scholarly agendas rather than develop or disrupt them.

In the area of Internet studies, as in many other sub-fields of media studies and the social sciences in general, Africa is often portrayed in terms of a lack, a challenge or a problem – as "synonymous with uncertain development, unorthodox economies, failed states, and nations fraught with corruption, poverty, and strife" (Comaroff & Comaroff, 2012, p. 113). Studies of the Internet in African societies consequently tend to foreground questions of access, development and democratic "deepening", in other words, positioning digital technologies in the first instance as solutions to problems. The assumption is that the Internet and ICTs in general are "passively received in African countries and act as a force for development" (Gagliardone, 2016, p. 3). It follows then that histories of the Internet within this paradigm are likely to follow a teleological approach – assessing African societies' progress on a pathway assumed to unfold uniformly regardless of context. In order to do justice to the differentiated nature of African societies and the agency and creativity of African Internet users to adopt and adapt technologies to suit their needs, African histories of the Internet should strive for heterogeneity, complexity and flexibility rather than assume that an overarching narrative is achievable. Furthermore, such histories would then be able to inform the development of theory from the South instead of serving as confirmation of theories developed elsewhere. As noted by Comaroff and Comaroff (2012, p. 113), the Global South has traditionally served as source for the raw material from which the Global North weaves its theories – usually a source of evidence rather than a source of theory. Africa, in such theoretical approaches, tends to be the place where you go to find "parochial wisdom", "antiquarian traditions", "exotic ways and means" and, especially, raw data which can be used to support theories developed in, and about, social realities in the Global North (p. 114).

What is needed from historiography of the Internet in Africa is therefore a recognition of complexity, contradictions and contestations. The tendency to "dehistoricize and decontextualise discordant experiences" as Mahmood Mamdani (2011) has put it, and the desire to universalise historical trajectories, have to be resisted in the interest of developing histories of the Internet that are truly international in character. The complexity characterising the various social, political and economic dimensions of the Internet in a diverse continent such as Africa is compounded by the complex nature of research about the information society in general. Studying the rapid development, adoption and adaptation of new technologies has been compared to "blurred snapshots of a moving bullet" (Norris, 2001, p. 26). In a continent that itself is undergoing rapid change, to the extent that older narratives of the "hopeless continent" have made way for more recent, positive assessments of "Africa Rising" (see Bunce, Franks, & Paterson, 2016), such complexity can be overwhelming.

As African histories of the Internet draw on scholarship in the broad field of ICTs, it should be borne in mind that scholarship in this area is itself contested (Chib, May, & Barrantes, 2015, p. v). These contestations have played themselves out in three main areas, namely access, impact and appropriation. A brief consideration of the contestations in each of these areas in turn can provide some contours for a historiography of the Internet in Africa.

Access

One of the major areas for research on the Internet in the Global South has centred around questions of access. The inequalities marking Internet access between countries and regions and within nations themselves have been a scholarly concern for decades, signified by a term that has become ubiquitous when talking about the asymmetrical distribution of online resources: the "Digital Divide". Further conceptual nuances have been noted such as the "global divide" (differences between rich and poor countries), the "social divide" (the gap between the wealthy and the poor within nations) and the "democratic divide" (pointing to those who manage to use the Internet and related technologies to make an impact on policy-making and public life, and those who remain excluded) (Norris, 2001, p. 4). Emerging from this emphasis on access was a related debate between cyber-optimists and cyber-pessimists, who respectively envisaged "the positive role of the Internet for transforming poverty in developing societies" and "skeptics who believe that new technologies will further exacerbate the existing North-South debate" (p. 9). The history of the Internet in Africa has been intertwined with the history of scholarly debates about these distinctions. As the Internet evolved, similar questions have been asked about social media applications such as Facebook and Twitter, as well as mobile media in African contexts (Ekine, 2010; Etzo & Collender, 2010). It has become clear that the links between economic development and Internet access show similarities with similar causes for the uneven distribution of older mass media like radio and television (Norris, 2001, p. 233), although more optimistic assessments have been hoping for a "leapfrog" effect where new media technologies may surpass the introduction of older platforms. The mobile Internet has for instance overtaken fixed line Internet, particularly in the Global South (Donner, 2015, p. 19). This means that access to the Internet is not as insurmountable a problem in regions like Africa than it used to be, and the question has now shifted from how to give access to people living in the Global South, to what happens after they have gained access – as it becomes easier to access the Internet, scholarship should be directed at exploring the heterogeneous ways in which people experience the Internet in their lives (pp. 36–7, 51). A history of the Internet in Africa therefore has to encompass various areas in which the Internet has been seen to make an impact – not only on a macro level but also on the level of the everyday. The use of the Internet on the continent seldom takes place in isolation, but in combination or in convergence with other media practices, as can be seen in the cases brought together by Willems and Mano (2017). For example, the use of social media by radio listeners in Ghana, where radio stations use social network sites like Facebook, micro-blogging sites like Twitter and web-enabled platforms like Whatsapp to connect with their audiences (Avle, 2017, p. 161). These listeners used to phone in their messages to the station but now send messages via one of these networked platforms (p. 161). The combination of "old" and "new" media in convergent practices such as these, indicate that the story of access is not adequate to understand the historical trajectory of the Internet in Africa. A history of the Internet in this context cannot exclude legacy media, nor should it be blind for ways in which present uses of the Internet and related platforms might mimic routines and habits from the past.

Impact

One of the predominant themes in scholarship on the histories of the Internet in Africa has been the potential contribution that it could make to development and the deepening of democracy on the continent. Despite the frequency of debates in this area during the history of the Internet in Africa, wide differences of opinion exist about how digital platforms can create political change (Hahn & Kibora, 2008, p. 88). The debates between those optimistic about the creation of "e-democracy" and those who are more cynical about the impact of digital media, largely hinge on whether structure (the lack of access, literacy and related factors) or agency (for instance, the creative ability of users to combine digital platforms with other forms of communication such as oral networks or legacy media) is foregrounded. The history of the Internet in Africa in relation to its political role seems to have taken the form of ebbs and flows of positivism or cynicism. Initial utopian visions from the 1990s of the potential of digital media for political change, often informed by political determinist views of how new platforms would invigorate political participation, were subsequently toned down in the light of structural challenges (Mudhai, Tettey, & Banda, 2009, p. 1).

This optimism was often based on technologically determinist assumptions that the introduction of new technologies per se will bring about social change and deepen democratic participation. In theorising the African digital public sphere, postulations of what ICTs might mean for African societies frequently drew on older modernisation paradigms of "development": a universal, linear trajectory of progress was assumed to be facilitated through media, consisting of various stages that could be "leapfrogged" by new technologies. However, when this optimism proved to be exaggerated, questions about access, inequality, power and quality of information returned (Mudhai et al., 2009, p. 1). In more recent years, due to the rise of the mobile Internet and increased affordability of connectivity for African users, a shift has again occurred towards ways in which users from the Global South can use the Internet – particularly via mobile platforms – for political action and activism (Donner, 2015, p. 97). But in this regard, it is again instructive to note that a simplistic teleological analysis of the Internet as having contributed to greater openness and transparency in African politics might lead to overly optimistic assessments of its impact. As Gagliardone (2016, p. 3) notes, the optimism that emerged in the 1990s about the potential impact of ICTs on African politics "has been partially eroded by the realization that traditional forms of politics are still able to shape or re-shape technology, even in countries with limited technical capabilities", as African states try to assert or re-assert control in the ICT sphere. Examples of such assertions include attempts to block mobile signals of reporters in the South African democratic parliament in 2015 (Pointer, Bosch, Chuma, & Wasserman, 2016), which evoked similarities with the oppressive tactics of the apartheid regime, or the Ethiopian government's extension of its legal powers to influence in the telecommunications and online sphere under the guise of anti-terrorism. The latter includes the conviction of journalists under the Anti-Terrorism Proclamation (Gagliardone, 2016, p. 138). The history of the Internet's "impact" on African societies is therefore not a simple, linear, teleological one from underdevelopment to development, or from authoritarianism to democracy, but weaves in and out between politics of the past and practices of the present.

Related to the contested history of debates about the Internet's role in African politics, are questions about its contribution to development. A range of applications of the Internet with the objective of "building inclusive, responsive civil societies and increasing participation" (Donner, 2015, p. 98), ranging from agriculture to journalism, finance and banking to medicine and education, conflict mapping to election monitoring, have been developed in Africa over the past number of years. Again here, the mobile Internet in particular has often been celebrated as a tool to provide African users with more social, political and economic power. While mobile platforms have made the Internet more affordable to African users, it has also given commercial players a stronger foothold in African societies. Donner (2015, p. 188) reflects on the challenge to older theories of ICT4D posed by the proliferation of applications such as Facebook, Twitter and Whatsapp in the Global South which may impact as much, if not more, on the experience of the Internet by resource-constrained societies than explicitly development-oriented applications might do.

The continued innovation of such platforms might feed into technological determinist views of the relationship between technology and African societies, or to teleological visions of history in which these innovations might be taken as indications of a linear trajectory of progress. To counter such simplistic understandings of the Internet's role in African societies, a focus on how the Internet is being appropriated, adopted and adapted in African settings is needed.

Appropriation

While measuring the assumed impact of the Internet on developing societies has been a prominent area of focus, an account of the development of the Internet in Africa should not only focus on how technologies change societies, but also on how societies change technologies in the process of adoption, appropriation and adaptation (De Bruijn, Nyamnjoh, & Brinkman, 2009, p. 13). These uses range from the use of Internet platforms to spread political gossip, jokes and humour in contexts where the African state controls mainstream media, to the conspicuous consumption and display of mobile phones, Facebook account or Twitter handles to position African Internet users as technology savvy, globalised and connected.

Underpinning technologically determinist ways of thinking about the history of the Internet in Africa, in particular development discourses, is not only theoretical assumptions that foreground transmission of information rather than the cultural ecologies within which they get adopted, but also one which sees African societies as in need of modernisation. More contextualised understandings of the Internet in Africa, especially how it converges with other communication forms, would emphasise the social and cultural ecology within which digital media are appropriated (see, e.g. De Bruijn et al., 2009; Willems, 2010). This goes not only for the "softer" uses of the Internet to facilitate social connections, conversations and conviviality, but also for the ways in which contextual factors influence the way in which digital platforms are used for activism, protest and political contestation. In these accounts, the social meanings, identity formations and everyday experiences of Internet users form the point of departure. The focus is not in the first instance on what technologies do to these societies, but what societies do to them, even amidst ongoing economic constraints and inequalities of access on the continent. The Internet in Africa has also given audiences the tools and sites to participate in a global media sphere, and they appropriate these tools to speak back to dominant global media narratives, for example when Kenyan social media users took to Twitter with the hashtag #SomeonetellCNN# to protest the way the American network covered an incidence of violence in 2012 (Willems & Mano, 2017, p. 9). The Internet, often accessed through mobile phones or in Internet cafes, has provided African users the agency to access information to which they may otherwise not have access due to cultural, political or social reasons. This information is then appropriated to assist them in negotiating their identities between spaces of belonging (e.g. to religious communities), tradition (e.g. gendered roles as wives and mothers) and modernity (e.g. as consumers of fashion and music). An example of such usage can be found in Mutch's study of Muslim women in Zanzibar's use of the Internet to "juggle the competing tensions" between the desire to be informed and globally connected with the need to retain their reputations in the communities in which they are grounded (2017, p. 238).

A focus on the social and the cultural dimensions of the Internet often highlights differences in the contextual appropriation of the Internet in African societies that differ from those in the more technologically saturated Global North, and therefore contradicts or problematises theory developed elsewhere. This brings us to the point made earlier in this article about knowledge production from the South: A history of the Internet in Africa cannot merely be one in which the historian seeks examples or validation of existing theories. Instead, an inductive, immersive approach to a contextually rich history of the Internet should be followed in which heterogeneity, contradiction and complexity should not be seen as problematic for the construction of a holistic historical narrative, but as contributing to its rich texture. In the African context specifically, the combination of tradition and modernity in the way audiences appropriate technologies into their everyday lives also necessitates a view of Internet "history" in a non-linear fashion, to enable the historian to understand how past traditions, historical loyalties and belongings intermingle with innovative, modern and imaginative ways in which the Internet is put to use in -everyday life.

This also means that differences between African countries are taken into account, rather than treating the region as a monolith. What are the differences and/or similarities between Facebook as a key site for activism in Zimbabwe and the use of Twitter and Whatsapp by student protesters in South Africa? What factors determine the use of the Internet by African migrants in South Africa, and how does the Internet facilitate their mobility across continental borders? Is there a difference between the ways political satire operates in the public sphere in Zimbabwe (e.g. the mysterious Facebook character Baba Jukwa poking fun at Mugabe), where there is less tolerance for mediated dissent, and

Internet memes making fun of South African president Jacob Zuma in a context where freedom of expression is better entrenched?

The multifarious uses of ICTs in the Global South have been described by the term "digital repertoire" (Donner, 2015, pp. 106–107) in an attempt to reflect the range of practices adopted and choices made between various media which stand in relation to one another in ways which are not in the first instance *determined* by cost, access or literacy but by the agency, skills and creativity displayed by users who choose between them within an information economy shaped by structural factors as well as other considerations like aesthetics (pp. 107–109). Historians of the African Internet would therefore be attentive to the ways in which these repertoires change over time, in relation to changing environments and under the influence of a wide array of social, political and economic conditions. Ethnographic approaches to historiography, informed by theories of domestication approach (Ling, 2004, p. 26) would consider the history of the Internet in Africa as part of everyday life, involved in ongoing processes of negotiation, adaptation and change. Another recommendation for a historiography of the Internet would be to use oral histories, diaries or self-documentation to establish how Africans incorporate technological changes and developments over time into their lives (Allen, 2012, p. 271).

Conclusion

Accounts of the political, social and economic dimensions of the Internet in Africa have been contested vigorously in past decades. Shifting points of focus – emphasising structure or agency in turn – as well as competing frameworks of optimism or cynicism have contributed to a multi-dimensional picture of African Internet use that often comes across as fragmented or contradictory. The challenge for Internet historiography focusing on Africa is to attempt a holistic grasp of these multi-facetted, complex and contradictory developments while acknowledging wide divergence in local specificities. At the same time, issues of access, impact and appropriation should be considered together as various dimensions of the historical development of the Internetin Africa.

Disclosure statement

No potential conflict of interest was reported by the author.

References

Allen, M. (2012). What was Web 2.0? Versions as the dominant mode of internet history. *New Media & Society, 15*(2), 260–275.

Avle, S. (2017). 'Radio locked on @Citi973': Twitter use by FM radio listeners in Ghana. In W. Willems & W. Mano (Eds.), *Everyday media culture in Africa: Audiences and users* (pp. 161–179). London: Routledge.

Bunce, M., Franks, S., & Paterson C. (Eds.). (2016). *Africa's media image in the 21st century: From heart of darkness to Africa rising*. London: Routledge.

Cohen-Almagor, R. (2013). Internet history. In R. Luppicini (Ed.), *Moral, ethical and social dilemmas in the age of technology: Theories and practice* (pp. 19–39). Hershey, PA: Information Science Reference.

Comaroff, J., & Comaroff, J. (2012). Theory from the South: Or, how Euro-America is evolving toward Africa. *Anthropological Forum, 22*(2), 113–131.

De Bruijn, M., Nyamnjoh, F., & Brinkman, I. (2009). Introduction. In M. De Bruijn, F. Nyamnjoh, & I. Brinkman (Eds.), *Mobile phones: The new talking drums of everyday Africa* (pp. 11–22). Leiden: Langaa & African Studies Centre.

Donner, J. (2015). *After access: Inclusion, development and a more mobile internet*. Cambridge, MA: The MIT Press.

Ekine, S. (Ed.). (2010). *SMS uprising: Mobile activism in Africa*. Oxford: Pambazuka Press.

Etzo, S., & Collender, G. (2010). The mobile phone "revolution" in Africa: Rhetoric or reality? *African Affairs, 109/437*, 659–668.

Gagliardone, I. (2016). *The politics of technology in Africa*. Cambridge: Cambridge University Press

Hahn, H. P., & Kibora, L. (2008). The domestication of the mobile phone: Oral society and new ICT in Burkina Faso. *Journal of Modern African Studies, 46*(1), 87–109.

Ling, R. (2004). *The mobile connection: The cell phone's impact on society*. San Francisco, CA: Morgan Kaufman.

Mamdani, M. (2011, April 21). The importance of research in a university. *Pambazuka News*. (Accessed October 12, 2016). Retrieved from http://www.pambazuka.org/resources/importance-research-university

Mansell, R. (2015). Foreword. In A. Chib, J. May, & R. Barrantes (Eds.), *Impact of information society research in the Global South* (pp. v–vii). Singapore: Springer Open.

Mudhai, F. O., Tettey, W., & Banda, F. (Eds.). (2009). *African media and the digital public sphere*. New York, NY: Palgrave Macmillan.

Mutch, T. (2017). Agency behind the veil: Gender, digital media and being 'Ninja' in Zanzibar. In W. Willems & W. Mano (Eds.), *Everyday media culture in Africa: Audiences and users* (pp. 220–246). London: Routledge.

Norris, P. (2001). *Digital divide: Civic engagement, information poverty, and the internet worldwide*. Cambridge: Cambridge University Press.

Pointer, R., Bosch, T., Chuma, W., & Wasserman, H. (2016). *Comparative analysis of civil society, media and conflict*(Mecodem Working Paper). (Accessed March 13, 2017). Retrieved from http://www.mecodem.eu/wp-content/uploads/2015/05/Pointer-Bosch-Chuma-Wasserman-2016_Comparative-analysis-of-civil-society-media-and-conflict.pdf

Russell, A. (2012, October). *Histories of networking vs. the history of the internet*. Paper presented atthe 2012 SIGCIS Workshop, Copenhagen, Denmark. (Accessed March 13, 2017). Retrieved from http://arussell.org/papers/russell-SIGCIS-2012.pdf

Willems, W. (2010). At the crossroads of the formal and popular: Convergence culture and new publics in Zimbabwe. In H. Wasserman (Ed.), *Popular media, democracy and development in Africa* (pp. 46–62). London: Routledge.

Willems, W., & Mano, W. (2017). Decolonizing and provincializing audience and internet studies: Contextual approaches from African vantage points. In W. Willems & W. Mano (Eds.), *Everyday media culture in Africa: Audiences and users* (pp. 1–26). London: Routledge.

Notes from/dev/null

Finn Brunton

ABSTRACT
I will discuss the digital materials that we do not want to archive, or
that do not want to be archived, that are particular to Internet
history: the trash, cruft, detritus and intentionally opaque hoard of
documents and artefacts that constitute our digital middens.
Middens are pits of domestic refuse filled with the discards and by-
products of material life: the gnawed bones, ashes, fruit stones and
potsherds, shells and chips and hair and drippings which together
constitute the photographic negative of a community in action and
an invaluable record for archaeologists. Using this analogy, I will
discuss two from my own research: the archives of spam, which we
would all rather forget, and the records of the communities and
marketplaces of the so-called "Dark Web," which would prefer to be
forgotten. I will also address the challenges of research with other
kinds of eccentric, troubling or speculative archives, like
blockchains, ephemeral imageboards and doxxes. I will close by
discussing ways that we can think of digital historiography, in
particular, in terms of these accidental, unwanted, averse archives.

Introduction: strange archives

This is a paper about strange archives: archives that want to disappear, archives that conceal other archives within them, archives that are produced as side effects and accidents
and by-products, archives of rejected material, archives that are trying to look like other
things, archives that are the negative space of archives that no longer exist, archives that
do not permit themselves to be read or try to refuse that permission. The goal of this
paper is to itemise and describe some of these strange archives, many of which are particular to the work of studying the history of networked digital media, and to consider questions they raise for us about accounting for and making use of their strangeness.

I would like to put three of these questions to you, each one framed by a section of this
paper. There are many more questions, of course, some of which I will bring up in passing
below, but these are the three I want to ask in the context of the first issue of *Internet Histories:*

- What can we do with these new "archives" of Internet history that we could not do
  with prior archival forms?
- What tools, approaches and ways of thinking are best suited to making use of them?

– Can we produce typologies, common sets of themes and shared problems among these disparate collections – and what else is out there?

First, to think about the properties of these strange archives of networked computing, I will put them in the context of the richness and complexity of our archival situation in Internet history, and the historiographic approaches that richness makes possible. Second, I will draw on the work that brought me to some strange archival spaces in the history of the Internet to present a way of exploring and using the "middens" I found there: accidental archives, collections of digital rubbish. Finally, I will lay out the start of a list of our strange archives in Internet history and outline their different properties for your consideration. I would like to begin with a seemingly simple, deeply vexing question: When does the history of the Internet start?

Part 1: beginning of the Internet age

The Internet age began behind a biker bar, the Alpine Inn Beer Garden in Portola Valley, about a half-hour south by the freeway from Menlo Park. A small plaque announces this, tucked away among the photos of Little League teams, next to a dartboard and across from a pinball machine ("Attack from Mars"): "BEGINNING OF THE INTERNET AGE," it says. It summarises the trip taken by the SRI International van on 27 August 1976: an interlink between two different networks, from a computer set up on a picnic table in Portola Valley by radio ("PRnet") to the Advanced Research Projects Agency Network (ARPANET), including Bolt, Beranek and Newman (BBN) in Boston and the University of Southern California in Los Angeles as endpoints, using the Transmission Control Protocol and Internet Protocol (TCP/IP). "This event marked the beginning of the Internet Age," says the plaque.

Is that true? It depends on your analysis – on what different historians and students of the history see as the most salient factors with the greatest explanatory power. In some ways, the really significant demonstration of internetworking came in November of the following year: a three-network connection over radio, ARPANET and satellite. The protocol in use in both tests was not what it would become when it was more widely adopted as Internet Protocol version 4 (IPv4), formally specified in a document in September 1981 (which supersedes a document from January 1980) (RFC 760, 1980; RFC 791, 1981). We could date the BEGINNING OF THE INTERNET AGE from when the new protocol was first put into general use: the cutover "flag day" of 1 January 1983, when all the nodes on ARPANET were obligated to switch their systems from the old protocol to TCP/IP, which is when this set of Internet standards became, well, standard.

Or we can push the history farther back. The standard did not materialise in the SRI parking lot in the mid-1970s, after all. We can trace the documents and collaborations back through the Network Working Group and the Request for Comments that introduces the term "internet" (at first a technical adjective, not a noun – "an internet system," as we might say "a robust system") in December 1974 (RFC 675, 1974). But there are still earlier systems which directly influenced the group, like CYCLADES in France and the work of Donald Davies in the UK, so why not start with those? We could write the history of *preconditions* – all those elements which had to be in place for the Internet to happen when and as it did. This could be a study of previous infrastructural layers and ideas that shaped the system (like Tung-Hui Hu's *A Prehistory of the Cloud*) or of the larger social and economic pressures – the market needs and demands – that set the terrain for the event (like James Beniger's *The Control Revolution*). Indeed, it could be something akin to an indirect history of the US military during the Cold War, with the funding it provided and the institutional challenges it presented: robust and resilient command-and-control that could run by wire or radio, linking airborne and shipboard computers with satellites, radar bases and the buried lines running into Cheyenne Mountain.

I give this litany not only to lay out the richness of Internet historiography, but to indirectly show the richness of our archives – of a piece with the archival richness of studying computing and digital technology generally. We have so many documents: formal papers and publications, memoranda, theses and dissertations, brochures and manuals and patent filings, oral histories, materials for salespeople, plus a galaxy of both hobbyist and professional magazines and journals. We can reconstruct events cinematically and visually, with an astonishing amount of video, ranging from contemporary documentaries (like 1972s *Computer Networks: The Heralds of Resource Sharing,* with Licklider, Kahn and Donald Davies – among others! – at fever pitch) to demos, to records of the software itself in operation. Even in cases not as thoroughly documented, we often have images, photos and screenshots. Finally, of course, we have the technology. We can often tinker with the machines themselves – and, of course, for huge variety of instances, we can emulate and explore the software, read the code and documentation and even reconstruct and run period hardware: it is possible to simulate a network of interface message processors (IMPs) from 1973 (a few years before the drive to Portola Valley) and tune their operation, which is like being able to book a direct flight to Jurassic Park (The IMP Guys, 2013).

There are many angles to assembling Internet histories that are missing from my list of approaches so far, including various kinds of *counter-histories*. We have to consider the space of alternatives against which the project could define itself and come to be defined – from protocols like Open Systems Interconnection (OSI) to other networks entirely, like Usenet, Bulletin Board Systems or Minitel, and networks that emerged in different contexts and did not expand beyond them, like the Soviet All-State Automated System of Management (Driscoll, 2014; Peters, 2016). We must account for the unrealised systems that informed aspects or fantasies of the project: Engelbart's oN-Line System, Nelson's Xanadu or clashing visions of remote time-sharing terminals or personal computers. We need to explore the negative spaces, the failures and dead-ends and missing, excluded, ignored or under-discussed pieces of the network's history that also had their role to play, shaping the whole arrangement like the shadowy planet in the three-body problem, which you can only observe by variations in other orbits. I crash-landed on one of these sunless worlds in 2007 and stayed there for six years.

Part II: = (REAL BANK LOGINS SPAM SUPPLYS) =

During my time excavating the world of garbage that became the book *Spam: A Shadow History of the Internet,* I became convinced of two things. First, that the history of "spam" online, in all its various meanings, was an important component of what the network became – affecting search engines, walled garden systems, email, encryption, distributed denial of service (DDoS) attacks, advertising models, specialised artificial intelligence, the politics of identity, you name it. Second, that it was very hard to properly tell that history, because the very technologies spam had shaped, had been built to eradicate it. It was a chronicle of notes from /dev/null, the device to which you direct data you want to never be written. For stretches of the period I was covering, I was essentially working on a Gnostic history. Much of what we know about the Gnostics comes through documents created by Church Fathers, theologians and Christian historians devoted to their eradication. Likewise, new spam techniques and technologies would become apparent through their citation and forwarding and copy-pasting by the people trying to evolve policy and software and law enforcement tools to make them stop. Many of the most technically interesting varieties of spam were notable for finding ways to render themselves invisible, unsearchable, un-indexable – dictionary attacks of phrasal salad, with images and HTML tricks to conceal themselves from documentation by their adversaries. They had an intriguing temporality, like *events* rather than objects, meant to get some action and disappear. The most prominent, documented parts of this history tended therefore to be especially memorable, peculiar or egregious examples – circulated, shared and referenced – a trophy case of monsters, no more representative of the larger phenomenon than the wall of a hunting lodge is of the local fauna.

The best things I found for reconstructing this history were *dumps*, literally and figuratively. A key archive for me was the Enron email corpus, a set of about 650,000 emails collected by the Federal Energy Regulatory Commission during their investigation of the company's fraud and market manipulation, which was dumped online in 2003 in a massive tranche of internal corporate media including trading floor phone calls and scanned documents. This collection of messages became one of the benchmark tools for training anti-spam systems – that is, for trying to determine the properties of "normal email." It was a flash-frozen Pompeii of email culture, and it had also become an important scientific artefact, used for many different training and machine learning systems like spam filtering. But it was also the story of Gerald and Lisa, two Enron employees whose disintegrating marriage was documented by their intra-office email exchanges – which introduces the theme of accidental inclusions in the accidental archive of the dump.

That was just the prelude to the archive of Premier Services, a mid-level spam company hacked by someone who called themselves "The Man in the Wilderness." Wilderness Man had a vendetta against Premier, so she, he or they captured several megabytes of data and dumped it all online: chat logs, screenshots of software in operation, budgets, the ins and outs of running the business. It was invaluable for understanding exactly how the spam business worked at that time, after the Web and AOL but before successful widespread automated spam filters. The hack, and the dump, was also a personal attack, including private photographs of the company's founder and employees and plenty of personally identifying information. (Pictures of the founder were used for proto-meme purposes, with mocking text added.)

I took to thinking of these and other haphazard, accreted digital archives as *middens*, the accumulations of by-products and junk and trash and bits and pieces of the working life of computers and communities. It seems like a useful metaphor for this kind of scholarly object. A midden is an archaeological site, the waste dump generated by people: discarded shells (shell middens are a major resource for the study of maritime cultures), potsherds and stone chips ("debitage," from fashioning tools), excrement, husks, peels and rinds, feathers, hair and ashes. When addressing the future, you deliberately leave etched runes, standing stones, red ochre, ziggurats, grave goods – but, just as important, you also accidentally leave the trash record of how you lived and how you got by, the document of manufacture, preparation, consumption, exclusion and waste. The production of what I think of as informational middens is peculiar to digital technologies, but not unique: textual and archival packrats have always existed, bless them, but the ease of digital information storage and transmission has produced many more of these dumps, with a huge variety of archival information within which a stratum of spam could be found – among many other things. Like middens, these dumps were often accidental, side effects: digging around for material meant to be discarded, material designed to be difficult to observe, index or search, was most rewarding when the "archive" had been created by intentions other than preservation alone, like revenge or legal discovery.

There was a related challenge: to document middens-in-process, as it were, with the data of current working communities and marketplaces, for whom any record was an accidental by-product of their activities. They had no desire to be observed. To understand the spam business, it was necessary to observe the credit card scammers, identity thieves and teams selling slices of botnet capacity to send email in million-message batches. Their Internet Relay Chat (IRC) channels and discussion boards were abuzz with people and bots making sales pitches and doing deals: " = (REAL BANK LOGINS SPAM SUPPLYS) = (SELL BANK LOGINS\PRICE DEPENDS ON BALANCE 10% FROM IT) = (BIG BASE!) = ." They maintained their own systems of records – some users got a +v, "verified," known merchants with good histories who would not rip you off (probably) – but kept no histories, no findable archives. They had to be documented in action.

Spam was an enormous mass of material for which no one wanted to keep records (except email filter developers and the Federal Trade Commission); around it were communities and groups who did not want their records to be kept. Spam had the invisibility of refuse, and spammers and their ancillary businesses had the opacity of deliberate secrecy. Given very different causes and effects, this shares an interesting family resemblance with other major motors of Internet adoption and use, like pornography, online gambling and file sharing – and the drug dens, pre-loaded debit card vendors, covert media libraries and scam sites (hire an assassin!) of the so-called Dark Web of onion sites, neither indexed nor cached nor added to the Internet Archive and generally short-lived indeed.

I approached these projects of accumulation, documentation, mirroring and digging from the perspective of trying to make them into traditionally viable archives, time-stamped and organised. The question I would like to raise now is whether there are other aspects of these middens – things particular to them, properties they have, as the dumps of data in which material meant to vanish is captured – that are worth thinking about. With that question in mind – how to understand a mirror of acropol4ti6ytzeh.onion as a historical record? – I want to turn to our final question. What other kinds of archives are particular and significant (if not always unique) to the work of Internet history? What are their distinctive properties?

Part III: password is lol

There are the archives of hacks and hacking. Not just the materials that the hackers produce, but the processes and media generated *by* them: the Pastebin announcements, the communiqués and ransom demands and launch screens that tell a company they have been compromised. Consider the pictures – pictures, really, since the computer is now locked, so instead of a screenshot we have an image, taken by a phone, of the screen – of the menacing skeleton announcing the "Guardians Of Peace" hack of Sony Pictures, or the exploding-head manifesto of the Impact Team takeover of Ashley Madison. There are ransomware lock windows, which – among other things – document the adoption of Bitcoin as the extortionist's currency of choice. And there are the archives of the aftermath, from the blackmail messages received by email addresses in the Ashley Madison database, to documents like Andrew "weev" Arnheimer's "Open letter to federal scum," a Pastebin text in which he demands recompense (in Bitcoin, natch) for his prison time, and that he is planning to use the Ashley Madison dump to expose the attorneys who put him away. Finally, there is the *context* of hacks, like the associated Twitter accounts in which hackers address fans, clients and adversaries alike. Consider two tweets from @DotGovs, whose username is "penis" and icon is the head of Buzz Lightyear from the *Toy Story* movies. ("Whose": it is actually a team at work, or so one person claimed; details remain murky.) One tweet immediately follows the other, both on 8 February 2016:

"watching keeping up with the kardashians"
"20,000 FBI EMPLOYEES NAMES, TITLES, PHONE NUMBERS, EMAILS, COUNTRY cryptobin.org/78u0h164 password is lol #FreePalestine"

I believe that being able to entirely explain all the details, references and context of these two tweets alone in a few decades will provide a superb window on the Internet history of our time. (The account has been suspended, of course, and is no longer available in official form.) Dumps like the hack of Premier Services are proto-doxxes, but doxxing is now a common strategy: how should we think about and approach these weaponised archives?

There are the archives of the ephemeral and anonymous: words and posts meant to disappear or become unavailable, deliberately or by negligence, and never to connect with any specific identity. Think of 4chan and its many imitators and knock-offs, and the rush to realise apps and platforms for self-destructing or anonymous communication (or, at least, the promise of it). Amateurs and professionals alike have been collecting and saving as much of this kind of material as possible – it is attractive in its very challenge to preservation – but beyond the difficulty of capture, it is interesting to understand an archive of material meant to vanish, or to conceal those using it. I tend to reflexively think of dissident and cryptographic groups in this light, but what about a history of the Low-Orbit Ion Cannon? It was software that exploited a structural flaw in the Internet (the denial of service attack), which was shared and applied by groups of volunteers seeking to aid Anonymous – and it leaked data about its users. Built for ephemerality – a DDoS attack is the flash-mob sit-in of digital activist tactics – and anonymity, it left behind a cache of accidental records that are valuable for themselves as well as for what they reveal.

What about the archives of materials that hope to go unnoticed? There are the detritus of hoaxes, frauds and scams – things which are meant to look like other things, and which seek, above all, to pass without awareness of what makes them significant: phishing messages, faux URLs, ersatz landing pages, alerts from cryptocurrency wallets to trick you into giving up your private key. There are archives of new kinds of marketplaces which hope to draw only the most marginal notice, because they thrive in the corners of far larger platforms which may wish to present themselves differently. There are, or were, Egyptian shepherds and butchers and Kuwaiti dealers in manga and anime using Instagram as a storefront, and term-paper-writing businesses and gun dealers on Facebook, communities to themselves seeking to avoid wider recognition to dodge moderation or deletion. (Even black markets had subgroups, like the assisted suicide community on the Silk Road, shipping Nembutal amidst all the various white/brown powders and sheets of acid.) A far larger case along these lines is the ad tech and online ad marketplace – not covert so much as *obscure*, the vast bazaar of microsecond analysis, bundling and auctions of browsing data to serve ads that shape so much of the experience of "content" on the web. And there are the archives of attempts to make things disappear. Deindexing, de-listing, burying, deleting, which sometimes leave their own records in the negative space of broken links or create a new kind of archival garbage in the obfuscating materials generated to bury search results: "to expedite the eradication of references to the pepper spray incident," as the "Brand and Reputation Enhancement" memo for the Chancellor of UC Davis puts it. (Stanton & Lambert, 2016; Helen Nissenbaum and I discussed obfuscating data in *Obfuscation*.)

Finally, on a completely different note, it is well worth thinking about new systems like blockchains as another class of novel archives: they are built to act as a shared, collective timestamping mechanism for their contents, unchangeable save by linear additions, an endless list churned out by a system that rewards its members for verifying past details. It is a set of chronicles (in the classic, historiographic sense of a chronologically organised and notated record of events) each of which contains in hashed form, the material that precedes it. Blockchains are rife with metadata and odd, encoded details – the Bitcoin blockchain, in particular, was quickly adopted by people using transactions to store other kinds of data in this accidental, distributed, resilient archive. Indeed, Brewster Kahle (among others) has proposed the broader application of blockchains to make the Internet itself its own backup system (2015).

From a specific event where we (but not our subject) began – with a van in Portola Valley in the afternoon in 1976 that is also, in a sense, on the Internet – to gigabytes of images and accidental caches of millions of messages accrued over decades, to secret marketplaces and timestamped public archives: over all of these hover other questions. What is the nature of the digital archive in particular? (We could start with Matthew Kirschenbaum, with Lori Emerson, with Lisa Gitelman....) How – practically and theoretically – to manage the preservational excess, the terabyte burdens placed on the archival community? (As I write this, the rush is on to protect enormous masses of data endangered by the new Republican administration in the United States – a story familiar from the scale of "data friction" discussed by Paul Edwards.) But, for this first issue of *Internet Histories*, I would like to close with the simple, complex question with which I opened my outline of strange archives: When does Internet history begin?

Disclosure statement

No potential conflict of interest was reported by the authors.

References

Beniger, J. (1989). *The control revolution: Technological and economic origins of the information society*. Cambridge, MA: Harvard University Press.

Brunton, F. (2013). *Spam: A shadow history of the internet*. Cambridge, MA: MIT Press.

Brunton, F., & Nissenbaum, H. (2015). *Obfuscation: A user's guide for privacy and protest*. Cambridge, MA: MIT Press.

Driscoll, K. (2014). *Hobbyist inter-networking and the popular internet imaginary: Forgotten histories of networked personal computing, 1978-1998* (dissertation). Los Angeles, CA: University of Southern California.

Hu, T.-H. (2015). *A prehistory of the cloud*. Cambridge, MA: MIT Press.

Kahle, B. (2015). Locking the web open: A call for a distributed web [Blog post]. Retrieved August 11, 2015, from http://brewster.kahle.org/2015/08/11/locking-the-web-open-a-call-for-a-distributed-web-2/.

Peters, B. (2016). *How not to network a nation: The uneasy history of the soviet internet*. Cambridge, MA: MIT Press.

RFC 675. (1974). Specification of internet transmission control program. Retrieved from https://tools.ietf.org/html/rfc675.

RFC 760. (1980). DoD standard internet protocol. Retrieved from https://tools.ietf.org/html/rfc760.

RFC 791. (1981). Internet protocol: DARPA internet program protocol specification. Retrieved from https://tools.ietf.org/html/rfc791.

Stanton, S., & Lambert, D. (2016, April 13). UC Davis spent thousands to scrub pepper-spray references from internet. *The Sacramento Bee*.

The IMP Guys. (2013). The ARPANET IMP program: Retrospective and resurrection (draft of December 2, 2013). Retrieved from http://walden-family.com/bbn/imp-code.pdf.

Archaeology of the Amsterdam digital city; why digital data are dynamic and should be treated accordingly

Gerard Alberts, Marc Went ⓘ and Robert Jansma ⓘ

ABSTRACT

One of the major initiatives in The Netherlands promoting the use of the Internet by private individuals was De Digitale Stad (DDS), which is the Amsterdam digital city. DDS was launched in January 1994 and soon evolved from an elementary bulletin-board-like system to a full blown virtual city with squares, houses, post-offices, cafés and a metro. Archaeology of the digital city makes it clear that there is no beaten track for preserving and, after two decades, unwrapping "born digital" material. During the research to reconstruct the digital city two routes were tried, one emulating the old system, another replicating it. The outcome, together with the harvest of two working systems, is a lesson, a concern and an appeal. From the experience of reconstructing digital heritage, we draw pragmatic lessons. Tools for digital archaeology are tried and contemplated. The lessons, however, do not unequivocally support the use of the notion "archaeology." The concern is one of the social responsibilities. Web archaeology, being part of contemporary history, confronts the researcher with such issues as privacy and the ethics of "young" data. A case is made for treating digital data dynamically.

Introduction

Participants in the digital city had an avatar. DDS, De Digitale Stad, that is the Amsterdam digital city, was much more than an Internet server, if only because the community shaping it had not settled for a definite meaning. The systems conveyed a sense of community building, and although there was not one but many communities, there was this one basic sense of being a virtual "citizen" expressed by the avatar. The DDS-team was self-conscious enough to adorn its second anniversary with a full backup of the system "to be studied by archaeologists in a distant future": The FREEZE, 1996.[1]

Two decades do not create a great distance. However, we do embark on the archaeology of DDS. Following the actors of 1996, the effort to read and resuscitate vintage digital material may be called "archaeology." The metaphorical expression does not come without repercussions. First, the lack of distance poses problems of contemporary history, hardly associated with the notion of archaeology. Second, notions like digital archaeology or web archaeology suggest a kinship to a media archaeology or to an archaeology of knowledge in the sense of Foucault (1969) or media theory (Ernst, 2013; Presner, Shepard, & Kawano, 2014, p. 84ff), which is hardly explored here. The present contribution is about digital, but very material, old tapes. Getting hold of the vintage tapes is one thing, reading them and making sense of the content quite another. Different tools were tried and developed. In the perspective of accessing the data for historical research and possibly museum presentation, major issues arise. Ethical issues, not unusual for contemporary history, hit the digital archaeologist in the face. More specific questions related to the technological aspect of DDS impose themselves, issues of security and integrity of the data. The question of privacy, perhaps not strictly related to technology, poses itself with new urgency.

Archaeologies, emulation vs. replica

The effort to reconstruct the digital city and have it in operation almost naturally proceeds along two routes: emulation and a replica (simulation). The two notions of emulation and replica have a long evolution of shifting meanings in art history. Here they are taken after their, equally unstable, meaning in computer science (Smith & Nair, 2005, Chapter 2). The resulting contradistinction adds a nuance, informed by computer science, to the discussion on emulation in electronic art (Jones, 2004).

Emulation is the effort to run the original code on a new platform. This does not come without compromise. The DDS-system as preserved does not easily "un-freeze". It will not run, primarily because the physical systems supporting it are not readily available. Migration to present day systems is tedious, but feasible. Getting the legacy software operational requires adaptations. The authenticity-question, as to what system one is "actually" running, always remains.

Replica, the look-alike remake by present day means, seemingly discards the authenticity-question – one is obviously not running the real system – and focuses on presence to the user, rather than on the system.

The difference is that the mimicking is on a different level and from a different perspective. The original sense of emulation is that of one artist out of admiration mimicking another. Here one computer system is thought to mimic the other. The agency is with the system; it is placed on level with the artist – in the original sense of emulation. The perspective is that of the system; the boundary is between hardware and software, or between layers of software. In a replica, the perspective is that of the user. Irrespective of what happens under the hood of the system, its surface performance for the senses is what counts. The boundary is between the user and the system. No sharp distinction is assumed between user and system, or between hardware and software. The crucial point here is that considering something either an emulation or a replica is a matter of perspective and comes with diverging expectations. Criteria vary from reconstructing the operation of the system to recreating the user experience. Recreation implies making the experience present, and is in that historiographical sense presentism. Does the archaeologist in her interpretation identify (with) the code or with the user? It seems that archaeologists by default choose the first; we are preoccupied with the authenticity of the code. We are, but in fact we show the alternative route as well.

What approach to choose and which tools to develop is contingent upon the goals set for such a project, which in turn depends on the context. Heritage has a community on the donating end, a group strong and dedicated enough to not throw away the material remnants, and on the receiving end, a group feeling strongly about the value of these materials. In fact there are several groups caring for the DDS heritage and their goals vary. For the joy of a one-time replay a system may be fired up and run with loose ends. For public access, by contrast, for example a museum exhibit, integrity and security of the system and privacy of personal data are key issues. The mere consideration of the latter purpose was one of the motives inspiring the alternative approach of building a new system from scratch with the same functionality, a replica.

Dynamic approach

If preserving and reconstructing data may be called web archaeology, what are the "scoops" and "brushes" in the digital practice? For the most part tools of digital archaeology require manual calibration and application; automated procedures are in their infancy. Working with legacy digital material brings home one crucial insight: whether the unearthed objects are data, scripts or full blown software; their archaeology involves getting the code to work. Born digital material is dynamic. Executing a script may yield different outputs each time it runs. Static material does not react, let alone react differently. The archaeologist will not be satisfied with images or screenshots.

This is in stark contrast to the existing practices of Web Archiving, viz. to preserve snippets of the Internet as pages, as snapshots. The maturing of the field of Web Archiving has been well captured in the volume edited by Julien Masanès (2006). The pioneering work of the Internet Archive and its Wayback Machine from the late 1990s has been broadened and institutionalised on a national scale in many countries. National Archives and Media Archives have automated their harvesting with crawlers and filters. The materials they gather, however, are static, or rather, are treated statically. Even if websites contain code, they are saved simply as pictures of pages. Today, the Internet Archive does more. It replays the harvested pages as much as it can. Our plea is to reinstate the pages as they were born, not starting from the resulting page, but from the server. Given the dynamic character of born digital material the archaeological approach should be dynamic. To put it differently: such material is called "born digital" to emphasise that its symbols are not just text. The text is considered as working code. And for working code, emulation and replica offer themselves as feasible approaches, each with their own tools.

De Digitale Stad: a local history

De Digitale Stad, the Amsterdam digital city, exemplified the electronic social network. It facilitated the exploration of all the possibilities to connectis, including almost incidentally access to the Internet. It was designed with the city metaphor in mind. On 15 January 1994, the digital city opened its gates. Beyond the practice of earlier FreeNets, De Digitale Stad appealed to its users to adopt the metaphor and create a true community. It allowed the users to be "citizens" or "netizens" and enter the unknown world of the Internet.

The project was initially funded for 10 weeks by the city of Amsterdam, on the assumption of bridging the gap between local politics and the ordinary citizens. The number of subscriptions skyrocketed. After the first 10 weeks, with the project clearly growing bigger than anyone had anticipated, DDS acquired further funding to continue beyond the initial experiment (Castells, 2001; Lovink, 2002; Rustema, 2001, pp. 42–67).

The first version of DDS was a bulletin board system (BBS), a static menu offering the user a choice of line numbers to continue towards further pages. Imagination was an essential asset for the user to walk the streets of the digital city.

The second version made a major step to change from the Gopher communication protocol, used in version 1, towards the newer HTTP protocol still in use today on modern web pages. Within weeks, yet another version of DDS was released. Through a major overhaul this version 3 had become a truly interactive system, embodying the metaphor of a city. The overarching metaphor was further detailed by such facilities as "post office", "city square" and "café." These allowed the "citizens" to navigate the city more intuitively. Users could fetch their mail at an email facility called "post office", they could set-up their own homepages called "houses" that were reachable by traveling across "squares", those were web pages linking between each other, or they could hang out in a "café", which we nowadays see as a chat room. The city metaphor was introduced and promoted the Internet as a common, a public space, which it hardly was in 1994/1995, when network services were mostly available in universities, libraries and as private facilities in large companies.

DDS grew amidst optimist expectations, expectations of technology having a democratisation effect. In the sense of spreading the technology itself among larger section of society it certainly had this impact. Hope that the technical facilities by themselves would bridge the gap between politics and public, and thus solve the representation and legitimatisation problems of politics soon evaporated. Such hopes were certainly played out in acquiring the initial subvention of DDS by the city of Amsterdam. The idea of a push-button direct democracy is a recurring dream, also in DDS circles. In the same vein but stronger and more specific for DDS were the expectations of an emerging community and a new kind of sociability. Conceiving DDS as a commons, as a public sphere, deeply motivated many of the early actors. Their motivation was even strengthened when in those very years in the US the Internet rapidly evolved in a commercial connectivity with a new kind of economy (Aspray & Ceruzzi, 2008). Lovink (2002) observes that not one but many communities shaped around the digital city and created their own niches subcultures. From recent research into the themes of the cafés and lists in DDS, one may infer that the electronic facilities did in cases serve as vehicles of emancipation.[2] Dennis Beckers and Peter van den Besselaar have in a series of publications shown the dynamics of the various groups involved in DDS-initiatives (Beckers & Besselaar, 1998; Besselaar & Beckers, 1998). Thus, while Lovink (2002) characterised the divergence between the communities as cultural differences, Beckers and Besselaar were more political in their analysis by pointing at divergence through conflicting interests.

At a more fundamental level studies in sociology, STS and media students have hinted at new kinds of sociability emerging in such connected commons as DDS. Castells, famous for his trilogy on the Information Age (1996), in The Internet Galaxy (2001) presented DDS and many other case studies as vistas on new forms of society. The more radical approach in this direction was Howard Rheingold's (1993) effort to continue where Dürkheim and Weber have left us with "Gemeinschaft" and "Gesellschaft." Reinder Rustema (2001) emulates Rheingold's search for a "society" beyond Gesellschaft by the example of De Digitale

Stad. Sociology has not yet come to conclusions, but without any doubt DDS is part of the empirical material to be reflected upon. Media studies on their part show that the industrial society is superseded by the platform society (Van Dijck, Poell, & Waal, 2016) – of which then DDS is not a forerunner or prime example.

Local frost and defrost

On 15–16 January 1996, the DDS servers were down for most of the night to allow for a full backup of De Digitale Stad. A full 1-on-1 disk copy of all the servers running DDS was created on 3 Digital Linear Tapes (DLT). DDS congratulated itself with a city frozen in time, preserved "to be studied by archaeologists in a distant future": the FREEZE. Further heritage material was gathered at "gravediggers parties" and the Amsterdam Museum installed a small exhibit on DDS.

In restoring old data, it soon came to light that the package would not simply unwrap, or defrost. The DLT Tapes holding the FREEZE did not easily render their content. After a good deal of searching for auxiliary hardware, the tapes had been read and converted into the more common format of compressed gzipped tarball (.tar.gz). Initial attempts to extract this tarball of 10 Gb failed because, for no apparent reason, it exceeded the available storage. After several tries, each time with more storage available, the files were finally extracted to a network attached storage (NAS) with 12 Tb of free space. The size of the completed extraction revealed why earlier attempts failed: the data filled little over 2.2 Tb of storage space. When searching for the cause why a 10 Gb .tgz file extracted to over 2.2 Tb (220x its own size), we detected four corrupted files, each over 500 Gb in size – quite possibly the effect of a "decompression bomb." Omitting these four files, the extraction returned to reasonable size, approximately 35 Gb. The project "DDS 3.0 operational" worked from these cleaned files.

Sockets

However, in an effort to understand what had gone awry in handing down the legacy files, and to make sure that no major parts of the original files were missing, we made a detour going back to the original servers, still extant in the Amsterdam Museum. Other than the FREEZE the content of these servers was not strictly dated, let alone of the same date as the FREEZE. Because of its historical significance, the original, but not necessarily operational, hardware is preserved at the store of the Amsterdam Museum. For the purpose of our research project, we were granted access. For just this one occasion the original hard drives were retrieved from these servers – and put back.

In order to read the 20-year-old hard drives, vintage equipment was needed, with the sockets of the cables as major obstacles. The original server had eight hard drives, connected using three different cable sockets. The interface was SCSI, which is a parallel interface subject to different standards. The solution was found with the help of a former system administrator digging up the fitting connectors from an old drawer. To read out the content of the hard disks a Linux live USB was set-up. The disks were connected one at a time. A full-disk-image was made – and preserved carefully.

This sidestep of the project greatly improved our understanding of the legacy material being studied, specifically the hardware. The newly retrieved content read from the original servers, showed sufficient overlap with the FREEZE of 1996 to confirm the adequacy of the cleaned files, but being of different date, was not included in our current reconstruction project.

Avatar generator

In January 2015, after the defrost and clean-up of the FREEZE had been achieved, first forays into the data were started. Since there was little indication of the structure of the stored file, except that the system was an old Sun SPARC system, investigations began with mapping the folder structures and sizes, and listing the installed software. The first observation was that the system was not as systematic as one might naively assume. In particular, there were no systematic locations for source code, if preserved at all, going with the installed code. Harsh lesson for the archaeologist: with the programs installed and running in 1996, there will not even be an indication of source code being preserved and, if so, where it might be stored in the system. Another harsh lesson, even the non-techies have to learn some jargon.

Software appears in various modes, basically "source code" and "binary." Programmes are written by the programmer – with the help of a whole factory of tools – written in a programming language. This written version is called source code. This is the version one usually refers to when discussing programs. Source code is just text, it does not work by itself. A program in source code is translated to fit on a system, in our case on the Sun SPARC station. The result of translation is an "executable" or "binary" code. This is the version that does the work. Hence, the digital archaeologist looks for the "binaries" to see what a system can do, which engines are available.

The tool doing the translation from source code to binary is called translator or "compiler." In some special cases and only for specific languages, a tool exists which can do the reverse translation, back from binary to source code, a "de-compiler".

Memories

In exploring the files, it was of great help that former "citizens" vividly remembered the avatars. This clue from oral history set the challenge of locating the relevant software. With the introduction of DDS 3.0, the system had become truly interactive and logging in became more than having access. Every user would now have an avatar representing him or her whilst "walking" through the digital city. A program would generate a small icon-like image representing the user, an avatar. Somewhere on the server there must be such a piece of software performing that function, the avatar generator. In 1995, for lack of memory space and operational speed, the system would not allow for pictures or other complex images to be inserted. Therefore, the avatar generator created simple but effectively distinctive images for every user, varying on a pattern inspired by a character from the Muppet show, Beaker.

Exploration of the frozen data yielded no such file as avatar or avatar generator. A further clue was to search for the programs governing registration to the system, because that was the procedure including the creation of an avatar. This lead to locating Apache and its original configuration file, from there the original registration page was traced. The registration scripts had been written in CGI PERL, easily readable, and thus the steps of registration could be traced.

Further recollections from oral history suggested that these icon images were never called avatars, but DoDoS, in an apparent play on the name of the system DDS. And "Dodo" is the extinct bird from Mauritius. So, the avatar generator would revive the extinct bird. The script, now located, had the name Dodo.cgi. This shows the development of terminology of the past 20 years. Where nowadays "avatar" is the appropriate jargon, it shows that this term was not as pervasive back in the day.

Soft lesson for the archaeologist: follow the challenges set by oral history.

The reconstruction project

With the avatar generator resuscitated in 2015, and several other chunks of software brought to life in 2016, we could not resist the temptation of trying to get the whole system back into operation, project "DDS 3.0 Operational." The project group soon split up and worked in two opposite directions. One part of the research focused on what seemed to be the most obvious thing to do, viz. to try and run the original software again. The other part focused on the idea of reinstating the user experience, regardless of the machinery behind the screen. This second route, to replicate the digital city, leads to rebuilding the system from scratch and working per modern technology and standards.

Preservation of the digital city

The goal of the FREEZE had been to preserve De Digitale Stad as it had existed and run two years after its introduction, to ensure for future generations the possibility to experience and to study the early days of the web. However, simply backing up one's data does not automatically result in preservation. A 1-on-1 copy may be historically accurate, but such a copy loses much of its attraction if it cannot be run, if the context of the original production server is missing. DDS ran on the Solaris SPARC computer architecture. Because Sun SPARC has become proprietary software and hardware from Adobe, with prohibitively high licensing costs, virtualisation seemed the road towards reconstructing an adequate remplacant context. It proved to be not that easy, since emulation of the SPARC architecture on a different system has usually low performance, particularly on the most common architecture in the 2010s, the x64 architecture.

Emulation

The one research direction was to revive De Digitale Stad in its original state, from the perspective of the software running it. Like a hyena going for the innards, the software archaeologist goes looking for the software that was run, the software that was executed to create the performance of the system. The search is for the executable files, or "binaries." Being familiar with the operating system, mostly Unix, and knowing how to identify and search for these files, binaries, archaeologists use such instructions as "grep" and "find" to trace the location of the executables in the FREEZE.

Lesson of exclusion: only close familiarity with the legacy system and its operating system will allow one to do the work of a web-archaeologist. To a large degree this is tacit knowledge.

Knowing which programs did in fact do the job is not enough to run them again. Binaries are executable only in a specific context, in this case the SPARC context.

At this point the web archaeologist, in general the software archaeologist, bereft from straightforward automatic tools like a Virtual Machine doing the work, must revert to more subtle and more individual methods. For the DDS 3.0 Operational project, a pragmatic decision was made with far reaching consequences. In spite of the dependencies – i.e. the points where the programmer had created constructions particular to the specific machine – we chose to emulate on an x64 architecture. The consequence being that the binaries on the old system (Sparc) are of no use and one has to create new binaries for the new system (x64). We had to go back to the source codes, the programmes as written, and would in that mode of the programme have to deal with the dependencies each individually. The task at hand was now to find the original versions of the software running in 1996 and compile these programs anew for the operating systems coming with the x64 architecture. Fortunately for this project a good deal of the source code, even if not systematically preserved, was retrieved scattered throughout the FREEZE. For future archaeology there is a use for systematic tools of de-compilation, in cases where there is no source code is available at all.

The positive side of emulating on an x64 architecture that this system is so common that one may expect it to survive for the foreseeable future. We are good, not for archaeological stretches of time, but at least for one or two generations. One may hope that the present work of getting a version of DDS running needs not be repeated from scratch in 20 years from now.

The downside is that corners of DDS with the heaviest dependencies are hard to restore. In particular, the system for authentication, logging in, was most specific for the SPARC architecture and has therefore been left out of the present emulation. By consequence the avatar generator, Dodo.cgi, was found and brought back into operation, but the programs constituting its context, logging in, are not. So, we can play and make avatar-wallpaper today, but we cannot have our DoDo walk through the system for us. When the former systems administrator was consulted on how to emulate this feature – which he had in fact programmed – his answer was: " consider not to." In terms of DDS 3.0 as it ran in 1996, one can only visit the city in the "guest" mode. In other parts of the DDS program functionality was restored by prag-matic patches. Thus, this emulation comes with compromise.

Along the route of emulation, the digital city has been restored as close to the original project as possible. In as far as it functions, it does revive with a feel of authenticity – so say DDS's former inhabitants. As an extra benefit the emulation preserves code of histori-cal interest and allows comparison to modern standards. It reveals the challenges as the DDS developers perceived them and the answers they chose when designing the early pieces of Internet. It makes the look and feel of born digital media accessible, including its inner workings and some of the thoughts behind it.

Replica

The other approach was to revive the digital city from the point of view of the end user, replicating the original system as closely as possible using current technologies of 2016. This was feasible because, compared to today's projects, the size of the digital city was rel-atively small and quite straightforward. Although providing static images only, the Way-back Machine did show the appearance of DDS to the end user. The programming for the replica was done in parallel to, and strongly inspired by, the emulation. While missing out on historical accuracy in the back-end software, the replica proves the feasibility of creat-ing a user interface very near to the original, and in practice indistinguishable from the emulation – so say again DDS's former inhabitants. The user will "walk" through the city without noticing it is not the original software. In that sense the experience is effectively preserved.

Major advantages of the replica are, beyond its technical maintainability and sustain-ability, its security. If one were to consider the creation of a publicly accessible version of DDS 3.0, for example as a museum exhibit, a replica would offer a doable solution; whether feasible in terms of museum practice, remains to be seen. As long as mainte-nance is kept up a replica can be secured and it could be filled with part of the legacy con-tent upon authorisation by the, former, users.

Tools

The archaeologist's brushes

If preserving and reconstructing data may be called web archaeology, what are its brushes and spades? Digging up the digital city has in large part been a manual labour. In fact relied heavily on the tacit knowledge typical of craftsmanship. It required familiarity with Unix and other operating systems. Key element in the tacit knowledge is practical insight in the way server systems were usually built up, preferably joined with expertise in today's systems. It took the joint forces of former system administrators who had not forgotten their trade and were willing to share, and archaeologists who are able to absorb. The latter are talented computer science graduates using some of their academic lessons and heavily relying on their experience of working as system administrators to pay for their studies. Their concerted effort has allowed for a "handmade reconstruction" of DDS.

But in a digital environment, should one not expect "systematic and automated tools"? Some tools do exist in the realm of software archaeology. For example, source code is compiled into executable code. For some situations, e.g. programs written in high level programming languages, tools do exist for the reverse process: decompilation to reconstruct source code from executable files. Further automated tools are dearly wanted, like excavation tools to help to recognise the various types of files.

Beyond the archaeological metaphor

As far as craftsmanship goes, the metaphor of archaeology sounds attractive and serves well. But in fact, what we are describing here has little to do with archaeology proper, but all with handing over, i.e. heritage through living tradition. It was not Pompeji but Amsterdam 1996 with its inhabitants still around today.

Once access is gained, from 2015 through unfreezing the FREEZE and now by its dynamic reconstruction, research is not solely focused on software. The floor is open for an analysis of the content. Approach and tools are quite different from the above. Whether historical, sociological, anthropological or phrased by media studies, the further research questions involve a completely different set of tools. Technologies of searching through data of filtering and of visualisation are available in the computer sciences and the data sciences. Some of the more sophisticated tools are being developed in a branch of data science going under the name of forensics.

In every part of the research on DDS, even in the most technical niches of the reconstruction process, the "archaeological" research is mingled with dialogue. Oral history helps. More than that, the intermingling reminds the researcher that in fact the historical approach is the umbrella underneath which it all makes sense: the dusting and scooping and fitting fragments together. Our archaeology of the web has all the benefits and the pitfalls of contemporary history. The takeaway message is that in spite of what the reconstructed operationality of the software may suggest to some, the historical distance remains. It is in the very process of reconstruction that the archaeologist is reminded of the ineradicable historical distance.

Personal data

Manipulating such "young data" on people acting as inhabitants of DDS two decades ago, and existing as fellow citizens today, may well produce a moment of shivers. The archaeologist finds herself swimming in a pond of personal information. Applied to the study of "young data" the metaphor of archaeology is brutally misleading. The work is social science or contemporary history and carries with it the social responsibilities tied to such sciences. Accessing young data poses major privacy issues.

In 1994 a major shift occurred that allowed people to share intimate experiences with the click of a button. Privacy was a difficult question and people did not, nor could they, predict the long-term implications of posting their information. Google, Facebook, Amazon and many other tech companies use these data to their advantage. Where users used to be proud "citizens" or "stakeholders in the commons", today they are seen as natural resources for those companies having evolved into platforms. The meaning of "data" has shifted dramatically in the past 20 years, from information bearing, to monetary gain. The notion of privacy has changed even more.

Purpose limitation

As a researcher in web archaeology, one will quickly find oneself dealing with legal and ethical concerns regarding the privacy of historical subjects. The web was first and foremost a communication medium and as such is filled with personal information of its users. Personal information is not just the information directly linked to one individual person. Any piece of information, that could possibly be linked to an individual, counts as personal information. Linking data to a username would link all these data to an individual, once that username has been linked to a person. By consequence, most of the web is subject to privacy laws, as most of the content is about, or created by, individuals – regardless of whether they can be directly identified through this content.

The ensuing legal considerations may vary greatly depending on national or state laws. And since the Internet hardly stops at national borders, legal considerations are complicated even further. Inside of the Netherlands, when handling personal data, the concept of "purpose limitation" (Dutch: doelbinding) is a core concept of the privacy legislation. Its purport is that personal data should only be used for the purpose for which they were acquired (Ketelaar, 2000). Medical data are to be used for health care only and not by insurance companies; income data gathered for taxes should not be shared beyond tax administration, etc. An exception to this rule is made if the purpose is historical research. However, leaning on this exception will only turn the legal consideration into an ethical one, which it already was.

By publishing web archaeological finds, the researcher will encroach on the privacy of the group being studied. And due to the freshness of the sources in the FREEZE, chances are that the group being studied is still alive and might object to the personal data being spread. Therefore, researchers must weigh the potential harm their research might cause, against the potential gain for society of including the personal data under consideration. The more so while, as researchers, we are inherently biased towards publishing. Therefore, other researchers must be consulted, and in an ideal world ethical committees should be installed overseeing projects of web-archaeology (Markham & Buchanan, 2012). In the DDS case, our provisional measure has been that any access to the retrieved data for the purpose of research is given under an agreement of confidentiality between the researcher and the Amsterdam Museum, procuring the source material.

Security

If for historical research, privacy issues may be addressed in similar ways as other research, with an extra caveat, because of the rapid changes in Internet practices, the discourse takes a different turn in museum context. Suppose the purpose were to create a public exhibit out of legacy web sources, not only should the above reticence towards the publication of personal information be taken into account, but technical matters need to be considered as well.

Systems built in the 1990s were not created with today's practices of collecting data in mind. Technologies of protection have evolved accordingly. The legacy systems, even if one wanted dearly, could not possibly be made secure and safe to the standards of the twenty-first century. This thought has considerably strengthened the inspiration to build a replica next to the emulation, which in terms of safety and security must be judged hopeless.

Treating digital heritage dynamically

The established practice of archiving the legacy of the web is to store "snapshots", that is take a momentary image of a website and download it. This can be done automatically by so-called crawlers and yields enormous haystacks of information on the history of the Internet. Not only the *Internet Archive* and the *Wayback Machine* operate like this, national libraries and archives have adopted and standardized this approach (Mason 2007). The *Internet Archive* will replay the pages thus harvested. In doing so, they are reducing websites to mere pages. But the Internet is not a book, its sites are generated dynamically, be it at a pace of once per day or ten thousand times per second. Upon return the visitor will find a new thing. Michel Serres (2015) reminds us what a parochial way of organising our knowledge it is to put it page by page, now that we could liberate ourselves from that format thanks to the very Internet. As early as 2003 Helen Tibbo (2003, p. 16) observed the dynamic nature of the web:

> A related problem is the Web's dynamic nature. Web archiving initiatives can only preserve "snapshots" of sites or domains at the expense of their dynamism, rather like insects trapped in amber. Once snapshots of Web content are located outside the active Web, it is arguably missing one of its most characteristic properties.

The appeal was picked up by Michael Day in (2006, p. 193). We urge to take consequence of the dynamic nature and call for an adequate, dynamic approach. Far from incidental, the complexity and dynamism of the web reflect its digital nature. And the way we conceive of this heritage should change accordingly. The web should be seen not just as text and image. It is working text: code or software. Preserving the web, thus conceived, may well burst the frame of archiving. In that sense web archaeology is a truly new field, an extension of archiving proper.

The dynamic character of a website's content expresses the underlying code. Whether simple CGI scripts, markups or complicated software, executable files lend the web its dynamic character. This code is the "working text." Without it the documents as the user sees them are different, static. The dynamic approach to web heritage implies to take the text on the surface inclusive of the underlying code, its context. To be able to contain the context of a web page one cannot assume static snapshots as a solution. To properly preserve web content for future research, it must be stored with its dynamic elements in mind.

Notes

1. In Dutch "gedeponeerd in een archief ter bestudering voor archeologen in een verre toekomst", in "De digitale stad bestaat (bijna) twee jaar". Post on the DDS, 1996. https://hart.amsterdam/nl/page/37138/gevondenfreeze http://web.archive.org/web/20100830120819/ http://www.almedia.nl/DDS/Nieuws/freeze.html
2. Unpublished reports of student work.

Acknowledgments

"History of Digital Cultures" is a regular graduate course by Gerard Alberts in the joint MSc Computer Sciences programme of University of Amsterdam and Free University Amsterdam. "DDS 3.0 operational" was a special course in 2016 taken by Marc Went, Robert Jansma, Ronald Bethlehem, Tim

Veenman, Kishan Nirghin, Millen Mortier and Thomas Koch. Reports on this work are available on [Re:DDS 1.0]. The authors further extend their gratitude to Tjarda de Haan and the team at Amsterdam Museum for support throughout the project and hosting the presentation, to Waag Society for facilitating our meetings, to Jesse de Vos and Dennis Beckers for guest lectures, to Theun van den Doel for tireless moral support, and most of all to former system administrators Michael van Eeden and Paul Vogel for immediate help and for sharing their implicit knowledge of the systems. We gratefully acknowledge the Digital Preservation Coalition for distinguishing *The Digital City Revives*, of which our *DDS 3.0 operational* is a part, with the 2016 National Archives Award for Safeguarding the Digital Heritage.

Disclosure statement

No potential conflict of interest was reported by the authors.

ORCID

Marc Went (iD) http://orcid.org/0000-0002-1133-5805
Robert Jansma (iD) http://orcid.org/0000-0003-1121-4189

References

Aspray, W., & Ceruzzi, P.E. (Eds.). (2008). *The internet and American business*. Cambridge, MA: MIT Press.

Beckers, D., & Besselaar, P. (1998). Sociale interactie in een virtuele omgeving: De Digitale Stad [Social interaction in a virtual environment: The Digital City]. In *Informatie & informatiebeleid 16-4*.

Besselaar, P., & Beckers, D. (1998). Demographics and sociographics of the digital city. In T. Ishida (Ed.), *Community computing and support systems — Lecture notes in computer science* (Vol. 1519, pp. 108–125). Berlin: Springer Verlag.

Castells, M. (1996). *The information age: Economy, society and culture (Vols. 3)*. Cambridge, MA: Blackwell.

Castells, M. (2001). *The internet galaxy: Reflections on the internet, business, and society*. Oxford: Oxford University Press.

Day, M. (2006). *The long-term preservation of web content*. In J. Masanès (Ed.), *Web archiving* (pp. 177–199). Berlin: Springer Verlag.

Ernst, W. (2013). *Digital memory and the archive*. Minneapolis: University of Minnesota Press.

Foucault, M. (1969). *L'archéologie du savoir* [The archaeology of knowledge]. Paris: Gallimard.

Jones, C. (2004, June). *Seeing double: Emulation in theory and practice. TheEerl King case study*. Paper presented at the electronic media group. Annual Meeting of the American Institute for Conservation of Historic and Artistic Works. Portland, OR.

Ketelaar, F.C.J. (2000). Elke handeling telt. archiefdiensten en de wet bescherming persoonsgegevens [Every act counts. Archival agencies and the law on the protection of personal data]. *Nederlands Archievenblad, 104*, 18–23.

Lovink, G. (2002). *Dark fiber: Tracking critical internet culture*. Cambridge, MA: MIT Press.

Markham, A., & Buchanan, E. (2012). *Ethical decision-making and internet research. Recommendations from the AoIR ethics working committee (version 2.0)*. AoIR. Retrieved from https://aoir.org/reports/ethics2.pdf

Masanès, J. (Ed.). (2006). *Web archiving*. Berlin: Springer Verlag.

Mason, I. (2007). Virtual preservation: How has digital culture influenced our ideas about permanence? Changing practice in a national legal deposit library. In M.V. Cloonan & R. Harvey (Eds.), *Preserving cultural heritage, Library trends, 56-1* (summer 2007) (pp. 198–215) [Special issue].

Presner, T., Shepard, D., & Kawano, Y. (2014). *HyperCities. Thick mapping in the digital humanities*. Cambridge, MA: Harvard University Press.

Rheingold. H. (1993). *Virtual community, homesteading on the electric frontier*. Reading, MA: Edison Wesley.

Rustema, R. (2001). *The Rise and fall of DDS: Evaluating the ambitions of Amsterdam's digital city* (Unpublished master's thesis). University of Amsterdam, Amsterdam. Retrieved from http://reinder.rustema.nl/dds/rise_and_fall_dds.pdf

Serres, M. (2015). *Thumbelina: The culture and technology of millennials*. London: Rowman & Littlefield International.

Smith, J., & Nair, R. (2005). *Virtual machines: Versatile platforms for systems and processes*. San Francisco, CA: Elsevier.

Tibbo, H.R. (2003). On the nature and importance of archiving in the digital age. *Advances in Computers, 57*, 1–67.

Van Dijck, J., Poell, T., & Waal, M. (2016). *De platformsamenleving. strijd om publieke waarden in een online wereld* [The platform society. The struggle on public values in an online world]. Amsterdam: Amsterdam University Press.

Doing Web history with the Internet Archive: screencast documentaries

Richard Rogers

ABSTRACT

Among the conceptual and methodological opportunities afforded by the Internet Archive, and more specifically, the WayBack Machine, is the capacity to capture and "play back" the history a web page, most notably a website's homepage. These playbacks could be construed as "website histories", distinctive at least in principle from other uses put to the Internet Archive such as "digital history" and "Internet history". In the following, common use cases for web archives are put forward in a discussion of digital source criticism. Thereafter, I situate website history within traditions in web historiography. The particular approach to website history introduced here is called "screencast documentaries". Building upon Jon Udell's pioneering screencapturing work retelling the edit history of a Wikipedia page, I discuss overarching strategies for narrating screencast documentaries of websites, namely histories of the Web as seen through the changes to a single page, media histories as negotiations between new and old media as well as digital histories made from scrutinising changes to the list of priorities at a tone-setting institution such as whitehouse.gov.

Introduction: digital history, Web history and website history

The Internet Archive and the Web archives of national libraries are thought as sources for "digital history", which refers to history-writing with Web-based materials (Brügger, 2012; Cohen & Rosenzweig, 2006; Internet Archive, 2017; Rosenzweig, 2003). The creation and maintenance of Web archives often are justified for digital history purposes, considering the wealth of online materials not only compared to other media but also because they encompass them. The argument for the specificity of Web archives thus lies in the growth of "born-digital" materials, in contrast to digitised ones of media archives. It also rests especially upon their use by future historians, when they come to write the history of particular periods, such as the 1990s. The value of the archived Web is thus often thought to lie in its special contents that are otherwise unavailable elsewhere and in its future use by historians, as Milligan notes:

> Imagine a history of the late 1990s or early 2000s that draws primarily on print newspapers, ignoring the [Internet] technology that fundamentally affected how people share, interact, and leave historical traces behind (2016).

Internet (and Web) history, on the other hand, may be distinguished from digital history, as it concerns employing the Web to tell its own story, in the tradition of medium or media history. Whilst there are exceptions, Web archives are not as often justified as sources for specific Internet and Web histories (Ben-David, 2016; Goggin & McLelland, 2017; Stevenson, 2016). Moreover, Internet histories may be written largely without them (Abbatte, 2000; Ryan, 2011). Indeed, be it for digital, Internet or Web history, actual historian use of Web archives remains limited (Brock, 2005; Dougherty et al., 2010; Hockx-Yu, 2014; Weltevrede & Helmond, 2012).

How to reconsider the value of Web archives to Web history? The point of departure here is to reintroduce a more specific type of Web history – website history – and put forward an approach to its study and at the same time a productive use of Web archives (Brügger, 2008). That is, the screencast documentary is both an approach to studying website histories and also a means to provide researcher use for Web archives, which itself is understudied (Dougherty et al., 2010). It takes advantage of the organisation of the Internet Archive, and especially the interface and query machine built on top of it to access its contents.

Whilst it recently has added a keyword search, for over a decade now, the WayBack Machine has had as its primary (and default) input field a single URL. Using digital methods, or tool-based methods to extract and analyse Web data and objects for social and cultural research, the screencast documentary approach put forward here captures the outputs of the WayBack Machine (list of archived pages with dates), screenshots the unique ones, and arrays them in chronological order so as to play back the history of the website in the style of time-lapse photography (Rogers, 2013).

In the following, narrations or particular goals for telling the history of a website are put forward. They offer means to study the history of the Web (as seen through a single website like Google Web Search), the history of the Web as media (such as how a newspaper has grappled with the new medium) as well as the history of a particular institution (such as the US White House or marriage, as seen through a leading wedding website). Arguably, the first is a form of Web and medium history, the second media history, and the third digital history, however much each also blends the approaches and blurs the distinctions.

It should be pointed out that the WayBack Machine of the Internet Archive is itself a Web-historical object. In a sense, it also tells the story of the Web, or at least a particular period of it, through the manner in which it primarily grants access to websites. By the default means by which it is queried and also how archived web pages are interlinked, the WayBack Machine of the Internet Archive has organised a surfer's Web circa 1990s rather than a searcher's Web of the 2000s or a scroller's of the 2010s (with a smartphone).

Here, it is argued that the WayBack Machine also lends itself to a particular historiography that is embedded in the screencast documentary approach, namely a single-site or site-biographical method of recounting history. Having developed that argument in brief, the piece concludes with how to put to use the WayBack Machine of the Internet Archive to tell single-site histories as screencast documentaries.

The WayBack Machine: surf the Web as it was, or use the Internet Archive as source

The WayBack Machine of the Internet Archive, with its original slogan "surf the Web as it was", was conceived and presented in part as a solution to the 404 problem, the response

Figure 1. Alexa toolbar, with WayBack icon to access the Internet Archive, circa 2004. Author screenshot.

code signifying that the file or web page is not found. With the Alexa toolbar installed in a browser (in the 1990s, see Figure 1), the Web browser user confronted by a 404 error message would receive a flashing WayBack icon on the toolbar that indicates that the missing page is in the Internet Archive. (If the button did not flash, there was no archived version, and the page had been lost.) In return for Alexa's solution to the 404 problem as well as the content at the Internet Archive, the user would aid in populating the archive. That is, when downloading the toolbar, permission would be given to have his/her browsing activity logged, and web pages or sites that a user visited would be sent to Alexa. If a site was not yet in the archive, a crawler would visit it, and thus grew the Internet Archive. Later, high-traffic and other significant sites would be earmarked for regular archiving.

The WayBack Machine's architecture, designed and launched in the mid-1990s, aimed to furnish an ideal surfer's experience, frictionless and without dead ends. Once onto a website in the archive, clicking links takes the surfer to the page closest in time, and if unavailable to the page on the live Web. The surfer jumps through time as if in an atemporal hyperspace, one of the earliest Web metaphors or structuring devices for a document universe without directories or search engines. The WayBack Machine thus sacrifices temporal matching for smooth navigation, and as such embeds a period in Web history, in an experience that could be described as more living museum of a surfer's space than historian's meticulous archive.

Apart from the "way it was" experience, the WayBack Machine is also suggestive of particular research practices and ultimately historiographical approaches. With respect to the research practices, there are largely two afforded by the interface. At archive.org, the http:// prompt invites the inputting of a single page URL so as to summon its history. At the outset, in other words, one is invited to submit a URL and pursue its history through two outputs, one of which shows minute changes to the contents of the pages in the archive (additions and deletions), and another that invites the exploration of a fuller arc, where one can click backward and forward arrows through larger chunks of the page's history.

In the original results page, asterisks next to date stamps indicate changed content on the web page. One may thus peruse a web page's history to spot the crucial, detailed change (or "diff" in computational language). As a research output, one perhaps would wish to put two or more pages side-to-side, highlighting the specific, telling diff, such as an infringement of one's intellectual property, which is a common use case of the WayBack Machine in the legal arena, discussed in more detail below.

> [I]n Telewizja Polska USA, Inc. v. Echostar Satellite Corp., the plaintiff alleged that the defendant was using the plaintiffs trademark name in violation of its intellectual property rights. In response, the defendant introduced the printout of the defendant's archived webpage dated before the plaintiff received the trademark of its brand (Gazaryan, 2013, p. 221).

The form of output navigation for exploring the fuller arc of history is the timeline (see Figure 2). Instead of pouring over the detailed changes, with the timeline, one makes

Figure 2. WayBack Machine banner that accompanies archived web page loaded in a browser. Example is Myspace.com, indicating the date it changed from a social networking to a music-oriented social entertainment site. Source: http://web.archive.org/web/20101116021305/http://www.myspace.com/ (accessed 28 December 2016).

a sweep through the interface and content of a web page over the years with an eye towards the broader themes, such as the introduction and subsequent locking down or removal of comment spaces and other interactive features on websites that once made new media new.

The interface to the Internet Archive thus creates at once a surfer's experience from a particular period in Web history whilst also affording modes of historical work that privilege focusing on the minute as well as the sweeping change to a single page.

Digital source criticism

Seen from the perspective of digital history (history-writing with Web materials), the Way-Back Machine also could be said to invite the user to seek a specific source, and scrutinise it for its veracity because it is a Web source. Here, with the WayBack Machine, one brings the Web, and its pages, into the evidentiary arena of source criticism. There are at least three sets of questions, or aspirations for the "digitally reborn" sources online now that they appear as web.archive.org URLs rather than in their original name space state (Brügger, 2012). Once captured and put back online, the archived web pages face tests, from a series of scholarly discourses, before they may employed as proper sources. In law do they count as duplicated sources, in the social sciences as valid and in history as sufficient substitutes for missing materials? From the start, one of the more popular use cases for the Internet Archive, apart from the 404-not-found error whilst surfing, has been as evidence (Howell, 2006). One could go back in time to a website for evidentiary purposes, checking for trademark and intellectual property infringements, as was the case with its first-time deployment in US courts in 2003 when print-outs from the WayBack Machine were introduced as exhibits (Eltgroth, 2009). Here, the questions concern the extent to which one can treat the archived page as a duplicate of the original one no longer online, or in a lesser test, at least warrant through testimony that it represents accurately the material the site owner put online. In the event, the archived website need not be a duplicate in code and data to be admissible; rather it only need to be an accurate representation.[1]

Apart from its authenticity in legal arenas, a web page faces scrutiny as a source for scholarly referencing purposes, in order to anchor an account of events, for example. In the very first place, the challenge put to the Web as source may rest upon its overall (historical) reputation problem, as a medium of pirates, pornographers, conspiracy theorists and self-publishers (Dean, 1998). As the fake news scandals surrounding the US presidential campaigns of 2016 pointed to anew, it is a space with and without professional editors, and has been subject to the question of its quality, even as the Web further domesticated, in its nearly thirty years of use (Thelwall, Vaughan, & Björneborn, 2005).

More to the point is the question of whether URLs should be referenced in the first place as sources, and if offline, whether a WayBack URL could stand in. Apart from the reputation problem, it is often argued that the Web's ephemerality, or perhaps its uneven maintenance, disproves its worthiness as source. Referenced URLs break, as links rot (Klein et al., 2014; Veronin, 2002). In this context, the WayBack Machine may be viewed as a set of well-tethered (rather than broken) source links. The Internet Archive thus becomes an early attempt at providing permanence to ephemeral Web sources, in a lineage of such attempts from the tradition of hypertext (permalinks in blogs and edit history retention in wikis) to that of library science (DOI numbers). Once accepted as not only references but reference-able, Web sources that break and are reborn in the Internet Archive face further tests. Are the archived ones "valid"? Such a determination relies, among other things, on whether the date stamps of archived web pages, including new archived versions, match the dates of the web pages when online, an issue studied by a series of authors (Dougherty & Meyer, 2014; Dougherty et al., 2010; Murphy, Hashim, & O'Connor, 2007). In the event, the Internet Archive has met validation challenges concerning web page (and thus content) age.

For referencing, a WayBack URL rather supplements than replaces an original URL. In a recent edition to the MLA style guide, even (original) broken URLs should be referenced, with access date, for the reader may be able to "evaluate the credibility of the site that published the source, or locate the source under a new URL" (Gibson, 2016, n.p.). In all, the MLA recommends adding the WayBack URL to the reference after the broken URL, rather than pruning the citation through the use of the archived URL only (Internet Archive, 2016).

For historians, a further test concerns whether a reborn website in the archive was ever online as such in the first place (Brügger, 2012). Websites reconstituted by the archiving appear to be damning critiques of their value as historical sources (Russell & Kane, 2008). Especially newspapers, as proverbial first drafts of history, are susceptible to hodge-podge archival reconstructions, where certain plugged-in content is saved at another time than the front page of the newspaper, and when one recombines it in the archive, the "digitally reborn source" becomes a novel artefact of its archiving process. Even given the missing original, the question steps beyond whether the incomplete, archived source is acceptable, in the spirit of save what one can. When writing digital history, or using the Web as historical source, being a scholar of the history of the Web (and dynamic websites), together with the history of its archiving (and the treatment of dynamic websites), becomes crucial.

Web historiographies in brief

As discussed above, the architecture of the WayBack Machine of the Internet Archive invites website or web page histories, given that one fetches the history of a URL through the interface, and peruses it looking for minor changes with the aid of the asterisks in the classic interface, or with a broad sweep, forward clicking month by month, examining the larger thematic changes to the life and times of the site.

Before introducing examples of website histories, in the style of Jon Udell's pioneering screencast documentary of the edit history of a Wikipedia page, it is instructive to mention that the biographical (in which a website history would fall) is among at least four dominant traditions of Web archive collection and usage. The second tradition is of a spe-cial collection, where typically elections, disasters and changes of power or transitions are archived, such as US elections and the installation of a new pope (Schneider & Foot, 2004). Here, the approach to Web historiography is event-based. In the archiving, there is also an attention cycle to consider, both the run-up to an election and transition as well as its aftermath. Archiving agility (especially for a disaster) is called for.

A third type of Web historiographical approach is embodied in the efforts by national libraries to demarcate and save "national" Webs, beginning with the preservation of the official public record and continuing often with a carefully considered definition of a website of relevance to national heritage (Jacobsen, 2008; Rogers, Weltevrede, Borra, & Niederer, 2013). For example, the Danish, pioneers in Web archiving, define a relevant national website as having at least one of four properties: in the top-level country .dk domain, written in Danish, about a Danish subject matter (e.g. the author Hans Christian Andersen) or material of relevance to the Danish or Denmark, the last type of which expands the material to such an extent that it becomes a matter of editorial selection, bringing the librarians back into Web content curation (after the demise of the online directories).

The fourth one, an autobiographical, is the most recent, and concerns Web properties that are essentially no longer considered websites, at least as we have known them to be as accessible without a password and residing for the most part on an open Web. Whether they are social media platforms or smartphone apps, they are difficult to collect and pre-serve, and improbable to make accessible at any scale, owing to the fact that they are per-sonal, behind user logins, or have other novel social and technical constraints. Here, the approaches to storing differ in that just the data are captured (e.g. by individuals-requested data dumps from Facebook) or by videorecording a user interacting with her mobile phone. The collection becomes the video together eventually with the smart-phone itself. More recently, at Rhizome, the digital arts collective, the "webenact" tech-nique, put online as webrecorder.io, has been developed to capture or record a social media user's pages so as to re-enact them or play them back. The work was developed on the heels of the critically acclaimed performance piece of the user of Instagram, Amalia Ulman (Rhizome, 2014).[2]

Website histories and the screencast documentary

From the standpoint of Web historiography, a website history or single-site biography may be understood as the unfolding of the history of the website, and with it a variety of stories may be told. First, the history of a website could be seen to encapsulate the larger story of the history of the Web. In one example discussed in detail below, the history of the changes to the front page of Google.com (in particular, the tabs) may be read as the history of the demise of the human editors of the Web, and the rise of the back-end, of the algorithm, taking over from the librarians. From the history of a website, second, one also may tell the story of the history of media, such as how a newspaper, a radio station, or a television channel grappled with the Web, over time (Bødker & Brügger, 2017). Has the old media form, so-called, embraced new media features, only to settle back into a digitised version of its original self? How have newspapers domesticated the blog, or tamped down the comment space where readers can talk back to the institution referred to historically as gatekeepers?

In a screencast documentary of the history of nytimes.com, the newspaper has experimented repeatedly with new media forms, beginning as a separate entity from the print version, without any reference to the print version or to subscriptions (Hermens, 2011). It was directed at a Web-only audience with such features as "cybertimes" and forums. Often these special new media forms would be jettisoned, though some have remained such as a curated comment space as well as novel newspaper navigation through "most emailed", "most viewed" and "recommended for you".

The third strategy is telling the history of an idea, individual, organisation, institution or other entity to which a website has been dedicated. Examining the evolution of the contents of the "issues" tab at whitehouse.gov shows at a glance how the priorities of the US presidential administration have changed, sometimes abruptly; after the 9/11 attacks on the World Trade Center and the Pentagon in 2001, most all issues on whitehouse.gov included the word "security", only gradually to broaden their scope in the years to come (Rogers, 2013). In another case, examining the history of theknot.com over a ten-year period, researchers found how a simple advice and registry site became a complex wedding planner, multiplying expenses and product placements, concluding that nowadays for weddings "no expense should be spared" (Livio, Mataly, & Schuh, 2012). Thus, one view on the evolution of the institution of marriage, and its commercialisation, may be reconstructed through a single-site history.

Techniques for making screencast documentaries of the history of a web page

There are practical aspects to creating a screencast documentary of the history of a web page. At the Digital Methods Initiative at the University of Amsterdam, colleagues and I have created tools and techniques to compile the archived versions of a web page, so as to assemble them chronologically as a movie. There are four steps: make a list of the archived pages, capture or download them, load them in a moviemaker and record a voiceover. In the first step, to make a list of the archived pages, use the tool, the Internet Archive WayBack Machine Link Ripper.[3] One enters the URL to be captured from the WayBack Machine (e.g. http://www.google.com), and the tool creates a list of links of its archived pages, removing duplicates by default, and providing options concerning the capture interval (e.g. daily or monthly). To study minute changes to the web page over time, one chooses daily snapshots, and for a fuller arc of history, monthly. In the second step, the WayBack Machine URL list (a text file) is subsequently inputted into a screenshot generator (such as the browser extension, Grab Them All).[4] Screenshots are made of each archived web page. The pages need to load in the browser for the screenshot to be made, so it is advisable to fine-tune the amount of time between screenshots so as to make sure the pages have loaded before the screenshots are taken. The third step is to load the screenshots into an image viewer such as iPhoto, and make a project in movie-making software such as iMovie (or Windows Movie Maker). Finally, the voiceover is recorded, and the movie is ready for playback.

For the voiceover, consideration should be made of the narrative strategy. In the "Heavy Metal Umlaut", Jon Udell establishes the literary and social value of the screencast documentary, previously known for software instructions of use (2005). In the screencast,

Udell deploys a simple narrative strategy that could be employed as a starting point. He opens with an overview of his subject matter, the revision history of the Wikipedia article on the heavy metal umlaut. Through a "quick flight" of the changelog (speeding up the chronological loading of the pages), he shows the growth and occasional vandalism of the article, speaking with awe about Wikipedians' vigilance (see Figure 3). Subsequently, he introduces four themes, and treats them one by one. The spinal tap theme concerns the typographical as well as factual question of the n-umlaut (or heavy metal umlaut). In the vandalism piece, he is impressed by the dedication shown by the Wikipedians, cleaning the graffiti and reverting other offensive edits only minutes after they have been made. He spends time talking about the organisation of the article, and how the table of contents matures over time. (The focus on the changes to the table of contents led colleagues and I to build a tool, the Wiki TOC scraper, that captures a Wikipedia article's table of contents, and, with the use of the slider, shows its changes over time.) Finally, Udell mentions issues of cultural sensitivity, and in particular how the look of the font and the n-umlaut is no longer associated with Nazism (as it was initially), but rather is described as Germanic. Without summarising the four themes, Udell concludes the screencast documentary by returning to the first edit and jumping to the last, making mention of the achievement of a "loose federation of volunteers", in this new type of content creation,

Figure 3. Screenshot from Jon Udell's "Heavy Metal Umlaut", screencast documentary (2005), discussion of graffiti.

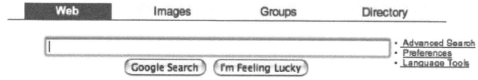

Figure 4. Google's Directory on Google's front page in 2000 (top), and receiving tab status in October of 2001 (bottom). Excerpt from Digital Methods Initiative and Kim de Groot, "The Demise of the Directory: Web librarian work removed in Google", Information Graphic, 2008, http://www.govcom.org/publications/drafts/GCO_directoryfall.pdf.

otherwise known as the wisdom of the crowd. In the edit revision history of a single Wikipedia article, it's as if Web history was made. The screencast thus captures the birth of user-generated content.

"Google and the Politics of Tabs" is the first single-site history made that follows in Udell's footsteps. It is the history of Google seen through its interface from 1998 until late 2007, and through it tells a larger story about the history of the Web (see Figure 4) (Rogers & Govcom.org, 2007). It makes use of all the available, updated Google front-pages in the Internet Archive, captured and played back, in the style of time-lapse photography. Google and the Politics of Tabs chronicles the subtle changes to the Google front-page real estate, showing the services that have risen to the interface, achieving tab status, and the others that have been relegated to the "more" and "even more" buttons. As its main theme, it tells the story of the demise of the directory (particularly, dmoz.org's), and how the back-end algorithm has taken over the organisation of Web information at the expense of the human editors and the librarians.

Conclusions: the value of capturing website histories

Website histories tell stories of the Web, media and cultural or political history. In terms of the stories to be told in the voiceover narrative of a web page history, one could be of loss; something of value has been taken, or replaced. In Google and the Politics of Tabs, which details a decade's worth of subtle changes to the Google.com's interface, ultimately, the algorithm has taken over from the librarian on the Web. Another is about transformation, or even continuity. Despite massive change around it, the object or subject has remained remarkably the same (or nearly so). Despite transformation, it has returned to its original form. As discussed above, the enthusiastic embrace of new media or its stubborn resistance is made the subject of the screencast by scrutinising how a newspaper, radio station, or television channel website has evolved. Has the old media form, so-called, radically embraced cyberspace and new media features, only to settle back (largely) into a digitised form of its original self, as in the case of nytimes.com? How have newspapers domesticated the blog, or tamed the comment space where readers once could talk back to the institution referred to historically as gatekeepers? Here, the story concerns incorporating new media into established practices. In each case, one is considering the overall narrative of change, concentrating on a limited number of story-lines, and leaving out the rest. The third strategy is to allow the history of an idea, individual, organisation, institution or other entity to unfold in the changes to a website. The wedding as institution could be simple, or it can be industrialised, as a website, theknot. com, and the Web is further monetised with the rise of e-commerce. One can thus build in the recipe of a great novel. Capture the life and times through the changes occurring to an institution – on its leading website.

On 20 January 2017, with the incoming Presidential administration, whitehouse.gov changed dramatically. A story in the *New York Times* opened: "Within moments of the inauguration of President Trump, the official White House website on Friday deleted nearly all mentions of climate change [...] part of the full digital turnover of whitehouse.gov, including taking down and archiving all the Obama administration's personal and policy pages" (Davanport, 2017). Capturing "transitions" such as the Papal in 2005 by the Library of Congress is an event-based Web historiography, pioneered in the websphere technique that curates a collection of thematically related and interlinked sites over a period of some months. One also may capture such transitions through website histories, where changed front-pages are made into screenshots (or otherwise captured) and played back as a screencast documentary or even as an animated gif. Here, the display of content removal tells the story of changes in political (and policy) priorities. One may also focus on additional sections or pages on the website, such as the changes under the "issues" tab, where after 20 January 2017, whitehouse.gov had such issues as "America First Energy Plan" and "America First Foreign Policy", which are distinctive in (sloganeering) style and substance to those on 19 January 2017 prior to the administration turnover (see Table 1).

Table 1. Top issues at whitehouse.gov. Source: WayBack Machine of the Internet Archive (archive.org).

19 January 2017
Civil rights
Climate change
Economy
Education
Foreign policy
Health care
Iran deal
Immigration action

20 January 2017
America first energy plan
America first foreign policy
Bringing back jobs and growth
Making our military strong again
Standing up for our law enforcement community
Trade deals that work for all Americans

The Internet Archive (and Web archives generally) are commonly thought of as sources for "digital history", however much actual historian use of Web archives appears to be limited (and is understudied). With such use, digital source criticism becomes a focal point with concerns about how in the archiving a "digitally reborn" source may be reconstituted in a form that never existed in the first place. Here is a particular case where digital history may draw from Web history, and its study of different forms of ephemerality (Chun, 2013). Indeed, Web archives have not necessarily been justified for the purposes of telling Internet and Web history, however much active use may be made of them by researchers in that field. Above, I reintroduced the notion of "website history" and put forward a particular approach to it (screencast documentary) that allows one to pursue a variety of histories: Web, media as well as digital history.

The screencast documentary approach derives from digital methods, or the use of tool-based methods for Web data extraction and analysis. The research affordances of the WayBack Machine are the point of departure, for it provides a list of stored pages (and an indication of which ones have new content, also known as the "diffs") that can be captured, and played back in the style of time-lapse photography. The website history, it is argued, could be seen in the Web historiological tradition of website biography, which is distinctive from event, national or autobiographical styles of collection and curation. Once captured, the website history may be narrated; in the examples given, the stories revolved around loss, continuity and transformation. They concern how the history of a single website may encapsulate the history of the Web, how so-called old media perpetuates itself in the new media, and how the transformation of an institution may be captured.

Notes

1. Until the burden was lessened in the late 1960s, when photographs were introduced to the courts of law, the fact finder was often asked to produce the negative together with the photograph so it could be authenticated and there was assurance it had not been doctored (Eltgroth, 2009).
2. See also docnow.io, which is a tool and a community developed around supporting the ethical collection, use, and preservation of social media content.
3. https://tools.digitalmethods.net/beta/internetArchiveWaybackMachineLinkRipper/.
4. There is also an option to download the html of the archived pages.

Acknowledgements

The author would like to acknowledge the work of Erik Borra, Anne Helmond, Michael Stevenson and Esther Weltevrede on the Digital Methods unit dedicated to 'The Website as Archived Object,' from which this article draws.

Disclosure statement

No potential conflict of interest was reported by the author.

Funding

This work was supported by the European Union's Horizon 2020 research and innovation programme [grant number 732942].

References

Abbate, J. (2000). *Inventing the internet*. Cambridge, MA: MIT Press.

Ben-David, A. (2016). What does the Web Remember of its Deleted Past? An archival reconstruction of the former Yugoslav top level domain. *New Media & Society, 18*(7), 1103–1119.

Bødker, H., & Brügger, N. (2017). The shifting temporalities of online news: The Guardian's website from 1996 to 2015. *Journalism*. doi:10.1177/1464884916916891.

Brock, A. (2005). 'A belief in humanity is a belief in colored men': Using culture to span the digital divide. *Journal of Computer-Mediated Communication, 11*(1), article 17.

Brügger, N. (2008). The archived website and website philology: A new type of historical document? *Nordicom Review, 29*(2), 151–171.

Brügger, N. (2012). When the present web is later the past: Web historiography, digital history and internet studies. *Historical Social Research, 37*(4), 102–117.

Chun, W. (2013). *Programmed visions: Software and memory*. Cambridge, MA: MIT Press.

Cohen, D. J., & Rosenzweig, R. (2006). *Digital history: A guide to gathering, preserving, and presenting the past on the web*. Philadelphia: University of Pennsylvania Press.

Davenport, C. (2017, January 20). With Trump in charge, climate change references purged from website. *New York Times*.

Dean, J. (1998). *Aliens in America: Conspiracy cultures from outerspace to cyberspace*. Ithaca, NY: Cornell University Press.

Dougherty, M., & Meyer, E. T. (2014). Community, tools, and practices in web archiving: The state-of-the-art in relation to social science and humanities research needs. *Journal of the Association for Information Science and Technology, 65*(11), 2195–2209.

Dougherty, M., Meyer, E. T., Madsen, C., van den Heuvel, C., Thomas, A., & Wyatt, S. (2010). *Researcher engagement with web archives: State of the art*. London: JISC.

Eltgroth, D. (2009). Best evidence and the Wayback Machine: Toward a workable authentication standard for archived Internet evidence. *Fordham Law Review, 78*(1), 181.

Gazaryan, K. (2013). Authenticity of archived websites: The need to lower the evidentiary hurdle is imminent. *Rutgers Computer and Technology Law Journal, 39*(2), 216–245.

Gibson, A. (2016, November 2). URLs: Some practical advice, MLA style center. New York, NY: Modern Language Association. Retrieved from https://style.mla.org/2016/11/02/urls-some-practical-advice/

Goggin, G., & McLelland, M. (2017). Introduction: Global Coordinates of Internet histories. In G. Goggin & M. McLelland (Eds.), *The Routledge companion to global internet histories*. New York, NY: Routledge.

Hermens, E. (2011). *The New York Times - a web historiography, screencast documentary*. Amsterdam: University of Amsterdam. Retrieved from https://vimeo.com/32319207

Hockx-Yu, H. (2014). Access and scholarly use of web archives. *Alexandria, 25*(1), 113–127.

Howell, B. A. (2006). Proving web history: How to use the Internet Archive. *Journal of Internet Law, 9*(8), 3–9.

Internet Archive. (2016). FAQ, San Francisco. Internet Archive. Retrieved from https://archive.org/about/faqs.php#265

Internet Archive. (2017). Internet Archive. Retrieved from http://www.archive.org

Jacobsen, G. (2008). Web archiving: Issues and problems in collection building and access. *LIBER Quarterly, 18*(3–4), 366–376.

Klein, M., van de Sompel, H., Sanderson, R., Shankar, H., Balakireva, L., & Zhou, K. (2014). Scholarly context not found: One in five articles suffers from reference rot. *PLoS ONE, 9*(12), e115253.

Livio, M., Mataly, J., & Schuh, M. (2012). *TheKnot.com - a website historiography, screencast documentary*. Amsterdam: University of Amsterdam. Retrieved from https://www.youtube.com/watch?v=5cxVXJthETA

Milligan, I. (2016). Lost in the infinite archive: The promise and pitfalls of web archives. *International Journal of Humanities and Arts Computing, 10*(1), 78–94.

Murphy, J., Hashim, N. H., & O'Connor, P. (2007). Take me back: Validating the WayBack Machine. *Journal of Computer-Mediated Communication, 13*(1).

Rhizome. (2014). *Amalia Ulman: Excellences & perfections*. New York, NY: Rhizome. Retrieved from http://webenact.rhizome.org/excellences-and-perfections

Rogers, R. (2013). *Digital methods*. Cambridge, MA: MIT Press.

Rogers, R. & Govcom.org. (2008). *Google and the politics of tabs, screencast documentary*. Amsterdam: Govcom.org. Retrieved from https://movies.digitalmethods.net/google.html

Rogers, R., Weltevrede, E., Borra, E., & Niederer, S. (2013). National Web studies: The case of Iran online. In J. Hartley, J. Burgess, & A. Bruns (Eds.), *A companion to new media dynamics*. Oxford: Wiley-Blackwell.

Rosenzweig, R. (2003). Scarcity or abundance? Preserving the past in a digital era. *The American Historical Review, 108*(3), 735–762.

Russell, E., & Kane, J. (2008). The missing link: Assessing the reliability of Internet citations in history journals. *Technology and Culture, 49*(2), 420–429.

Ryan, J. (2011). *A history of the internet and the digital future*. London: Reaktion.

Schneider, S., & Foot, K. (2004). The Web as an object of study. *New Media & Society, 6*(1), 114–122.

Stevenson, M. (2016). Rethinking the participatory web: A history of HotWired's 'new publishing paradigm,' 1994–1997. *New Media & Society, 18*(7), 1331–1346.

Thelwall, M., Vaughan, L., & Björneborn, L. (2005). Webometrics. *Annual Review of Information Science and Technology, 39*(1), 81–135.

Udell, J. (2005). Heavy metal Umlaut, screencast documentary. Retrieved from http://jonudell.net/udell/2005-01-22-heavy-metal-umlaut-the-movie.html

Veronin, M. A. (2002). Where are they now? A case study of health-related web site attrition. *Journal of Medical Internet Research, 4*(2), e10.

WayBack Machine. (2017). WayBack Machine of the Internet Archive. Retrieved from http://www.archive.org/web.

Weltevrede, E., & Helmond, A. (2012). Where do bloggers blog? Platform transitions within the historical Dutch blogosphere. *First Monday, 17*(2).

Breaking in to the mainstream: demonstrating the value of internet (and web) histories

Jane Winters ⓘD

ABSTRACT

This short article explores the challenges involved in demonstrating the value of web archives, and the histories that they embody, beyond media and Internet studies. Given the difficulties of working with such complex archival material, how can researchers in the humanities and social sciences more generally be persuaded to integrate Internet histories into their research? How can institutions and organisations be sufficiently convinced of the worth of their own online histories to take steps to preserve them? And how can value be demonstrated to the wider general public? It touches on public attitudes to personal and institutional Internet histories, barriers to access to web archives – technical, legal and methodological - and the cultural factors within academia that have hindered the penetration of new ways of working with new kinds of primary source. Rather than providing answers, this article is intended to provoke discussion and dialogue between the communities for whom Internet histories can and should be of significance.

The realisation of the Internet's potential to connect not just computers but individuals, families, communities and nations – through the growth of the web – has transformed our lives over the last two decades. Our histories are increasingly both created and consumed online, for an audience of millions or for an audience of only one or two people. The ease with which it is possible to write and post information online, the speed with which one can react to news and contribute to ensuing debates, has dramatically altered – in scale and type – the group of people whom we might now describe as creators, publishers or authors. While some voices are, of course, excluded from this discourse,[1] and others still are hidden or devalued, many more have taken advantage of new technologies and social forums publicly to share their lives, thoughts and beliefs.[2]

Consequently, after little more than a quarter of a century, the web already constitutes an unprecedentedly rich primary source, combining information from personal blogs, to formal reportage, to the communications of local and national government. It is where we socialise, learn, campaign and shop. All human life, as it were, is vigorously there. And while the live web is extraordinarily ephemeral, much of this data – an ever more important historical record – persists in web archives (Jackson, 2015).[3]

It might seem obvious that one could not begin to write the history of the late twentieth and early twenty-first centuries without recourse to web archives. Yet, researchers in the humanities, and historians in particular, have proven reluctant to engage with the histories of the web and the Internet, to explore web archives, to learn how to work with a new kind of source.

There are many practical reasons for this historical blind spot, which are more or less difficult to address. The most significant barrier to working with web archives is, quite simply, that it is difficult; it requires skills that many historians do not have, and in the short term may be unwilling to learn; it involves acknowledging a degree of ignorance with which otherwise seasoned researchers may be uncomfortable. The various methodological and theoretical challenges have been well enumerated, even if we are far from having solutions for them all (see, e.g. Brügger, 2013; Brügger & Finnemann, 2013). The multiplicity of national legal frameworks which regulate access to and reuse of web archives are a considerable hurdle to even the most dedicated scholar, but can seem an insurmountable problem to the more casual user. In the UK, for example, legal deposit legislation guarantees a comprehensive crawl of the .uk domain at least once a year, but it also ensures that anyone interested in studying the results of that crawl has to go to a reading room in one of the six UK copyright libraries and work through the archive web page by web page. The Internet Archive's Wayback Machine (http://archive.org/web/) does not have the same restrictions on access, and now supports searching on the text of archived home pages rather than simply by URL, but reuse remains a problem and rich analytical access is still a very distant prospect.[4]

There is no doubt that these are real issues, but there is something else at work too. It is not the case that large numbers of historians are trying to work with web archives, struggling and then giving up. Lack of awareness is a far more important criterion. Researchers in the humanities are used to working with digitised historical sources that they access online, and to reading much of their secondary literature on the web too, but they do not seem ready for the archived web itself as a focus of research, as embodying important histories. There are some indications that this is beginning to change. In February 2016, for example, the Mile End Institute (Queen Mary University of London) partnered with the Foreign Office Historians to organise a conference on "Contemporary political history in the digital age". Reflecting on the event, Helen McCarthy noted that "Part of the reason historians have been late to the party is because for all but the most contemporary of scholars, the vast bulk of relevant source material is still paper-based". In other words, it has been possible just to ignore this new, and difficult, material. But she concludes that, with more and more government business being transacted digitally, on the web, "historians just have to – well, just go out and start doing it. To grasp the full possibilities and challenges of the digital archive, we need to begin to work with born digital sources" (2016). In this instance, it is specifically political history that is being described, and this is where engagement with all kinds of born digital data is most likely to be seen first. The drift away from the analogue that can be seen in the sphere of government will leave historians with no option but to turn to web archives and other repositories of the digital. In the UK, for example, this is evidenced by a government commitment that "In the future our services will be fit for the 21st Century – agile, flexible and *digital by default*" (my emphasis; Maude, 2013).[5] But while political historians may necessarily have to lead the way, scholars working in other fields can also come to recognise the value of web archives.

The Big UK Domain Data for the Arts and Humanities project (BUDDAH; http://buddah. projects.history.ac.uk/)[6] suggests that looking up only briefly from the analogue is all that is required for humanities researchers to be persuaded of the value of web archives. BUDDAH recruited 10 early career researchers from different humanities disciplines who had never encountered web archives before and asked them to develop research projects which captured some of the stories in the archives. Their conclusions were striking: "I found that the UK Web Archive has … enormous potential as a research tool for literary researchers … There is a liberating sense, when working within the archive, of exploring both the past and the future, simultaneously – of entering uncharted territory while also rediscovering forgotten artefacts" (Cran, 2015); "Web archives are inordinately rich, rewarding and immense sources of information, but they are also something new and unique. The old methods and mindsets of both historians and archivists will have to be abandoned or at least revised" (Deswarte, 2015); "As our contemporary lives turn more and more to the digital, so too will our historical research, and the BUDDAH project has shown that, with the correct training and the right tools, web archives can be an incredibly useful research resource" (Taylor, 2015). These researchers, however, had access to a team of experienced scholars, archivists and developers, who could help them to explore this new digital landscape. The real challenge is to communicate the same value to a much wider audience, who will have to navigate the archives largely on their own.

Increasing the number and range of case studies which showcase the richness of information in web archives is an approach which has been shown to work – it clearly helps to address the "what's in it for me?" question that motivates so many scholars. But what about a more general background awareness of value? It is here that the media, and newspapers in particular, have an important role to play. In recent months, the news cycle has begun to make the case for the significance of web archives. To my knowledge, the first time that web archives found their way in to the mainstream media in the UK, in the news rather than technology pages, was in November 2013, when it was reported that the Conservative party had deleted more than a decade's worth of speeches from its website. The story was given an added news angle because one of those speeches was by the then Prime Minister David Cameron praising the Internet for "making more information available to more people". It was noted in *The Guardian* newspaper that "In a remarkable step the party has also blocked access to the Internet Archive's Wayback Machine, a US-based library that captures webpages for future generations, using a software robot that directs search engines not to access the pages" (Ramesh & Hern, 2013). The need to explain what the Internet Archive was – and this was just three years ago – indicates quite how new this seemed to most people. On this occasion, the British Library was able to say that it had been archiving the Conservative party website since 2004, so the material had been preserved as a part of the national historical record. A more frivolous example is the announcement by the BBC in May 2016 that it would be taking down its BBC Food website, removing 11,000 recipes from the public domain. The combination of the BBC and cooking, both staples of British culture, caused uproar and the Internet Archive was again able to come to the rescue. One popular tabloid newspaper, *The Mirror*, reported: the "BBC Food website is closing down – here's how to make sure you don't lose all your favourite recipes" and included a link to the relevant pages in the Internet Archive (Curtis, 2016). This time no explanation was needed.

Finally, there have been two very recent examples of web archives in the news. First, in the UK, most of the content on the website of the EU Referendum Leave campaign, including a number of claims which were proven to be inaccurate, was removed and replaced with a page just saying "Thank you". Newspapers again directed everyone to the Internet Archive (https://web.archive.org/web/20160620174917/http://www.voteleaveta kecontrol.org/); that particular history could not be so easily erased. Then in the USA, there was controversy surrounding the taking down of Melania Trump's website, which contained a claim that she had received a degree in design and architecture from a Slovenian university. Strikingly, when this was covered in *The Independent* newspaper, the Internet Archive was introduced as a research resource, with no accompanying explanatory text – a reporter simply noted that the information about Melania Trump's education "has been consistent since at least 2006, according to archives of the site captured by the Internet Archive" (Revesz, 2016).

Significant in all of these examples has been the requirement for quick and easy access to data that has disappeared from the live web. And it is here that the Internet Archive has a huge advantage over national archives which can only offer restricted access. Journalists are an important user group, especially when it comes to raising awareness, but they are very unlikely to go to a physical library to pursue a story about the web. The rapidly changing news cycle demands a rapid response to emerging stories. Being able to link straight to an archived web page is much more effective than having to include a paragraph of text explaining that a website has been archived but can only be viewed in a handful of libraries – especially when there is a growing expectation of instant, seamless access. Returning to those deleted Conservative party newspapers, the damaging effect of restrictions arising from legal deposit is made explicit in *The Guardian* coverage. While the British Library's work to archive the site is acknowledged, the report notes that "the British Library archive will only be accessible from terminals in its building, raising questions over the Tory commitment to transparency" (Ramesh & Hern, 2015). There is no doubt that in this case, archiving and preservation are not viewed as sufficient – access is key. This is, of course, a journalist's rather than a historian's perspective, but historians are not immune to preferring sources which are readily available.

I described the BBC Food incident above as relatively "frivolous", and compared to high politics perhaps it is. But the story gained so much publicity because it affected the daily lives of a large number of people. Much-loved and well-used family recipes were apparently about to be removed from the web forever. And it is as web archives become directly relevant to our social, cultural and working lives that they will truly begin to break in to the mainstream. One area of activity where this is increasingly likely to be the case is the law. In May 2016, for example, a federal judge in the USA ruled that the Wayback Machine was a legitimate source of trial evidence, in this instance in a case involving trademark infringement. The main criterion for his decision was that, while the archiving process might miss some data, it did not add or create material that had not originally been present (Bychowski, 2016).[7] There will be more and more examples of this as the web comes to represent the public face of businesses and institutions. How, for example, would a university prove not just what its course handbook contained at a particular date but when and how that information was publicly accessible?

Another topic of debate which is likely to affect public understanding about and aware-ness of web archives is the growing interest in the individual "right to be forgotten". This is broader than the European Court of Justice ruling against Google in 2014, which (in very simplified terms) allowed individuals within the European Union to request that certain information about them be removed from the search engine's index (Google Spain SL, Google Inc. v. Agencia Española de Protección de Datos (AEPD), Mario Costeja González, 2014). For most of human history, even for elites, there was very little chance of leaving any kind of trace in the documentary record. Being remembered at all, beyond one or two generations, generally indicated either great achievement or the chance survival of evi-dence – in essence, luck. The opportunity to be remembered, and the consequent con-cern about the type of legacy that might be left, are now open to far more people if one discounts the narrative of a "digital dark age" that appears with regularity in the press (another opportunity to demonstrate the value of web archives).[8] Web archives are a part of this new landscape, and the relationship between the right of nations to preserve their heritage and the right of individuals to decide how they want to be remembered (or not) will no doubt be negotiated in forums both public and private.

Contested though they may be, web histories are very much here to stay. They are not, however, the whole story when it comes to the record of our digital lives. If historians are already lagging behind in their engagement with the archived web, how much greater will be their difficulty in coming to terms with social media, apps and other forms of born digital data which fall outside the scope of web archives? Some of this information is imperfectly captured by current web harvesting methods, often appearing as a tantalising ghost presence in the archive, an indication of what we do not have. Still more of it is inac-cessible or missing altogether, and will never be susceptible to archiving within the frame-works that we have developed for the web. Some of this data is in the hands of businesses, who will only preserve it for as long as it retains commercial value; some is explicitly designed to disappear almost as soon as it is created – ephemerality is built in to the DNA of Snapchat, for example. The voices of individuals, and particularly of the mar-ginalised, may be louder here than they are on the web, so it is all the more important that we look beyond web archives and seek other digital challenges. A web archive does not, and cannot, contain all of our digital data, but it is at least part of the picture. And the relative maturity of web archiving means that there are lessons to be learnt for those seek-ing to negotiate the complex and evolving digital landscape to piece together twenty-first century life.

Notes

1. In the UK, for example, in 2014 it was found that "21% of Britain's population lack the basic digi-tal skills and capabilities required to realise the benefits of the internet. Around a third of small and medium enterprises (SMEs) don't have a website, and when we include voluntary, commu-nity and social enterprises (VCSEs) this figure rises to 50%" (Maude, 2014).
2. Even though he is referring specifically to Wikipedia, O'Sullivan's description of '"participatory" knowledge, a redefining of the public sphere', is applicable here (2009, p. 10).
3. In the digital sphere, terms like "archive" and "curation" have come to be used in ways that would not be recognisable to a professionally trained archivist. Many of our understandings about the creation, purpose and functioning of archives simply do not apply when we are deal-ing with the "archiving" of the web. The review and transfer procedures that have been

developed for paper records, for example, are clearly very different from automated harvesting. There is no paper equivalent to the transformation that occurs when a live web page is converted into an archival format such as WARC or ARC. New and more meaningful vocabularies will undoubtedly develop, but for the moment it is "web archive" that has gained currency.

4. The Internet Archive has made a number of datasets available for more complex analysis on a case-by-case basis, for example, to the British Library (data from the .uk domain crawled between December 1996 and April 2013; https://www.webarchive.org.uk/shine) and to the Alexandria team at the University of Hannover (http://alexandria-project.eu/), but this is not scalable; nor can the data be republished.

5. There is a noticeable looseness about the terminology used here, with a tendency to treat "online" and "digital" as pretty much synonymous (Maude, 2013). The focus of government strategy is clearly on engaging with its citizens via the web.

6. The BUDDAH project, a collaboration between the School of Advanced Study, University of London, Aarhus University, the British Library and the Oxford Internet Institute, was funded by the Arts and Humanities Research Council (Award no. AH/L009854/1).

7. Indeed, Thomson notes that, as early as 2004, "Archived information from websites is being admitted into evidence just as information from active sites is being admitted" (Thomson, 2011, p. 25; n. 49).

8. There are far too many examples of this digital doom-mongering to list them all, but recent examples include Fox (2016), Ghosh (2015) and Knapton (2015).

Acknowledgments

I am grateful to the anonymous peer reviewer of this journal for helpful comments and suggestions.

Disclosure statement

No potential conflict of interest was reported by the author.

Funding

This work was supported by the Arts and Humanities Research Council [grant number AH/L009854/1].

ORCID

Jane Winters (iD) http://orcid.org/0000-0001-5502-5887

References

Brügger, N. (2013). Web historiography and internet studies: Challenges and perspectives. *New Media & Society, 15*, 752–764.

Brügger, N., & Finnemann, N. O. (2013). The web and digital humanities: Theoretical and methodo-logical concerns. *Journal of Broadcasting and Electronic Media, 57*, 66–80.

Bychowski, S. (2016, May 16). The internet archive Wayback machine: A useful IP litigation tool, but is it admissible? Retrieved from http://www.trademarkandcopyrightlawblog.com/2016/05/the-inter net-archive-wayback-machine-a-useful-ip-litigation-tool-but-is-it-admissible

Cran, R. (2015). All writing is in fact cut ups: The UK Web Archive and Beat literature. Retrieved from http://sas-space.sas.ac.uk/id/eprint/6101

Curtis, S. (2016, May 17). BBC Food website is closing down – here's how to make sure you don't lose all your favourite recipes. *The Mirror*. Retrieved from http://www.mirror.co.uk/tech/bbc-food-web site-closing-down-7991786

Deswarte, R. (2015). Revealing British Euroscepticism in the UK web domain and archive case study. Retrieved from http://sas-space.sas.ac.uk/id/eprint/6103

Fox, J. (2016, March 23). The digital dark ages are upon us. *Bloomberg View*. Retrieved from https://www.bloomberg.com/view/articles/2016-03-23/the-digital-dark-ages-are-upon-us

Ghosh, P. (2015, February 13). Google's Vint Cerf warns of "digital Dark Age". *BBC Science and Environ-ment*. Retrieved from http://www.bbc.co.uk/news/science-environment-31450389

Google Spain SL Google Inc. v. Agencia Española de Protección de Datos (AEPD), Mario Costeja González (2014, May 13). Retrieved from http://curia.europa.eu/juris/document/document_print.jsf?doclang=EN&docid=152065

Jackson, A. (2015). *Ten years of the UK Web Archive: What have we saved?* [PowerPoint presentation]. Retrieved from http://blogs.bl.uk/webarchive/2015/09/ten-years-of-the-uk-web-archive-what-have-we-saved.html

Knapton, S. (2015, October 11). Vital information could be lost in "digital dark age" warns professor. *The Telegraph*. Retrieved from http://www.telegraph.co.uk/news/science/science-news/11922192/Vital-information-could-be-lost-in-digital-dark-age-warns-professor.html

Maude, F. (2013, December 10). Foreword. *Government Digital Strategy*. Retrieved from https://www.gov.uk/government/publications/government-digital-strategy/government-digital-strategy

Maude, F. (2014, December 4). Foreword. *Government Digital Inclusion Strategy: December 2013*. Retrieved from https://www.gov.uk/government/publications/government-digital-inclusion-strat egy/government-digital-inclusion-strategy

McCarthy, H. (2016). Political history in the digital age: The challenges of archiving and analysing born digital sources. *The Impact Blog*. Retrieved from http://blogs.lse.ac.uk/impactofsocialscien ces/2016/03/31/political-history-in-the-digital-age-born-digital-sources/

O'Sullivan, D. (2009). *Wikipedia: A new community of practice*. Farnham: Ashgate.

Ramesh, R., & Hern, A. (2013, November 13). Conservative party deletes archive of speeches from internet. *The Guardian*. Retrieved from https://www.theguardian.com/politics/2013/nov/13/con servative-party-archive-speeches-internet

Revesz, R. (2016, July 28). Melania Trump's website vanishes from internet after rumours swirl over her university degree. *The Independent*. Retrieved from http://www.independent.co.uk/news/world/americas/melania-trump-vanishes-biography-website-online-disappears-rumours-plagiar ised-speech-education-a7160856.html

Taylor, H. (2015). Do online networks exist for the poetry community? Retrieved from http://sas-space.sas.ac.uk/id/eprint/6105

Thomson, L. L. (2011, December 1). *Admissibility of electronic documentation as evidence in U.S. courts.* (Human Rights Electronic Evidence Study). Retrieved from http://www.crl.edu/sites/default/files/d6/attachments/pages/Thomson-E-evidence-report.pdf

For a dynamic and post-digital history of the Internet: a research agenda

Leopoldina Fortunati

ABSTRACT

The making of history of technology is in itself a challenge, but making Internet history is a goal that is likely to be overly ambitious, given the breadth and complexity of such a technological artefact and of social relations that it entails. One way to reduce the difficulties presented by this objective is to think in terms of urgent research directions. In this short article, I propose eight themes that I think are unavoidable for scholars who want to accept the challenge of doing research on the history of the Internet.

The making of history of technology is in itself a challenge, but making Internet history is a goal that is likely to be overly ambitious, given the breadth and complexity of such a technological artefact and of social relations that it entails. One way to reduce the difficulties presented by this objective is to think in terms of urgent research directions. In this short article, I propose eight themes that I think are unavoidable for scholars who want to accept the challenge of doing research on the history of the Internet. While there is a certain arbitrariness and lack of comprehensiveness to the choice of themes, I hope that these themes can provide some good starting points for discussing research agendas for contemporary Internet researchers.

First, the new wave of the Internet studies needs to put in perspective the materiality of the Internet, how the Internet was and is made of, and how it works (Brügger, 2002). To begin, considering and analysing what materially Internet was, is and has become over time, both at the level of its infrastructure and at the level of the services and networks, is an important task. This technological artefact is made of a physical support consisting of a network of cables and optical fibres, in which the data can move. Private companies, that agree to use common and standardised protocols with the purpose to provide data navigation, act as Internet providers. Other private companies that produce content and data preside to the immaterial level of the Internet. All these companies are part of what Christian Fuchs calls "digital capitalism" (2016) that has its own history. Obviously, the picture becomes complete only if we include in it the World Wide Web, one of the most important services of the Internet that allows to navigate and benefit a huge ensemble of professional and amateur content (multimedia and not) as well as of the presence of research engines and web browsers. The picture, however, becomes meaningful only if we include in it the networks of individuals groups, movements and firms that are in communication among them, organise them or do business with them. The material practices of use of this artefact as well as the social representation of it, the emotions that are posited inside it, the attitudes towards it and the perceptions of it are the fields of investigation where it is necessary to multiply our efforts of theorisation, investigation and historicisation.

Second, Internet regulation and ownership is another crucial issue to monitor and to which historical studies of the Internet should pay a specific attention – because it establishes a framework affecting the freedom of Internet users and the range of their human rights (Goggin, 2015). For example, let us consider the Internet Assigned Numbers Authority (IANA). So far, IANA was responsible for interpreting numerical addresses on the Web to a readable language. The regulatory framework has now changed, moving from a US control of the Internet to a non-profit organisation, the Internet Corporation for Assigned Names and Numbers (ICANN), a multi-stakeholder body based in Los Angeles that includes countries such as China and Russia. It is too early to understand the possible effects of this transition from an Internet governed by the US to an Internet governed by a multi-stakeholder. For now, it suffices to say that Internet researchers have to keep under their radar this transition, because this theme certainly encompasses many other issues to analyse.

Third, we need to explore more concerning how the Internet is used, when, where, how and by whom for communication, information, knowledge, teaching and learning, sociability, political organisation and business. Social networks and applications are now the lens through which it makes sense to do this investigation. The Internet use entails various forms of labour relationships: waged labour, voluntary work, work for free and often the form of the labour relationship is hidden or mystified (Terranova, 2000). For example, the Internet is largely occupied by social networks and, in turn, it nourishes the world of applications that are the current gateway through which Internet users manage to perform a lot of tasks and activities. In particular, almost a million and half applications are currently downloaded or updated, and in many cases bought and used by people. Social networks and applications have the apparent function to provide mediated solutions for a wide range of problems. However, their real "nature" behind these apparent functions is as private firms that make money with the service they offer.

Fourth, Internet researchers should avoid a flat or descriptive history of the Internet: the development of the various platforms and services provided by this technological artefact can be grasped effectively only if we reconstruct and interpret the historical dynamics that has generated them. Internet, like any other technology or object, is a place of power and counter-power and/or empowerment (Fortunati, 2014). Thus, we should look at this technology as at a terrain of confrontation, struggle, negotiation and mediation between social groups or political movements and even individuals with different interests. Internet evolution has been the fruit of many forces: army, industry, market, but, especially, initiative, creativity and innovation of users all over the world. What is important is to reconstruct when the technological initiative has been predominant and when users' social and political agency has produced radical changes or trends in this technological artefact. To take just one example: the transition from forums to blogs and to social networks can be read in terms of a technological evolution; or, alternatively, can be read trying to identify the social subjects who have provoked this evolution with their behaviour. Only in the second case, we will be able to grasp the social meaning of this evolution in reconstructing the reasons and motivations behind users' behaviours.

Forums have been one of the first opportunities for people to express their own opinions and to discuss online. The main purpose of people contributions was to influence the agenda setting both of the online newspapers and of the news websites. Although their expectations, it turned out that the relationship between the readership and the newsroom has never taken off. Users were often reminded that the online place belonged to someone else (the owner of the online newspaper or news site) who dictated rules and limits of readers' messages by means of a webmaster. This figure generally selected, and gave a title to, the messages to be published according to the net-etiquette and traditional journalism rules (no bad words, curses, insults and so on), recommending people to write short comments (no longer than 30 lines) (Fortunati, 2009). Furthermore, editorial staff regulated the agenda setting of the forums by launching the themes, which later on were discussed by users. Very soon, people understood that, in addition to the limitations to which their conversation was subject, their comments were read maybe with interest only by other users – but that they were not able to influence the journalists and the newsrooms of the online newspapers. This brought many users to abandon the forums and create their blogs, where the online space belonged only to them and of which they had full responsibility. From 2001 to 2007, blogs enjoyed a big success (Jenkins, 2006). In 2011, it seems that there were 150 million blogs. However, the new freedom enjoyed by bloggers suddenly revealed its dark face in the sense that for bloggers it was difficult to find an audience and thus the majority of bloggers suffered of social and communicative isolation. The reaction to this isolation was a new migration on the part of users to social networks, where the possibility to reach an audience increased considerably.

Analysing the interests, the motivations and the reasons behind users' behaviours enables us to understand that the social relationships that have developed over time among the various Internet stakeholders have shaped this technological artefact in a very different way according to the various temporalities. However, as Gerard Goggin argues, this also applies to the various geographical areas. The Internet is not the same all over the world, because the influence of culture, of political activities and social practices is different and we need a historical research describing, for example, other histories in detail other than American Internet histories.

Fifth, it is necessary to avoid telling a unilateral story of the Internet. To do this, it is important to reconstruct a history of this technological artefact considered inside the network of personal technologies we use in our daily life. It is important for Internet researchers to not study this tool in a vacuum and to be aware that it is a part, although very important, of the media system. My concern here is specifically the vision that describes the Internet as a metamedium, a totalising reality that has cannibalised the old media (television, radio and newspapers, telephone) (Agre, 2008). In this vision, the Internet, with its incredible force would have stormed analogue mass media and the telephone and would have sucked them into the metamedium of the digital world. The Internet, as the key place of the digital, would represent the new because it manages to do better what that the analogue did before, worse. If this is the present, then the future is presented as the site of the triumph of the digital on the analogue, what is perceived as outdated, retrograde (Lehman-Wilzig & Cohen-Avigdor, 2004).

Such a view is wrong because, in addition to overlooking the crucial role of users' subjectivity, it is prisoner of an opposition between digital and analogue, and between the Internet and the traditional media, which proves to be false (Ludovico, 2012). In fact, the digital does not do better what the analogue did and continues to do but it does so in a different way. Internet presents different characteristics and capabilities from traditional analogue media, and this diversity is the element that must be fully understood and analysed. Understanding this diversity can put us in the position to understand how and to what extent the Internet has benefitted from other media and what in turn it has offered to them. On the one hand, the radio and the phone have brought the contribution of voice, still largely absent on the Internet; the cinema and the television, their ability to handle moving images and stories; and the press, its knowledge of the layout and of how information is produced. Overall, traditional media has offered to the Internet content, decades of experience in the production of languages and communicative, informative and aesthetic modes.

On the other hand, the Internet has shown the capacity to penetrate the analogue world of the old media and to hybridise with it. There is a lot of the analogue in the digital and, vice versa, for building digital products such as books or newspapers, the production process has to incorporate a lot of digital (O'Sullivan, Fortunati, & Taipale, 2017). It would be interesting to study the different phases of this production process in which the analogue still flourishes and those in which the digital is recognised as more suitable, convenient and so on. And to study it in the various contexts such as the work places (Sellen & Harper, 2002), the education world with the text-books and all the experiments that are exploring new strategies to put together the advantages of the Internet and of the paper, the information world with the print and online newspapers. Beyond the technical and structural aspects, the contemporary audiences are increasingly transmedia and, in addition to being more educated, experienced and proactive, they are able to take the best from the characteristics of each medium. A true story of the Internet today cannot but tell the interweaving with the stories of the other media because the technological ecology in which we live includes all of them. Indeed, in people's daily life, the various media constitute a dynamic network that led to a division of the communication and information labour among them.

At the same time, Internet has extended the traditional media networking capabilities to a potentially global audience and able to be proactive, a space and a time with less and/or different limits. Observing the processes of convergence and divergence among the various media over time allows us to understand to what extent the Internet has become interconnected with the television, the radio, the press and the telephone. Moreover it allows us to understand how difficult it is today to draw the lines of demarcation between them and how fluid is the hybridisation and specialisation in the media landscape. A vision that supports only the dominance of the Internet in the media environment fails to grasp the dynamics that has developed among the various media and that is subject to a continuous change. There is a power relationship among the various media, which is continuously shaped and re-shaped by the preferences and practices of Internet use and which brings to varying trends of convergence or divergence under the dominance of a medium. Contrary to what this vision proposes, it is instead clear that the dominance in the media environment is expressed today by the smartphone, which swept aside the desktop computer as the prerogative of the highest Internet access.

In this framework, special attention should be accorded to the study of the historical relationship between the Internet and the mobile phone, as this seems to configure itself today as the most essential relationship for the Internet. Smartphones have benefitted enormously from the contribution given to them by the Internet. Through the access to the Internet, mobile phones have transformed themselves from a device dedicated essentially to intimate communication to a tool capable to be open to any service, platform and application, such as Whatsapp. At the same time, smartphones have become open to a relation with the physical space in a richer way. Already in 2002, a research foresaw that the merging between the mobile and the Internet would be held in the name of the dominance of the mobile phone on the Internet (Fortunati & Contarello, 2002). More recent data confirm that the access to the Internet is more frequent on the mobile phone than on the fixed-line Internet (ITU, 2015). The secret for explaining mobile current dominance in this specific relationship lies in the human body: the mobile follows the body in all its movements and respects its freedom of moving, while the fixed-line Internet obliges the body to be steady. Thus, the mobile phone gives to the fixed-line Internet the possibility to move, have legs and feet and being present where people go and are. Mobile phone gives to the Internet the possibility of becoming embodied in the aura of the human body and acquiring movement by upsetting the fundamental steadiness of users' body and the chain of micro gestures that the use of the fixed-line Internet implies. Mobile phones entertain with their users a more intimate and close emotional relation and this distinctive sign of the mobile phone extends also to the Internet once this is incorporated into the mobile phone. As it has drawn more closer to the human body, this has afforded the Internet the possibility to acquire a new life and a different relationship with emotion. The Internet has become a big repository of written or visual emotion, often expressed in a disconnected way from personal identity.

Sixth, another important aspect to investigate further at the historical level is in regard to sociability. Here one thing that the Internet has represented, especially in the last years after the advent of social networks, is the place in which the self of the humankind has had the possibility to network for the first time on a very large scale. One of the roles of the Internet has been and is to provide a place where humankind networks, supports, maintains and experiences many different forms of sociability: from friendship to contacts, from business relationships to dating, from sexual relationships to religious ones, to the social relationships in self-help communities and so on. On the positive side, this possibility has diminished the mental and psychological distance among people. A sole-minded humankind is developing and this is unique for its experience. Jung's idea of collective unconscious is now embodied in a precise place and that is the Internet. Probably also, a specific collective personality has developed in the Internet over time, as well as a multicultural and multilinguistic awareness of the differences that characterise the humankind. The Internet has become a matrix of the encounters of many cultures, languages, interests, business, practices, knowledge, information and communication. As consequence, the Internet has represented an important window on reality since we have begun to have visibility of others and their lives on a global scale. Literature and media have been so far the places where we could imagine or experience somehow people's life. Now, social networks offer the possibility to read and look at the people's lives from their own perspective. On the negative side, social media have become the place where everyday life is often represented and communicated in a superficial manner, where hate speech (including misogyny, racism and bullying) could be developed without too many barriers and where fake news propagate virally and uncontrollably, just to make some examples.

Seventh, it is important to reflect and carry out historical, multidisciplinary research on how the Internet sensorium has transformed over time. Even now, silence is dominant in the Internet, which is still largely a written world. The most important activities in the Internet still seem to be reading and writing, whereas listening and speaking are set forth as marginal. Just the sensory impairment alone, as well as the lack of expression and communication that go with it, give a precise idea of the conflictual relationship with the material human body that the Internet entertains. This impairment is not something of irrelevant since it builds a social reality which under develops orality and the capacity to listen. We know instead that the human voice is important, for example, for intimate relationships, and also for social and political movements that have the problem to raise the voice for making their protest to be heard by those in power. This habit of not exercising the listening in the Internet has strengthened probably also people's incapacity of listening in their everyday life. The mediation of the technology of writing within the technology of the Internet has contributed to expel from this technology the presence of the human body and thus of life. The Internet presents a double technological mediation as it implies technology-mediated communication and written communication. The presence of writing in the Internet is so strong that the use of the Internet has influenced greatly also the use of the mobile phone that from an oral communication device has become a written device. One explanation can be that advanced by Fortunati and Baron (in press), who have argued that written forms of mobile communication have been successful because they are less direct and invasive than speech, since they are asynchronous and can be ignored more easily than a voice call. Nevertheless, there is in the last years an increasing penetration of voices – through, for example, YouTube, tutorials, Skype, podcasts, Whatsapp vocal messages and so on – which limits, in a certain sense, the empire of silence.

Eight, another important element to monitor, also longitudinally, and discuss is the increasing robotisation to which the Internet has been submitted. As is well known, a high percentage of the Internet traffic (60%) is occurring today between machines (Zeifman, 2016). The introduction and development of bots, which are software designed to perform various functions, is treating the possibility to understand really how many visits by humans a website receives (Gehel & Bakardjieva, 2017). The role of bots on astroturfing (Bakardjieva, 2015) as well as on destroying and rebuilding reputations, introduces an issue of manipulation. The premise is that computer-mediated communication is a form of human communication mediated by a computer and thus lacking a series of cues on the identity of the interlocutor and on the characteristics of the context in which the interlocutor is located. Given this premise, bots can access the Internet through the same channels used by human users such as webpages, chat systems, videogames, etc. Moreover, bots act as spiders of search engines that monitor the Internet with the purpose to discover content and websites or as programs that scour the net looking for information to be used for spam campaigns.

A historical reconstruction of this process would enable us to understand in more detail why there has been the need of developing a strategy of contrast to these kinds of programs, such as providing tests that bots could not elude when they seek to deceive virtual systems by posing as users. The classic tools of contrast are the tests one needs to take in the webpages that offer the chance to sign up and submit users' data. Users are required to pass these tests in order to prove that they are not a robot and consequently that they are humans. These tests are called Captcha (Completely Automated Public Turing Test to Tell Computers and Humans Apart) and in reality are a public and completely automatic Turing test that has the purpose to distinguish bots and humans. Practically, a Captcha test usually consists of the request to rewrite the content of a distorted word or an image or a number of images. Recently, vocal or auditory Captcha have been introduced, whose meaning can be de-codified only by a human user (Abrich, Berbenetz, & Thorpe, 2011; Gelernter & Herzberg, 2016).

These tests create the paradoxical situation in which the presentation of the self becomes secondary for a human being in respect to the need to demonstrate of not being a robot. So far, the presentation of the self was performed in order to delineate the uniqueness of a specific human being from the other human beings and to convey the rich data of his/her personal identity, with the purpose of distinguishing one particular identity from the other human identities. After the advent of bots, people are required by a machine to express their identity in terms of being a human in opposition to being a robot. It is a sort of reversal of the situation which had affected automata and androids, accused in ancient time of cheating on their identity because their features so imitated human beings as to be mistaken for them. The automation of the Internet entails also its new penetration into the physical space: the Internet of Things. This is a new frontier that will connect not only individuals but also objects, opening many social and psychological issues also requiring the full attention of Internet researchers.

Disclosure statement

No potential conflict of interest was reported by the author.

References

Abrich, R., Berbenetz, V., & Thorpe, M. (2011). Distinguishing between humans and robots on the Web. Retrieved from https://www.academia.edu/3293658/
Agre, P. (2008). The Internet and public discourse. *First Monday*, *3*(3).
Bakardjieva, M. (2015). Rationalizing sociality: An unfinished script for socialbots. *The Information Society*, *31*(3), 244–256.
Brügger, N. (2002). Does the materiality of the internet matter? In N. Brügger & H. Bødker (Eds.), *The internet and society? Questioning answers and answering questions* (pp. 13–22). Aarhus: The Centre for Internet Research.

Fortunati, L. (2009). Online newspapers interactivity and e-participation: A balance. *Communication, Politics & Culture, 42*(2), 65–86.

Fortunati, L. (2014). Media between power and empowerment: Can we resolve this dilemma? *The Information Society: An International Journal, 30*(3), 169–183.

Fortunati, L., & Baron, N. (in press). Evolving patterns of mobile call openings and closings. In A. Serrano (Ed.), *Between public and private in mobile communications*. New York, NY: Routledge.

Fortunati, L., & Contarello A. (2002). Internet-mobile convergence: Via similarity or complementarity? *Trends in Communication, 9*, 81–98.

Fuchs, C. (2016). *Critical theory of communication: New readings of Lukács, Adorno, Marcuse, Honneth and Habermas in the age of the internet*. London: University of Westminster Press.

Gehel, R. W., & Bakardjieva, M. (Eds.). (2017). *Sociobots and their friends. Digital media and the automation of sociality*. New York, NY: Routledge.

Gelernter, N., & Herzberg, A. (2016). Tell me about yourself: The malicious Captcha attack. In *Proceedings of the 25th International Conference on World Wide Web* (pp. 999–1008). Montréal, Québec, Canada. doi:10.1145/2872427.2883005

Goggin, G. (2015). Communication rights and disability online: Policy and technology after the world summit on the information society (WSIS). *Information, Communication & Society, 18*(3), 327–341.

ITU (International Telecommunication Union). (2015). ITU releases 2015 ICT figures. Statistics confirm ICT revolution of the past 15 years. Retrieved from http://www.itu.int/net/pressoffice/press_releases/2015/17.aspx#.V81PGJiLS1s

Jenkins, H. (2006). *Fans, bloggers, and gamers*. New York: New York University Press.

Lehman-Wilzig, S., & Cohen-Avigdor, N. (2004). The natural life cycle of new media evolution. Intermedia struggle for survival in the internet age. *New Media & Society, 6*(6), 707–730.

Ludovico, A. (2012). *Post-digital print: The mutation of publishing since 1894*. Eindhoven, NE: Onamatopee.

O'Sullivan, J., Fortunati, L., & Taipale, S. (2017). Innovators and innovated. Newspapers and the post-digital future beyond the "Death of Print". *The Information Society, 33*(2), 86–95.

Sellen, A., & Harper, R. (2002). *The myth of the paperless office*. Cambridge, MA: MIT Press.

Terranova, T. (2000). Free labor: Producing culture for the digital economy. *Social Text, 18*(2), 33–58.

Zeifman, I. (2016). Bot traffic report. Incapsula. Retrieved March 16, 2017, at https://www.incapsula.com/blog/bot-traffic-report-2016.html

Tell us about...

Valérie Schafer

Notwithstanding Andrew Russell's warnings within this first issue to refrain from adopting a hagiographic relationship to Internet pioneers and core actors – and definitely keeping them in mind – we could not resist the opportunity to share their viewpoint with you. So, after the perspectives of historians on Internet history and its actors, it is their turn to give us a little bit of theirs...

By means of open and sometimes slightly "shifted" questions (for example, on their enthusiasm as Internet users rather than developers – in fact in the early days of the Internet, they are usually "user-developers" –, or what they would change or relive in the history of the Internet), well-known pioneering actors Vinton Cerf, Steve Crocker, Abhaya Induruwa, Dennis Jennings, John Klensin, Gérard Le Lann, Paul Mockapetris and Ted Nelson address a vast array of issues and topics which fully align with those of our journal: protocols and technical architectures, the applications and uses of the Internet, its evolving governance, the complex and collective processes, genealogies and trajectories of innovation, as well as national and transnational issues across continents and countries, from the United States and France to Sri Lanka.

Although our approach is different from the full-fledged academic interviews that will then fill this section, in these short and crossed interviews we have tried to capture a bit of the early Internet "spirit" as these actors perceived and lived it. One can certainly note the absences in this mixture of perspectives, among which the notable absence of women – not because we have neglected to contact them, but because they did not reply. However, a number of original viewpoints come out of the following pages, telling us a great deal about collectives, communities, a *Zeitgeist* where ideas, innovations and actors circulated. These pioneers unveil an effervescent, nascent world, the memories of which include technical issues as well as human, political and societal ones.

It is now time to leave the stage to Vinton Cerf, Steve Crocker, Abhaya Induruwa, Dennis Jennings, John Klensin, Gérard Le Lann, Paul Mockapetris and Ted Nelson, but not before thanking them warmly for having indulged in this short exercise with benevolence and generosity.

Valérie Schafer for the Editors

Tell us about ... one of your best memories as a pioneer/key actor in Internet and/or Web history...

Ted Nelson, who launched the Xanadu project, which, according to Pierre Lévy was the "absolute horizon of hypertext", opens the list of these souvenirs by going back to the mid-1960s.

> In 1965, shortly after my presentation at the ACM national conference, I got a direct call from the director of information processing research for the Central Intelligence Agency. He came to my house and said they would fund my work. I was excited - I thought I would get a great setup, and that I would give my government a system they badly needed, thus improving our nation's understanding and policy.

Steve Crocker, whose pivotal role in ARPANET and the RFCs is readily acknowledged, goes back to the end of the 1960s.

> I was one of the graduate students at UCLA that put the first node on the Arpanet. I helped develop the initial suite of protocols for the Arpanet, created the RFCs and formed and led the Network Working Group, the forerunner of today's IETF. I also spent three years at DARPA. I've watched network technology and use take off from the initial four nodes in the western part of the U.S. to become an intimate part of lives around the globe.

> In 1973, the Arpanet was in full bloom. The Internet, i.e. interconnection of multiple independent networks, was envisioned but not yet underway. Nonetheless it was already evident how the net was changing the lives of the people who were connected to it. As a program manager at DARPA, I interacted with a number of different parts of the U.S. military. One day at a meeting I introduced two Air Force captains to each other that I had been working with separately. After I introduced them to each other, I stepped back and they continued to talk. When they finished, they asked each other for their email addresses instead of their military system phone numbers (Autovon) I knew each of them had. I knew then network connectivity would become universal.

From ARPANET to the Internet, three key dates have persisted in **Vinton Cerf**'s memory within a path he has largely contributed to trace. Two of them are particularly well known by historians, and considered as fundamental steps in Internet history:

> November 22, 1977 – First demonstration of a three-network Internet using the Defense Advanced Research Projects Agency networks: ARPANET, Packet Radio Net and Packet Satellite Net.

> May 1974 – Publication of the first paper describing TCP and the architecture of the Internet in IEEE Transactions on Communications, May 1974

> January 1, 1983 – the day we officially declared the Internet operational.

The Seventies are indeed an effervescent period – French pioneer **Gérard Le Lann**, at the time working within the Cyclades project, launched at the *Institut de recherche en informatique et automatique* in 1971, remembers it well...

> Between October 1972 and April 1973, I had built a large simulation program (in Simula-67) for studying the dynamic behaviours of the Arpanet NCP protocol and the early versions of the Cyclades protocols. They suffered from unexplained erratic dysfunctions (e.g. blocking, losses, memory overflows). Causes and remedies were found, notably how to reliably open and close end-to-end connections despite losses or excessively long delays, and the sliding

window mechanism for end-to-end error and flow control (elimination of reassembly lock-ups). My Cyclades colleagues were the first to know, Hubert Zimmermann in particular. Updated versions of the Cyclades protocols were implemented end of 1973. I visited Vint Cerf at Stanford (Digital Systems Lab.) in April 1973, showing him my simulation results. Vint invited me to join his Arpanet team, which I did until summer 1974.

I vividly recall the numerous brainstorming meetings with Vint, at his house in Palo Alto, sitting on the ground for examining the large print outputs of the Simula-67 programs, and combining my findings with the on-going revisions of NCP undertaken by the Arpanet community (Robert Kahn, BBN, etc.). These novel schemes became essential constituents of the original TCP protocol. Great times in what was not yet named Silicon Valley!

The official launch of the Internet in the early eighties, and its distinction from ARPA-NET, opens up the way to the network of networks' steady rise within civil society, led by the scientific and academic world and the development of local and regional networks – as reminded by **Dennis Jennings**, the first Program Director for Networking at the National Science Foundation in 1985–1986 ...

One of my best memories is the trip that I made to Cornell University to talk about the NSFnet plans.

The first thing I remember about that trip is that the weather was exceedingly hot (July or August 1985, I think) and I travelled in shorts and a short sleeved shirt - and the airline lost my luggage! So I had to go into Cornell and meet the people there the following day in the clothes that I had travelled in! Not my style at all.

More importantly, after my talk about the emerging plans for NSFnet, the Cornell people gave me a presentation on their ideas for NYSERNet, the New York State Education and Research network. At the end of the presentation they asked me whether the NSF would be interested in assisting with funding. I was very enthusiastic, because I realised that the development of State and Regional networks would greatly leverage my limited NSF budget, and, more importantly, would expand the community of teams of networking experts working on the vision of a US national research and education network of networks - or internet. I confirmed my enthusiastic personal support (with, as usual, the caveat that I could not speak for the NSF, and that the NSFnet programme had its own procedures to follow). This meeting stimulated me to publish the NSF Solicitation for Proposals for Regional Networks as part of the NSFnet programme.

Since the eighties, the interest in networks is evident in several countries and progressively extends to all continents. **Abhaya Induruwa**, who developed a Local Area Networking strategy in 1986–1987, funded by a Japanese government grant and implemented within the Department of Computer Science and Engineering which he founded in 1985 at the University of Moratuwa (Sri Lanka), and who then proposed to set-up Lanka Experimental Academic and Research Network (LEARN) in April 1989 to the Sri Lankan government, notes that one of his best memories is

... meeting great Internet pioneers like Vint Cerf, George Sadowsky, Ben Segal, Randy Bush, etc., in the early nineties and getting inspiration to make the seemingly impossible possible. In the late eighties I started building an Internet in Sri Lanka literally with no money. My struggles bore fruit in 1995. Never in my wildest dreams did I imagine that, two decades later, I would be fortunate to share space on the Internet Hall of Fame with such Internet greats!

Tell us about one of your best memories as an Internet or Web user ...

Email, Mosaic, medical applications: those who have contributed to the Internet's first steps – oftentimes among the first in their countries – are, in the early days, designers-users. Asking them what impressed and enthused them, and not just what they contributed to, led us to discover...

... the enthusiasm of one of the Internet's founding fathers, **Vinton Cerf**, in front of the Web and of Mosaic:

> Seeing the avalanche of content arrive on the Internet via the WWW after the introduction of the MOSAIC Browser by Marc Andreessen and Eric Bina at the National Center for Supercomputer Applications at the University of Illinois at Urbana-Champagne.

That of **Steve Crocker**, faced with the power of a governance he contributed to build himself, by organising the Network Working Group and initiating the Request for Comments (RFCs):

> In September 1994 I gave a talk at the Indian Institute of Science in Bangalore, India. Afterwards I was introduced to a graduate student who had built an impressive system that combined several pieces of technology. I asked him how he had learned how to do all of this. He said he downloaded and read the RFCs and put all the pieces together. I was struck by the power of system of protocols, documents, and open access we had set in motion 25 years earlier.

Gérard Le Lann's, for the open, networked communication the Internet made possible:

> As a user, I have two best memories. The first one (chronological order) may seem incredibly naïve to contemporary readers: my first email from the West Coast to the East Coast. That was in 1973. The second one is my first experience in distributed co-writing. In 1982, from Rocquencourt, France (IRIA premises), I had to write a few chapters for a book (Distributed Systems - Architecture and Implementation, An Advanced Course, D.W. Davies and B.W. Lampson Editors), to be shipped to Maynard (MA), USA (B. Lampson was with Digital Equipment Corp.), and corrected interactively on-line. At that time, IRIA had access to the Internet via the MIT (MA). It worked very smoothly.

And the same taste for "real-time", but in another field, retraced by **Abhaya Induruwa**...

> ... organising a workshop in Colombo, Sri Lanka in September 1995 on the « Use of Internet for Medical Practitioners » and demonstrating data from Visible Human Project in real-time. For those who had previously seen and used WAIS and Gopher, accessing and displaying images in full colour, and in real-time, was a sensational experience.

Or the plurality of uses allowed, as reminded by **Dennis Jennings**, by performance improvements:

> In summer 1985 I had dial-up access to the ARPANET. One of the frustrations of using the ARPANET at that time was that the IMPs (routers) could only hold a cache of a small number of addresses (64 I was told!) and increasingly often the address of the site one wanted to access was not in the cache and there would be a long delay before connectivity could be established (the DNS was being designed at around that time by Paul Mockapetris). One day that summer the cache and software was upgraded to support double the number of addresses. Performance was suddenly greatly improved!

Should you choose one date/event in Internet history that you would like to live again, and one that you would like to change, what would they be?

Speaking of happiness and regrets with pioneers, technology is never very far away, as testified by **Steve Crocker**:

> We made a major mistake in the design of some of the early protocols when we allowed addresses to be communicated as ordinary data. The File Transfer Protocol (FTP), for example, passes the address of one of the parties to another as part of the data instead of the control. We should have used a bit of encapsulation and indirection to treat addresses as objects. If we had done so, the transition from IPv4 to IPv6 would have been manageable and nearly seamless. I remember feeling queasy when FTP was designed, and I had tried to do something different within the underlying Host-Host protocol. (The Host-Host protocol, later called the Network Control Protocol, was the predecessor to TCP). My particular proposal was not accepted by the community and there wasn't clear recognition of the importance of treating addresses as a special object. I wish we had been able to articulate the importance of treating addresses as objects.

and **Vinton Cerf** ...

> I think it would not work but I would have chosen a larger IP address space than 32 bits if I had realized that we would have hand-held smart phones and the Internet of Things. As it is we have to move to IPv6 and its 128 bit address space as quickly as we can. I also wish it had been feasible to introduce public key cryptography sooner into the system.

Notwithstanding the moments of "grace", as **Abhaya Induruwa** recollects:

> What would be a date/event in Internet History that I would like to live again ...the day in 1986 when we connected a Radio Shack TRS80 running Xenix at the University of Moratuwa to a similar computer at the University of Colombo using UUCP over a 300 baud modem connected to a telephone line. The moment we saw the login prompt from the remote computer on our screen at Moratuwa ... Little did we realize that this moment marked the beginning of the computer networking era in Sri Lanka. Some important milestones followed such as the first Ethernet LAN in a Sri Lankan University (at the University of Moratuwa) in 1987; first Internet based email (LEARNmail) in 1990; first IP WAN (LEARN) in 1994 and finally, after less than a decade from this moment, connecting LEARN to the Internet in 1995.

or **Gérard Le Lann**:

> The inception of one of the very first distributed algorithms, published in 1977 - IFIP Congress 1977[1], is one of the most exciting moments in my scientific carrier.
>
> The discovery of synchronization problems in networks where two distant processes (end-to-end connections) shall interact correctly through time varying and lossy channels prompted me to look at the general problems arising in systems where n (n > 2) processes need to coordinate their behaviours, despite differing individual views of "current system state" and no central locus of control. The Distributed Computing discipline emerged from Computer Networking in 1976. I could "sense" that this terra incognita was a mine of fascinating problems. This is the reason why my research interests bifurcated from network protocols to distributed algorithms at that time. It turns out that those algorithms devised in the late 70's and the 80's are at the origin of numerous system solutions implemented nowadays in the Web, in large databases, in search engines or in clouds.
>
> A date/event I would like to change: the overlooking of anonymity requirements in Arpanet/Internet communication protocols, requirements, which are now so much essential with mobile networking. Voluntary (e.g. beaconing as suggested for autonomous/automated

vehicles) or unintended disclosure of – and reliance on – IP addresses or MAC addresses is a risk-prone feature, especially when enriched with time-dependent geolocations. It would have been wise to offer at least two options with TCP/IP-based communications, public (well known) naming and anonymous naming. Privacy rests on the ability for every process to compute names that are unique, in a certain geographical zone or/and during a certain time interval, no third-party involved.

That was a terribly hard-to-solve problem in the 70's, with static processes in wired/managed networks. Nowadays, with mobile processes forming ad-hoc short-lived or long-lived open networks, that problem is even more difficult.

Beyond these moments of technical doubt or clear success, there are human adventures too, as **Ted Nelson,** who coined the term hypertext in 1965, testimonies:

In 1988, when our Xanadu Project got major funding, a programmer threatened to quit because my partner Roger Gregory, who was in charge of development, had become tyrannical. I did not ask Roger his side of the story, and acted swiftly to reduce his authority. If I had not done this, Xanadu might have been the international hypertext system, instead of the World Wide Web.

That is the day I would like to live again, and change.

However, there was the feeling to contribute to an adventure, either grasped at the right time or with some delay. **Paul Mockapetris,** who created and developed the Domain Name System (DNS) since 1983, recalls:

One of my happiest moments was when RFC 974, the specification for email routing over DNS was published.[2] This was the first application of my invention, DNS, which I didn't do myself, and proved that others were on the way to adoption.

I'd like to relive the transition from ARPAnet to TCP/IP protocols that happened January 1983. This culminated years of work and thought that essentially replaced all of the network architecture.

If I could change one decision, I probably should have joined the start of Internet commercialization when I finished my tour at ARPA.

It was also about slightly modify one's path, or changing temporalities and mindsets, **Abhaya Induruwa** reminds us:

What would be one that I would like to change … the date we finally connected Sri Lanka to the global Internet … it would have been better if we were able to do this earlier than 1995. In the eighties I was influenced by the trends in the UK and Europe and their efforts in trying to steer ahead with ISO-OSI so my first proposal in 1989 for a country-wide network for Sri Lanka was obviously based on X.25 technology. By the early nineties it was clear that X.25 was disappearing and TCP/IP was here to stay. In January 1992 I reformulated the proposal encompassing TCP/IP technology and resubmitted it to the Sri Lankan government. I now feel that I should have gone with TCP/IP from the beginning notwithstanding the push in Europe towards X.25. Would that have brought Internet to Sri Lanka sooner? That is something I can't tell and it is a hypothesis that we'll never be able to test.

… as well as **Dennis Jennings:**

I returned from the US, after my 15 months at the NSF and 4 months at the Consortium for Scientific Computing in Princeton, in the summer of 1986. Back in Europe I found the period from 1986 to 1991 to be pretty miserable for those of us who were interested in providing networking services for research and education. Networking in Europe was controlled by the technologists on the one hand, and by the PTTs/Governments/European Commission on the other. This combination of experts focussed on technology and officials willing to provide funding only for ISO/OSI protocols and for the use of low speed public packet switched (volume charged!) networks, was an absolute disaster - and ultimately doomed to failure since the approach could not address the end-to-end, workstation to workstation, environment actually used by researchers. While the USA stormed ahead with an increasingly high speed, high functionality, pervasive Internet for research and education, Europe stagnated.

I tried my best to change that, but I was unable to penetrate the closed minds of the technical experts and the funders. I wouldn't like to live that period again, but if I had to live that miserable period again, I would like to be successful in changing the minds of those involved.

Internet history is ...

What are the actors' perspectives on the field of Internet history? Often summarised by an optimist and ecumenical vision, a relationship between past and present that may enlighten the current issues, they warn us that it may also lead to a "presentist" look, rewritings, oblivion...

Fascinating, tells us **Abhaya Induruwa** ...

... fascinating. It is short but its impact on mankind is unparalleled. During a short period of time it has touched the lives of every human being on this planet in one way or another ... and it is just the beginning! From a humble beginning connecting four university computer centres who would have thought the Internet will grow to connect billions of people and tens of billions of things ... signalling the beginning of a new wave: the Internet of Things that is transforming the Internet to a whole new ball game.

A fascinating history for **Gérard Le Lann,** as well, but not without its pitfalls...

A fascinating topic. We have not seen yet all the implications of the advent of the Internet. Given the very deep consequences of what is and has been a fantastic journey in human history, it is no surprise that the Internet history is being written and re-written over and over. Trustable accounts have been provided by most actors of the Arpanet/Internet revolution. Unfortunately, the Internet history is also tainted by mistaken articles and biased interviews produced by improvised "experts."

... and shadows, as noted by **Ted Nelson**:

Internet history, like all history, is a fading tangle of misunderstandings that becomes more and more inaccurate.

While **Dennis Jennings** points out the risks of oblivion, memory biases, of the writing of history itself...

Internet history is a collection of the memories of all the participants. It varies from person to person, and the history remembered varies depending on the point in time and space at which one started to participate in the development or use of the Internet. For example, there were many precursor networks and technologies that are now forgotten, not just the ARPANET, and the ARPANET network wasn't the Internet, or even part of the Internet, until 1 January 1983.

... **John Klensin** underlines the forgotten trajectories, the paths that were left unquestioned, and the variety of genealogies and contributions to a history that cannot be constrained within narrow perimeters. In particular, he goes back to the messaging applications, the history of which he knows well – before serving on the Internet Architecture Board from 1996 to 2002 and 2009 to 2011 and being its Chair from 2000 to 2002, he was involved in the design and implementation of some key email systems and gateways, contributed to the design of contemporary email protocols, and served as working group chair or document editor for IETF Working Groups focused on messaging and email extensions to support a broader range of writing systems.

> For email specifically, there are a number of under-reported covered areas that are not going to be covered by anecdotes about specifically Internet history. Craig Partridge's IEEE piece[3] covers the Internet-specific history rather well, but there were many other email, forum, and discussion systems that grew up in parallel. The mail systems were ultimately integrated via gateways and the like, but, in the process, their design ideas and that of Internet email, evolved. As far as I know, there has been no careful look at the impact of Minitel on modern e-mail and messaging. I think most historians, especially outside Sweden, have vastly underestimated the importance of Jacob Palme's work on COM and its descendants, but simply dismiss them as a path not taken. The bulletin board systems and netnews were important too. While there were mailing lists on the ARPANET and Internet rather early, most of the important developments in list management and distribution derive from the work of Hank Nussbacher and, later, Eric Thomas on BITNET and EARN. Similarly, there was what we would now call instant messaging capability in the Unix "talk" protocols and, even earlier, in the SEND (and SAML and SOML) capabilities of early SMTP. Those never really took off but a good history and analysis of why not would be interesting.

> Even X.400 and the work leading up to it are relevant in that regard. While the protocol itself died a painful and probably well-deserved death, the influence of many of its design ideas have been underreported, partially because they are not considered "Internet" and we might be better off had we picked up one or two more of them.

John Klensin notes the dangers of the "unique and only inventor" figure, very familiar to historians ... in particular when it comes to the recent controversies concerning the paternity of email:

> Part of what makes all of this difficult for trying to reconstruct the history is that, with rare exceptions, almost any "who invented that" question asked in the 60s or 70s would have gotten an answer along the lines of "collaborative effort, lots of ideas in the wind, and everyone building on the ideas of everyone else." It has only been in recent years that (sadly from my point of view) there has been a scramble to figure out who invented what or to claim individual credit for particular developments.

This (hi)story, that has become for many a matter of recognition, is a collective one – as reminded by **Vinton Cerf**...

> ... a story of a grand global collaboration to create an information access and communication resource intended to benefit every person on the planet.

... and turned towards the future, for **Paul Mockapetris**,

> dedicated to recording what happened, but more importantly pointing out principles which we can apply again and again in the future.

It is time to leave the last word to **Steve Crocker**:

Internet history has progressed from a history of the technology to a history of modern communication. It is now intimately entwined in all aspects of our lives, so "Internet history" will shortly be indistinguishable from "human history."

… a gargantuan program and "construction site", indeed, for historians of today and tomorrow. We invite you to share it with us, and this journal, as issue after issue unfold.

Notes

1. https://www.rocq.inria.fr/novaltis/publications/IFIP%20Congress%201977.pdf
2. https://tools.ietf.org/html/rfc974
3. Partridge, C. (2008). The technical development of Internet email. *IEEE Annals of the History of Computing*, *30*(2), 3–29.

Disclosure statement

No potential conflict of interest was reported by the author.

Index

Note: Page numbers in *italics* refer to figures
Page numbers in **bold** refer to tables
Page numbers with "n" refer to notes

Abbate, Janet 8
access, Internet 11–12, 107; in Africa 132–133; in Arab region 98; *see also* digital divides
ADSL 31
Advanced Research Projects Agency Network (ARPANET) 10, 17–18, 21, 27, 32, 107, 139
aesthetics 40
affordance 65–66
Africa, histories of the Internet in 130–132; access 132–133; appropriation 134–136; contribution to development 134; differences between countries 135–136; digital repertoire 136; heterogeneous use of Internet 131, 132; impact 133–134; multi-levelled historiographical approach 130; optimism 133
Africa Rising 132
aimless connectedness, in social media 63
Alberts, Gerard 6, 146
Alexa toolbar 162, *162*
algorithms 52
Allagui, Ilhem 5, 97
Amara, Roy 66
Amazon 35
American mind 41, 42
American Online (AOL) 29, 90, 121
American Revolution 17
American Standard Code for Information Interchange (ASCII) 120–121
angel investors 93
Apple 87n7
appropriation of Internet, in Africa 134–136
Arab uprisings 98, 101; *see also* Middle East, Internet in
archives 18–19, 36, 138–139; ad tech and online ad marketplace 144; beginning of Internet age 139–140; blockchains 144; dumps 141, 142; ephemeral/anonymous 143; hacks 142–143; middens 141–142; PLATO 62; public

accessibility of 54–55; richness of 139, 140; spam 140–141; unnoticed 143–144; *see also* Web archives
argument-by-technology 72
artefacts 53, 86; maintenance costs of 55
arts 40
ASEAN (Association of Southeast Asian Nations) countries 98
Association of Internet Researchers 2
asymmetrical model of Internet development *see* Middle East, Internet in
authority, and digital networks 50
autonomy 22, 53
auxiliary sciences 54
Ayyadurai, Shiva 53

Baran, Paul 17
Barlow, John Perry 22
BBC 175–176
behavioural economics 35
Berners-Lee, Tim 17, 29
big data 51
Big UK Domain Data for the Arts and Humanities (BUDDAH) project 175, 178n6
Bitcoin blockchain 144
Bitzer, Donald 61
blasphemies 21–22
blockchains 144
blogs 100, 101, 181, 182
born-digital materials 51, 54, 148, 160, 174; public accessibility of 55
bots 185–186
Bourdieu, Pierre 87n2
Braman, Sandra 5, 70
Brand, Stewart 22
Brief History of Everything, A (Wilber) 20
British Library 175, 176
Brown, Doug 63
Brügger, Niels 1

Brunton, Finn 138
bulletin board system (BBS) 107, 149

cable broadband 31
Cameron, David 175
Captcha (Completely Automated Public Turing
    Test to Tell Computers and Humans Apart)
    186
category errors 19
Catholic Encyclopedia, The (Delehaye) 16
censorship, and Internet access 12
Cerf, Vinton 17, 18–19, 21, 74, 75, 188, 190–192
Chinese *see* Han character-based scripts
Clark, David 19, 73
Closed World, The (Edwards) 17–18
cloud computing 31
collective unconscious 184
commercial networks 27, 83
common language 30–32
communities: building *see* De Digitale Stad
    (DDS); and cultural history 40, 41, 43, 44;
    design, Internet 72, 75; PLATO as online
    community 63–66
community of innovation 63
compartmentalisation 32
compilers 151
CompuServe 27, 29, 35, 90, 121
Computer-based Education Research
    Laboratory (CERL), UIUC 60, 61
computer-mediated communication (CMC) *see*
    multilingualism; PLATO (Programmed Logic
    for Automated Teaching Operations)
computer memory: De Digitale Stad 151–152;
    and multilingualism 122
computer programs 52–53
content: Internet as 10–11; user-generated 35
contentious digital culture 101
contextualism 22
corporate governance 93
Cowan, Ruth Schwartz 42–43, 44
crawlers 157, 162
Crocker, Steve 189, 191, 192, 195–196
cultural history 39–40, 45; electrical grid 43;
    industrialized kitchen 42–43; railway 41; and
    symbolic transformation 41–42; television
    43–44
culture 12, 13, 80; anthropological sense of 81;
    and Internet development in Middle East 98,
    99, 101–102; monoculture, cyberspace as 36;
    relation to technology 86–87
cyberculture 80
cyber-Islamism 100
cyberspace 30–31, 33, 35; as monoculture 36;
    narrative layers 33
Cybersyn 10
CYCLADES 31, 139

dangers of Internet 22
Davies, Donald 139

Declaration of Independence of Cyberspace 22
de-compilers 151
decompression bombs 150
De Digitale Stad (DDS) 48, 49, 50, 52, 53,
    146–147; avatar generator 151; dynamic
    approach 148; emulation 147–148, 153–154;
    FREEZE operation 55, 146, 150, 151, 152, 156;
    local frost and defrost 150–152; local history
    148–150; memories 151–152; personal data
    155–156; preservation of digital city 152–153;
    purpose limitation 156; reconstruction project
    152–154; replica 147–148, 154; security 156;
    sockets 150–151; tools 154–155; treating
    digital heritage dynamically 157
Defense Advanced Research Projects Agency
    (DARPA) 17, 21
definitions of Internet 8–13; content and social
    space 10–11; locally situated experience
    11–12; politics of history 12–13; technology
    8–9
Delehaye, Hippolyte 16
Delphi method 66
democratic divide 132
design flaws, of Internet 21
design process, of Internet 70–71; RFCs as
    historical data 71–73; shared vision 75; social
    use of history outside 75–76; social use of
    history within 70–71, 74–75; subcultures
    within community 75; technical use of history
    within 70, 71, 73–74
Després, Rémi 19
digital archaeology 146–147
digital capitalism 180
digital dark age 177
digital divides 98, 106–107, 132; changing
    character of Internet 109–113; early 2000s
    110, 113; evolution of research 108–109;
    Internet diffusion 107; Michigan State of the
    State Survey Internet questions (1997–2016)
    111–112; mid- to late-2000s 113; 1990s 110;
    OxIS Internet questions (2003–2013) **114**;
    personal computing, pre-Internet diffusion
    110; research, patterns in operationalising
    115; second-level 108; study approach
    107–108; survey instruments 110; technology,
    digital divide policy and research timeline
    109; 2009–2016 113
digital economy 103
digital gap 98
digital history 160, 163, 164, 170
Digital Linear Tapes (DLT) 150
digital literacy: and language 121; in Middle East
    100
digitally reborn sources 163, 164, 170
Digital Methods Initiative, University of
    Amsterdam 166
digital networks *see* net histories
digital repertoire 136
digital source criticism 163–164, 170

Domain Name System (DNS) 121, 125
double-byte character sets 124
double entry bookkeeping 86
doxxing 143
drift (infrastructure) 9
Driscoll, Kevin 5, 47
dumps 141, 142, 143
Dutton, William H. 5, 106
Dynabook 29
Dyson, Esther 17

e-commerce 11
economic regulation, and precorporation 93
economics, and Internet development in Middle
    East 98, 102–103
e-democracy 133
electrical discourse 43
electrical grid 43
Electronic Information Exchange System (EIES)
    66
Elmer, Greg 5, 90
EMAIL 53
Emergency Management Information Systems
    and Reference Index (EMISARI) 66
Emerson, Ralph Waldo 41
emotions 184
emulation, De Digitale Stad 147–148, 153–154
Engelbart, Douglas 29, 66
Enron, email corpus of 141
Entrepreneurial State, The (Mazzucato) 17
ephemerality 22, 55, 143, 164, 177
E-rate programme 108
ethics: De Digitale Stad 155–156; and digital
    archaeology 147; and net histories 53
Ethiopia 134
ethnography 136
EU Referendum Leave campaign 176
European Court of Justice 177
Everything Engine 53
evolution, of Internet 181–182

Facebook 32, 35, 90–91, 92, 144; changes to
    interface and core user services 94; data
    collection 94; financialisation of 92, 93; IPO 93;
    open graph protocol 94; per worker company
    valuation 93; precorporate era 92–94;
    prospectus 92–93, 94; social graph algorithm
    93; value of 92–93
fake news 30
Father Knows Best (TV series) 42
FidoNet 55, 121
filter bubbles 11
financialisation 90, 91–92; of Facebook 92, 93
Fincher, David 93
Foreign Office Historians 174
format, of data 52
FORUM (conferencing platform) 66
forums 181–182
Fortunati, Leopoldina 6, 180

France Telecom 35
freedom of speech 35, 100
French National Science Foundation 57n7
From Counterculture to Cyberculture (Turner) 75

Gates, Bill 84
GCC (Gulf Cooperation Council countries)
    countries 98, 100
gender: and industrialisation 42; and Internet
    access 12; and television 44
General Electric Information Services (GEIS) 27
GeoCities 27, 49, 54, 55
global divide 132
globalisation 130
Global South see Africa, histories of the Internet in
Goggin, Gerard 1, 50, 182
Google 32, 34, 35, 92; European Court of Justice
    ruling against 177; and multilingualism 125;
    Usenet collection 52, 54
"Google and the Politics of Tabs" 168, 168
Gopher 35
Gore, Al, Jr. 84, 92
group communication tools 61–62
Guardian, The 176
Gutenberg press 30

habitus 87n2
hacks 142–143
hagiographies 15, 16–18
Han character-based scripts 119, 120, 121–123,
    126; multilingual character coding 124–125
"Heavy Metal Umlaut" 166–168, 167
hiragana syllabary 124
histories of networking 19–21
Hobbes' Internet Timeline (Zakon) 74, 75
homework gap 108
homophones 123
HTML see Hyper Text Markup language (HTML)
human subjects research 53
Hyper Text Markup language (HTML) 121

icons 126
ICT for Development (ICT4D) initiatives 130
idealism 40, 43, 82
imagined affordances 66
immateriality, and social media companies 92,
    94, 95n5
incorporation 91–92
Independent, The 176
Induruwa, Abhaya 190, 191, 192, 194
industrialisation 42–43
information, movement of 34
information and communication technologies
    (ICTs) 131; in Africa 133; and globalisation
    130; in Middle East 98, 100–101
information revolution see technological
    revolution
information superhighway 83
information theory 34

informatisation 72
infrastructure(s): cultural history of 40–41, 44, 45; electrical grid 43; industrialized kitchen 42–43; Internet as 9–10, 40; railway 41; and symbolic transformation 41–42; technical 42; television 43–44
infrastructure studies 9
initial public offering (IPO) 93
Instagram 144
internationalisation, and Requests for Comments 72
International Packet Network Working Group (INWG) 76
International Telecommunications Union 28
Internet Advisory Board (IAB) 76
Internet Archive 27, 52, 148, 157, 160; and Web archives 175–176; and Web history 161–163, 170; see also Wayback Machine
Internet Archive WayBack Machine Link Ripper 166
Internet Assigned Numbers Authority (IANA) 181
Internet Corporation for Assigned Names and Numbers (ICANN) 85, 125, 181
Internet: culture 39–40, 44; discourse 43; governance 79, 81, 85; study 2
Internet diffusion 106, 107; digital inequality before 110; in Middle East 100
Internet Engineering Task Force (IETF) 71, 76, 122
Internet histories, value of 173–178
Internet of Things 186
Internet Relay Chat 62, 63
Internet service providers (ISPs) 90
Internet Society (ISOC) 74
internetworking 21, 51, 84, 139
interviews, oral history 18, 19
Inventing the Internet (Abbate) 17

Jansma, Robert 146
Japanese see Han character-based scripts
Jennings, Dennis 190, 191, 193–194
Jobs, Steve 84
Johansen, Robert 66
Jones, Steve 5, 60
Jung, Carl 184

Kahn, Robert 17, 21
katakana syllabaries 124, 125
Kay, Alan 29
Kenya 135
Keywords (Williams) 82
kitchens, industrialized 42–43
Kleinrock, Leonard 18
Klensin, John 194–195
Korean see Han character-based scripts

labour 181
landscape, American 41
language: multilingualism 119–126; of Requests for Comments 72

Latzko-Toth, Guillaume 5, 60, 64–65
Leave it to Beaver (TV series) 42
Legends of the Saints, The (Delehaye) 16
Le Lann, Gérard 189–190, 191, 192–193, 194
Levilion, Marc 19
locally situated experience, Internet as 11–12
Low-Orbit Ion Cannon 143

Machine in the Garden, The (Marx) 41
McLelland, Mark 5, 50, 119
McMaster, John Bach 17
Magaziner, Ira 79–80, 81, 85, 86
magazines 44
Make Room for TV (Spigel) 43
Marvin, Carolyn 43, 44
Marx, Leo 40, 42, 44, 45, 81
materialism 40, 41, 42, 43
materiality, of Internet 180–181
media: hybridisation in 183; traditional, and Internet 182–183; and Web archives 175–176; see also social media
memory 54
messaging 35, 55
metamedium, Internet as 182
methods/approaches, Internet history 3–4
micro-histories 90–91
middens 141–142
Middle East, Internet in 97–98; conceptual implications 98–99, 99; culture 98, 99, 101–102; economics 98, 102–103; and Internet development in Middle East 98; politics 98–101
Mile End Institute (Queen Mary University of London) 174
Milligan, Ian 1
Mills, David 19
Minitel 29, 31, 35, 83
Mirror, The 175–176
mobile phones 30, 102, 183, 184; in Africa 130, 132, 133, 134
Mockapetris, Paul 193, 195
modems 31
Modern Family (TV series) 44
modernisation 133
More Work for Mother (Cowan) 42
multilingualism 119–120; ASCII 120–121; character coding 124–125; language problems on early Internet 121–123
multiplayer games 61
myth and symbol school 81

narratives 47–48, 49, 53, 87n5, 129–130
National Science Foundation Network (NSFNET) 83, 107
National Telecommunications and Information Administration (NTIA) 115; Connected Nation 113; Falling through the Net 108, 110; Nation Online, A 108
national Webs 165

neglect/decay of historical materials 54
Nelson, Michael E. 5, 106
Nelson, Ted 29, *65*, 189, 193, 194, 195
Net Effect, The (Streeter) 83, 87n6
Netherlands, the *see* De Digitale Stad (DDS)
net histories 49–51, 55–56; new sources 51–54
net neutrality 19, 31
nettime 56n4
network attached storage (NAS) 150
network revolution *see* technological revolution
network society 11, 22
Network Working Group 139
newspapers 164, 166; and Web archives 175–176
NLS (oN-Line System) 66
nostalgia 54
Notes 61–62, 64, 65, 66
novelty 80

online community, PLATO as 63–66
online information systems, comparative design of 33
online systems 29, 30, 33
Open Systems Interconnection 19
oral histories 18, 136, 155
ownership, Internet 181
Oxford Internet Survey (OxIS) 108; Internet questions (2003–2013) 113, **114**

Paloque-Berges, Camille 5, 47
Parker, Sean 93
periodisation 10, 90
persistence (infrastructure) 9
personal data, De Digitale Stad 155–156
physical interface, and Internet access 11–12
place, Internet as 40
PLANET (conferencing platform) 66
PLATO (Programmed Logic for Automated Teaching Operations) 60–62; as community of innovation 63; conflicts 64–65; contemporaries of 66; imagined affordances 66; inclusivity in 64–65; openness of 63–64, 65; reframing of 61; research context and methods 62; social affordances of 65–66; as social computing platform and online community 63–66; terminal *65*; users 63–64
policies 34
political activism 11
political history 174
politics: of history 12–13; and Internet development in Middle East 98–101; and Internet in Africa 133
popular history 51
Postel, Jon 17, 74
precorporation 91–92; Facebook 92–94
pre-Internet history *see* PLATO (Programmed Logic for Automated Teaching Operations)
pre-market period, of Internet companies 91
Premier Services 141

preservation of historical materials 32, 35, 36, 54–55
primary sources *see* Requests for Comments (RFCs)
printing press 86
privacy 12, 30; De Digitale Stad 155–156; and net histories 53
protectionism 98, 100
public institutions, networks sponsored by 54
public sphere: African 133, 135; De Digitale Stad as 149; Internet as 11, 13
purpose limitation 156

QWERTY keyboard 122

Race on the Line (Green) 20
railway 41
Ranke, Leopold von 16
ransomware 143
recursive public 72
reframing of device 61
registry, Internet 75
regulation, Internet 181
Reisdorf, Bianca C. 5, 106
religious language 17
replica, De Digitale Stad 147–148, 154
Requests for Comments (RFCs) 70–71, 139; as historical data 71–73; joke 75; social use of history outside design process 75–76; social use of history within design process 70–71, 74–75; technical use of history within design process 70, 71, 73–74
revisionism 15–16, 22; American Revolution 17; obstacles to 18–19
Rhizome 165
"right to be forgotten" 53, 177
Roberts, Larry 18
robotisation 185–186
Rogers, Richard 6, 160
romaji 123
Romanisation, of East-Asian languages 123
romantic individualism 83, 84–85, 87n6
ruby characters 124
Russell, Andrew L. 15, 47

Salam Pax 100
Savarin, Eduardo 93
Schafer, Valérie 1, 188
scientific hagiography 16
Scott, Jason 55
screencast documentaries 161, 165–166, 170; of history of a web page 166–168, *167*, *168*
search engines 90, 125, 177, 185
Securities and Exchange Commission 93
security: De Digitale Stad 156; lack of 21
sensorium, Internet 185
servers 35
smartphones 30, 102, 165, 183, 184
snapshots 157

sociability 184
social capital 11, 12
social computing *see* PLATO (Programmed Logic for Automated Teaching Operations)
social constructivism 17, 65–66
social divide 132
social groups 9, 10, 181
social machines 34
social media 165, 184–185; in Africa 132–133, 135; aimless connectedness in 63; in Arab world *see* Middle East, Internet in; precorporation in *see* precorporation
Social Network, The 93
social networks 71, 181, 182, 184–185; *see also* Facebook
social relationships, in PLATO 63
social space, Internet as 10–11
social web 64, 110
Sociology of Culture, The (Williams) 40
software 52–53; De Digitale Stad 151
Soul of the Internet, The (Randall) 18
source code 52, 151
sources: born-digital materials 51, 54, 55, 148, 160, 174; digitally reborn 163, 164, 170; digital source criticism 163–164, 170; historical 51–54
South Africa 113, 134
space: cyberspace 30–31, 33, 35, 36; and net histories 50; social space, Internet as 10–11; virtual space, Internet as 10
spam 140–141, 142
SPARC system (Sun) 151, 152–153
Special Interest Group for the History of Computer and Information systems (SIGCIS) 57n6
Spigel, Lynn 43–44
Stanford Research International (SRI), Network Information Center (NIC) 76
State Broadband Initiatives Program 108
State of the State Surveys (SOSS), Michigan State University 107; Internet questions (1997–2016) 110, **111–112**, 113
stock bubble 83, 85
stoke-order method 126
Streeter, Thomas 5, 12, 51, 79
structure of feeling 80–82; Internet-associated 82–85; theory of culture's relation to technology 86–87
subjectivity 42, 43
surveillance 22, 30, 100; and Internet access 12
survey instruments, digital divide 110
symbolic transformation, and infrastructure 41–42
systematic reviews 107
systems theory 9

Talkomatic 62, 63
TCP/IP (Transmission Control Protocol/Internet Protocol) 9, 17, 19, 21–22, 121, 139

technical innovations, and digital divide research 115
technological determinism 98, 129, 130, 133, 134
technological revolution 102
technology 61; adaptation 132, 134–136; and digital divide policy/research **109**; evolution 181; innovation, and digital divide research 115; Internet as 9–10; relation of culture to 86–87; spam 140–141, 142
telecommunication sector, in Middle East 101
Telenet 27
teleology 19, 47, 129–130, 131, 134
teletext 52
television 43–44
Tesla, Nikola 29
Thoreau, Henry David 41
time: and net histories 50, 53; online history by *28*
time-capsule effect 55
tools: De Digitale Stad 154–155; group communication 61–62; information 34
translator 151
Triwibowo, Whisnu 5, 106
Trump, Melania 176
Tunisia 101, 103
Turner, Fred 39
Twitter 92, 135, 143; archive 55
Tymnet 27
typewriters 122

Undersea Network, The (Starosielski) 20
Unicode/ISO 10646 code 124
United Arab Emirates (UAE) 102
Unix-to-Unix copy (UUCP) networks 49
URLs 164
Usenet 52, 54, 55
use of Internet 181
user(s) 48, 50; behaviour of 181–182; -generated content 35; in Middle East 99, 100, 101, 102; PLATO 63–64
US National Aeronautical and Space Administration (NASA) 72–73
US National Science Foundation (NSF) Future Internet Architecture project 73
US Securities Act 93

Vallee, Jacques 66
value proposition of social media 92
virtual space, Internet as 10

"walled gardens" 35
Wasserman, Herman 5, 129
Wayback Machine 148, 154, 157, 161–163, *162, 163*; digital source criticism 163–164; URL list 166; and Web archives 174, 175, 176
Web 27, 35, 36, 121, 180; addresses 125; dynamic nature of 157; national 165
Web 2.0 27, 100

Web archaeology 146–147

Web archives 160, 161, 164–165, 170, 173–174; access to 174, 175–176; barriers to working with 174; Big UK Domain Data for the Arts and Humanities (BUDDAH) project 175; case studies 175–176; lack of awareness of 174; and media 175–176; reuse of 174; right to be forgotten 177

Web archiving 148

Web browsers 90, 107, 124, 125

"webenact" technique 165

Weber, Marc 5, 26

Web historiographies 164–165

Web history 161; digital source criticism 163–164; value of 173–178; Wayback Machine 161–163, *162, 163*

Web page history, screencast documentaries for 166–168, *167, 168*

website history 161, 165–166; value of capturing 168–170

Went, Marc 6, 146

When Old Technologies Were New (Marvin) 43

Where Wizards Stay Up Late (Hafner) 47

whitehouse.gov 166, 169, **169**

Whitman, Walt 41

Whole Internet User's Guide and Catalog, The (Krol) 74

"Why We Post" project 20

Wikipedia 34

Wikis 29

Williams, Raymond 40, 80, 81, 82, 87n2

Winters, Jane 6, 173

wires 33

Woolley, David 63, 64

word wrap 124–125

world brain 28, 29

World Internet Project (WIP) 107, 108, 110, 113

World Trade Organization 99

World Wide Web *see* Web

wrong discourses 53–54

Yahoo! 54, 125

Zuckerberg, Mark 93